Best wishes for Xmas
. the him,
D...

The Wisest Fool in Christendom

By the same author

★

THE MURDER OF SIR THOMAS OVERBURY
THE STORY OF ENGLAND

JAMES VI OF SCOTLAND AS A BOY
Artist unknown

THE WISEST FOOL
IN CHRISTENDOM

The Reign of King James I and VI

by

WILLIAM McELWEE

FABER AND FABER
24 Russell Square
London

First published in mcmlviii
by Faber and Faber Limited
24 Russell Square London WC1
Printed in Great Britain by
Ebenezer Baylis and Son Limited
The Trinity Press, Worcester, and London

Contents

★

Contents

Illustrations

★

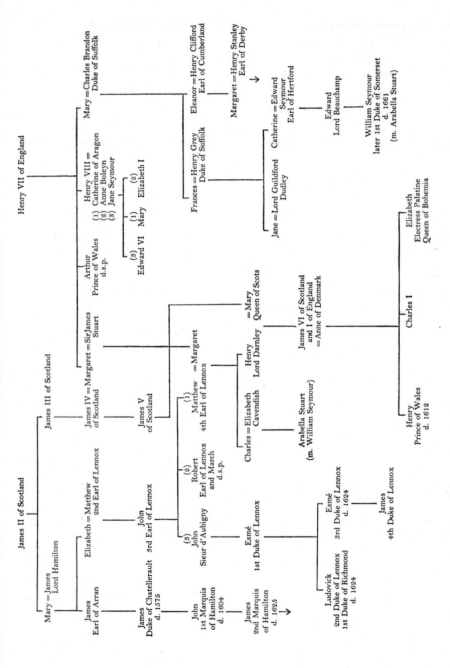

CHAPTER I

The Scottish Inheritance

*

All the proper conventional rejoicings marked the birth of James Stuart in Edinburgh Castle on the morning of June 19th, 1566. The Castle guns fired their salute and bonfires on the ramparts high above the city sent the news out to Scotland. All the proper nobles and great officers of state were present, the proper congratulatory messages and deputations were received, and the proper toasts drunk; and Sir James Melville, experienced, long-headed, and impeccably loyal, was sent off to carry to Queen Elizabeth at Greenwich the news which even she must seem to welcome that the Queen of Scots was 'lighter of a fair son'. But it was all, really, little more than an elaborate make-believe: one of the last moves in the desperate game which Mary Stuart was playing to keep her throne. A few ordinary folk in Scotland may have drunk a sincerely loyal toast in hope for the future. For most of the powerful interests and individuals in the kingdom the baby represented a new and unwelcome complication of a political and religious situation already critically dangerous. Almost a majority of the nobility had wished, for one reason or another, that he might never be born. The formal congratulations of Superintendent John Spottis-woode on behalf of the General Assembly of the Kirk of Scotland, then sitting, could not conceal the fact that the birth of an heir to the throne who would inevitably be baptized a Roman Catholic was a disaster for the religion which was rapidly winning a hold over more than half Scotland. Elizabeth of England would never be able to mask her jealousy and suspicion of the child whom, to the end of her life, she refused openly to recognize as her successor. Even the child's father, Henry, Lord Darnley, had done his malignant best to prevent the birth of the son who blighted his best chance of seizing his wife's throne for himself.

13

The very first ceremonial entry of the child into the world, on the afternoon of the day of his birth, showed how little real cause Queen and people had for rejoicing, or for confidence in the future. For Darnley himself had been sedulously propagating, by bawdy songs and hints, the rumour that James was in fact the bastard son of David Rizzio, the Queen's Italian secretary whom he had helped to murder in her presence four months before. It was vital to Mary that he should undo as much as possible of the harm he had already done, and she summoned him formally to acknowledge the child in the presence of her half-brother, Moray, the Earls of Mar, Atholl, and Argyll, her Privy Council, and her ladies. In a bitter little scene of recrimination Darnley, sullen, drunken and degenerate, was forced to acquiesce while she formally protested, as she should answer for it at the great Day of Judgement, that this was his son, begotten by none but him. It was not an auspicious start for any child, with Darnley goaded and embarrassed, reminding the Queen of her promise to 'forgive and forget all', and Mary unable to refrain from reminders and reproaches. Both she and Darnley knew that he had meant her, too, to die on the night of Rizzio's murder, and these were things which James himself would never be able altogether to forget. For, as Mary herself told her husband, 'he is so much your son that I fear it may be the worse for him hereafter'.

Though the historically important part of the life of James VI and I was lived in England, it is in these Scottish beginnings and against this background that it must first be studied. For James was born and brought up wholly and entirely as a Scotsman, and it has been a matter of pride to Scots ever since that the 300-year feud of their nation with England was ended not, as had once seemed probable, by an English conquest, but by the peaceful acquisition of the English throne by the King of Scots. Nevertheless, if nationalist prejudice be set aside, it must be admitted that the importance in history of James Stuart, only child of Mary, Queen of Scots, lies above all in the impact of his personality on an England whose institutions and politics were already diverging sharply from the continental pattern of which they had once seemed to form a part. His reign in England was the decisive period which committed the nation to a series of constitutional experiments out of which modern parliamentary democracy was to be evolved. There are few civilized nations today, at any rate of those which claim a 'western' civilization, which must not admit a large debt, for good or ill, to the political struggles of seventeenth-century England. Compared to this the reign of James VI in Scotland was unimportant in the history either of the nation or of the world. But the character and idiosyncrasies of James himself were Scotland's particular contribution to this phase of British history—the only immediate and decisive effect of the union of the crowns; and these were formed and hardened by the pattern of Scottish history and politics long before he crossed the Tweed.

Though packed with colourful incident and often easily romanticized, only too much of Scottish history in the fifteenth and sixteenth centuries presented a picture of squalid anarchy. North of what was later to be called the Highland Line—the southern edge of the great hills which cut off the remote north and west—the clans pursued a pattern of life which changed little with the centuries. Their feuds and private wars were endless, and, to any but themselves, meaningless. They wrung a sparse subsistence from a backward agriculture and from fishing, raided their weaker neighbours for cattle and sheep, and bred at every social level fighting men as fierce as any in Europe. Many of their chieftains had acquired feudal titles and incurred some feudal obligations. But the intense closeness of the clan organization coupled with the inaccessibility of the northern glens and western islands had made it impossible for the Scottish kings to assert any permanent authority or establish the rule of law in the Highlands, and for generation after generation the power and independence of a Huntly or an Argyll had proved themselves unbreakable. On the southern fringe of the kingdom a similar turbulence and lack of government had often to be tolerated, though for a different reason. Only a fierce fighting population grouped round powerful and largely independent local magnates could hope to hold off the ceaseless English raids across the Border. In between these two areas of lawlessness lay the narrow belt of the Lowlands, containing some of the richest agricultural land in Britain and the first beginnings of commercial and industrial development, largely concentrated in the capital at Edinburgh. Thus what prosperity there was in sixteenth-century Scotland lay permanently at the mercy of raids from north or south, and the slow progress of Scottish civilization was, moreover, ceaselessly interrupted and sometimes halted altogether by the large-scale devastation of English invasion.

In fact the task which medieval monarchy had set itself everywhere in Europe of reducing feudal anarchy and decentralization to a uniform law and order, had in Scotland been hardly attempted. There was no large class of prosperous merchants and lesser landed gentry whose wealth and backing would have enabled the Stuarts to do for Scotland what the Tudors did for England. The practice known as 'backing of parties at the bar', the packing of a law court with armed supporters which in England was known as Maintenance and had been stamped out by Henry VII, still flourished in Scotland a hundred years later and made it impossible to enforce the most elementary justice. A Scottish Parliament was largely dominated by the very feudal nobles whom it was the Crown's main task to subdue; and the course of Scottish history was almost entirely determined by the feuds and jealousies, ambitions and greed of a handful of mostly conscienceless feudal lords.

Against these the Stuart kings had fought a long and luckless battle. There had been moments of brilliant promise, when the Crown had seemed at last to be dominating the factious, disruptive forces which impeded all progress. But each had ended in the sudden, violent death of the sovereign and in a long minority in which all the ground gained had been lost again; since 1437 only one of them had been old enough to be properly aware of his own accession and none had lived into the prime of life. Battle and murder had accounted for most of them. James's grandfather, James V, had died of despair after the shameful defeat of his army by the English at Solway Moss in 1542, leaving to his week-old daughter, Mary, a situation even more dangerous than that which he himself had inherited at the age of seventeen months when his father had been killed at Flodden Field in 1513. For by then the politically disruptive force of Protestantism had penetrated Scotland to complicate the feuds and rivalries of clans and nobles with the basic dispute of two mutually intolerant religions. Henceforth a certain pattern and coherence were given to Scottish history by the struggle between two main and evenly balanced parties: Catholics who

MARY STUART, QUEEN OF SCOTS
Artist unknown

clung to the 'auld alliance' with France as the only safeguard against English ambition and hostility; and the Protestants who would seek support in England for their religion, even if it meant risking the national independence of Scotland. Thus home and foreign affairs, religion and politics, became inextricably confused, and were to remain so until the peaceful accession of James VI to the English throne in 1603.

This was the basic situation which had confronted Mary Stuart when she had returned from France in 1561 at the age of eighteen to pick up the threads of Scottish government. She herself had spent nearly the whole of her life abroad, sent away for safety in 1548 after a series of English invasions designed to bully the Scots into betrothing their infant queen to the young King Edward VI of England. This English policy had, in fact, defeated its own ends. Scottish nationalism was forced back to the traditional reliance on France, and the Queen Mother, Mary of Guise, a Frenchwoman and a staunch Catholic, was able as Regent to hold the country somewhat precariously to this course until her death in 1560. Mary Stuart, meanwhile, was betrothed and finally married to the Dauphin, and for a brief year, from 1559 to 1560, the union of the Crowns for which the English had striven so long was accomplished by the French. In 1560 Mary was Queen of Scots, Queen Consort of France, and in the eyes of every loyal Catholic in Europe rightful Queen of England. But then her husband died leaving her at the mercy of a mother-in-law whom she found intolerable. For reasons of policy and for the sake of a more secure future she abandoned the direct claim to the English crown, hoping thereby to persuade Elizabeth at least to recognize her formally as her heiress. She was thus uncommitted to any party alliance or policy when she landed at Leith on August 19th, 1561, to claim her kingdom in Scotland. But she was committed to a religion. She had announced in advance that she would leave the Scottish Estates to make what religious settlement they pleased. But in a country half-way through a religious reformation such a statement meant nothing; and her own personal determination to adhere to the Catholic faith and worship made her attempted impartiality almost meaningless. It made inevitable the bitter hostility of John Knox, the most formidable of all the Calvinist missionaries from Geneva, whom Elizabeth had just passed through England under safe-conduct with the deliberate intention of making things difficult for the Scottish Catholic party. Already Knox had provided the extremist Protestants with a rallying point in his new *Book of Discipline*; and he as much as anyone was ultimately to bring Mary to ruin.

For a very brief space it had seemed that Mary, like almost all her Stuart predecessors, might start her effective reign by achieving something of a national recovery. Though she was not beautiful, she had the assets of a great charm and vivacity and tremendous courage. She had a good brain and had been beautifully educated, and once she had set her mind on an objective she could pursue it with relentless determination. But only too often she lacked the statesmanship to select the right objectives. In the tangle of selfish and unprincipled intrigue which constituted Scottish politics—in that world of 'bands' and killing affrays and shifting, meaningless alliances—she could often more than hold her own. But she sought for diplomatic prestige abroad, and at home power for its own sake, and she had none of the almost painful longing to give her subjects good government which was characteristic of her cousin, Elizabeth. She was no judge of men and her intelligence was at the mercy of her passions. Thus in the five years which had elapsed before the birth of her son the brilliant promise of the opening year had degenerated into a bare struggle for political survival. She had probably set herself an impossible task in the first place: a political stability based on religious toleration such as Henry IV was only able to achieve in France after thirty years of intermittent civil war. The bitter intolerance of Knox and his vociferous minority, the underhand support from England for every subversive move against her, and above all the treachery and incompetence of the men on whom she had to rely, had combined to defeat her; and the crowning disaster had been her marriage to Darnley.

Darnley was heir to a younger branch of the Stuarts who, thanks to two judicious marriages, stood close to the succession to both Scottish and English crowns. His father, the fourth Earl of Lennox, but for the doubtfully legitimate Hamiltons, was Mary's heir presumptive, and his mother had the best claim after Mary's to succeed the Tudors in England. He was thus on paper a very suitable consort for the Queen of Scots, in spite of

18

having been brought up in England. It has been alleged that Elizabeth knew Darnley for the brutal, ill-mannered, drunken degenerate that he was the moment that he appeared at her court in 1564 and deliberately sent him north to tempt Mary to her ruin. It seems more likely that she saw only the good-looking athlete—the 'fayre, yollye yonge man' who so impressed the Scots court with his good manners when he first arrived at Wemyss—and that she calculated merely that his obvious weakness and lack of intelligence would at least give Mary no added strength. It was clear that Mary must marry, and Darnley alone, of the acceptable candidates, would not commit her to any dangerous cause either at home or abroad. His vanity and stupidity showed themselves quickly enough in Scotland to alienate most of his friends, but not, it seems, to the Queen, who fell in love with him and on July 24th, 1564, formally married him. Two incidents of that day reveal the impossibility of the situation in which she had involved herself. She attended her nuptial mass alone, since Darnley was cultivating Protestant favour; and the Proclamation declaring her husband King was received in stony silence by all save the bridegroom's father.

So all the elements were grouped for the final tragedy from which the life of James VI took its inauspicious start. Within three weeks of the marriage Mary's selfish, treacherous half-brother, the bastard Earl of Moray, whom she had at first wholly trusted and who had steadily betrayed her, came out in open rebellion in the name of the Protestant Kirk. Behind him there lay the implacable hostility of Elizabeth, who had contributed £3,000 to his war expenses, and the discontented Protestant lords who waited to see how the cat would jump; while in Edinburgh Knox preached a long, offensive sermon in front of Darnley in which he reminded his congregation that God had justly punished King Ahab for not taking order with the harlot, Jezebel. Surprisingly, for the moment, Mary's system held together. She really had managed to identify Scottish patriotism with a government which dealt equally faithfully with Catholic and Protestant rebels, and not even Knox could turn out the citizens of Edinburgh when Moray entered the city at the end of August. Their call to 'all such men as would receive wages for the defence of the Glory of God' met with little response, in spite of the promise of 'good pay'. They got, Knox recorded sadly, 'no comfort or support, for none or few resorted to them'. The Protestant lords kept quiet, and in a brisk, unspectacular campaign in the Borders known as the Chase-about Raid Mary drove Moray into England, where he was promptly and sanctimoniously disowned and denounced by Elizabeth.

But the triumph was superficial and short-lived. Her very success drew together all those enemies who saw their own lawless independence threated by it, and they found their opportunity in that very Darnley marriage on which Mary had hoped to rely for comfort and support. She had needed a man, if only as a soldier. For, though she delighted in campaigning, was 'never dismayed', and regretted only 'that she was not a man to know what it was to lye all nyghte in the feeldes', she could not well command her own troops. Instead she had acquired a petulant debauchee for whom her first passion quickly waned. Whether she first rebuffed him or he neglected her is a question which cannot now be easily determined. On this, as on all other issues connected with Mary Stuart, the evidence has got overlaid by the furious partisanship of historians. The known fact is that within six months Mary and Darnley were wholly estranged. He no longer attended Council meetings and she had a stamp made for his signature on public documents. *Henricus et Maria* on the coinage gave way to *Maria et Henricus,* and she absolutely refused to grant him the Crown Matrimonial which would have made him King of Scotland for his lifetime as well as hers. Undoubtedly Darnley behaved badly, consoling himself with bouts of drunkenness and infidelities. Undoubtedly, too, Mary allowed herself too intimate a friendship with her French Secretary, the Italian David Rizzio, who flaunted her favour and his promotion very injudiciously. By Christmas they were irreconcilable; and for Darnley it was the last straw that Mary already carried a child who would, if it survived, cut him out of the succession to both the crowns he coveted.

This was the situation out of which there grew the most celebrated of all the brutal and dramatic episodes of Scottish history, the murder of Rizzio at the Queen's supper table in Holyrood on March 9th, 1566. The bands that drew together round Darnley for this plot contained all those who could colourfully pretend alarm at the threat to Scottish Protestantism: Morton and the Douglases; old Lord Ruthven, a huge, brutal, embittered and dying man, who was prepared to assure anybody that the enterprise was 'conform to Christ's book'; Maitland of Lethington, the only statesmanlike brain in Scotland, and another of the men in whom the Queen had once reposed an absolute trust; and her half-brother and his exiled friends who hung about in New-castle waiting for the next chance to stir up trouble. It is not certain that Knox knew of it, though he certainly pronounced it 'worthy of all praise' after the event. European rumours of a forthcoming anti-Protestant league between Scotland, France, Spain and the Emperor gave some colour to the plot, though Mary at that moment was in fact in trouble with the Pope for refusing to countenance plans which would involve her in shed-ding her own subjects' blood. The real causes lay in the impend-ing Parliament which was likely to seal Mary's triumph by for-feiting the lands of Moray and his friends and by pronouncing some sort of tolerationist religious settlement, and in the fact that Mary, by marrying the Earl of Bothwell to Janet Gordon, Huntly's sister, had, temporarily at any rate, united in her sup-port the two most powerful men in Scotland. Darnley's colla-boration was won by playing on his already insensate vanity and jealousy with rumours and bawdy songs suggesting that Rizzio—Seigneur Davie—and not himself was the father of Mary's expected child.

So there occurred, before he was even born, the first attempt on the life of James VI. For there can be no doubt that the deliberate choice of the Queen's supper party for the murder was to make it a direct attack on her and her unborn son. At the very least her reputation would be tarnished and a slur of illegi-timacy cast on the child. It was more than likely that the shock of the sudden irruption and of seeing her secretary dragged literally from her skirts to be despatched outside the door would cause her to miscarry—perhaps even kill her; and some of the conspirators certainly meant to make sure by killing her out-right, apparently accidentally, in the confusion of overturned lights and struggling men. But, though Rizzio died, the con-spiracy failed. Huntly and Bothwell cut their way out of the Palace and Mary's level-headed courage saved her child's life and her own. In the bloodstained disorder of her bedroom, with her palace in the hands of her enemies and even her women kept from her, she began at once to save what could be saved from the wreck of her life. The power of Huntly in the Highlands and of Bothwell on the Borders was still unbroken, and if she could once get clear of Holyrood she could fight back with every chance of victory. It is a measure of the success of her conciliatory policy of the past five years that the Protestant citizens of Edinburgh beat to arms at once on her behalf and were with difficulty pacified from a window by Darnley.

Before the night was out she had won back to her side her cringing husband, terrified of the consequences of his own actions. Her two-faced brother, Moray, when he rode in prudently late the next morning, was easily detached from a conspiracy which had clearly failed with a promise of pardon and reinstatement. By simulating the beginnings of a miscarriage— the very event for which the plotters had been hoping—she more or less forced them to withdraw their guards from her private apartments. So she was able to slip out in the night with Darnley, who dared not stay with the friends he was engaged in betraying, and ride the thirty-odd miles to Bothwell's castle of Dunbar and safety. Within a week she was back in her capital and Rizzio's murderers were scattered in hiding or in exile; and by the time her child was born she had once again apparently restored the situation. The reconciliation with Darnley and Moray was outwardly complete, and there was only the ugly little scene in Edinburgh Castle on the afternoon of James's birth to recall the fact that her marriage was irretrievably ruined and what chance she might ever have had of establishing herself securely in power almost certainly destroyed.

For the six months that elapsed from James's birth to his christening at Stirling in December, 1566, the outward calm prevailed. The baby himself was shuffled out of the way, safe indeed in Stirling Castle for the next twelve years under the guardianship of the Earl of Mar, but handed over to a wet nurse, Helen Litell, who had a reputation as a drinker, and so neglected in what was probably an early attack of rickets that his shambling walk and weak legs were to be a subject of mockery for the rest of his life. His father detested him for robbing him of all his expectations, and his mother was fighting for her political life; only Lady Mar had any time or thought for the child as a human being. But since as a political factor—as the heir presumptive to two crowns—he was of enormous importance from the moment of his birth, his christening had to be a very grand affair indeed, and the slur which had been cast on his legitimacy made it doubly necessary that it should be nobly celebrated. None of his godparents, the King of France, the Queen of England, and the Duke of Savoy, could be expected to appear in person, but the embassies and the presents they sent with their proxies were impressive. The Comte de Brienne came with thirty gentlemen in his train bringing a necklace of pearls and rubies and two lovely ear-rings; Lord Bedford brought a train of forty and a heavy silver-gilt font. The Duke of Savoy sent a feathered, jewelled fan, but was content to be represented at the ceremony by M. du Croc, the resident French Ambassador.

The proper entertainment of delegations such as these put a fearful strain on meagre Scottish resources. But for these few days native barbarism and stringency were made to conform to the standards of the French court in which Mary had been educated. Moray and Argyll and Bothwell were dressed in new 'taffetie' suits at the Queen's expense, Moray in green, Argyll in red, and Bothwell in blue with shoes of cloth of silver. There were music, Latin elegiacs, and masques, a torchlight procession and dancing, two magnificent banquets, and fireworks from the castle guns of 'shot fire balls, fire spears, and all other things pleasant for the sight of man'; and the christening itself was a defiant last assertion of the dying Catholicism of Scotland, with Archbishop Hamilton of St Andrews and the Bishops of Dunkeld, Dunblane, and Ross in pontifical robes 'such as had not been seen in Scotland these seven years'. With all proper pageantry the heralds proclaimed Prince James Duke of Rothesay, Earl of Kyle, Carrick, and Cunningham, Lord of the Isles, and Baron of Renfrew. For three short days in the Palace of Stirling Mary allowed herself the illusion that life could still be civilized and urbane, showed off her French and her dancing and her charm, ignoring the sinister little indications of lurking trouble: the fact that Bothwell stopped at the door of the Chapel Royal with the rigidly Puritan Earl of Bedford, and that Darnley sulked in his room, boycotting a ceremony at which nobody was any longer prepared to treat him as a king. Darnley's father, the Earl of Lennox, was still scheming on his behalf for the Crown Matrimonial and a real share in the government. But Bedford had strict orders to show Darnley no 'more respect in any way than to the simplest gentleman present', and Brienne and du Croc had been similarly instructed, so the wretched young man remained out of sight, though he can never have been wholly out of Mary's mind.

In fact, though the ceremonies at Stirling apparently marked yet another triumph in Mary's dogged fight for power and security, the past six months had already brought her to the crisis which was to destroy her. She had never really recovered from the shock of Rizzio's murder. Though love for her son and a passionate desire for revenge had kept her going until James was safely born, she had lost the courage which had sustained her alone against the treachery of her nobles and the venomous denunciations of the preachers. 'The injury she received is exceeding great,' du Croc had written, 'and her Majesty will never forget it'; and as Sir James Melville, one of her few entirely faithful servants, put it, 'there were overfew to comfort her'. It was her tragedy that the man to whom she turned for comfort was the Earl of Bothwell.

Bothwell was clearly something more than the mere soldier of fortune—the brutal, arrogant, successful, male animal that has so often been painted. The fighting Border magnate who could hold his own with both English and Scots had to be all that and more: a reckless, swashbuckling adventurer, who never refused a gamble or a challenge and who never played for safety; a man who attracted women easily and as easily abandoned them. But he had also commanded the King of France's Scottish Guard, and must in the world of the French court have acquired at least a superficial polish and civilized manners. He was in fact well educated and a great reader. Had he not possessed at least this veneer of civilization it is inconceivable that he would have gained over Mary the hold that he did, however much she may have become in the end the slave of her own sensual passion. But it was undoubtedly as the man of action—the reliable and successful manipulator of men and events—that he first appealed to her. He stood out in clear-cut contrast to all the elements which were making her life intolerable: Darnley's effeminacy, Maitland's skilful, crooked intrigues, and the careful, selfish double-dealing of Moray. He was without fear and without scruple, but in the slippery, treacherous world in which she had been living for five years he none the less offered her something that seemed genuinely dependable; something that would not break in her hand at the critical moment. He policed her English Border. His troops and his quick thinking capacity as a man of action had alone saved her after Rizzio's murder. It is not surprising that she turned to him as the only force on which she could reconstruct her government in Scotland. It is not surprising, either, though it was tragic, that she also fell headlong in love with him.

The known facts of Mary's last year as Queen of Scotland are clear and straightforward enough. On December 24th, a week after his son's christening, Darnley learnt that Mary had pardoned the survivors of Rizzio's murderers, and he fled at once to his father's house in Glasgow where, in the heart of Lennox's own country, he could alone feel reasonably safe. Half the nobility of Scotland were out for the blood of the man who had betrayed them, and by then the Queen had certainly been shown at least one of the 'bands' Darnley had signed with the murderers and knew that it had not been merely a sudden, blind passion of jealousy that had driven her husband to collaborate with them. On his way to Glasgow he fell ill with smallpox, and while he lay between life and death Bothwell was busy weaving together another 'band' from among the implacable enemies whom Darnley had betrayed and whom Mary had now allowed back into Scotland. The Queen was sick and sad, with 'a sorrow,' du Croc wrote, 'which she cannot forget', and the air was thick with plots. It was widely known that Bothwell was aiming to marry the Queen and become King of Scotland himself, while Lethington stated quite openly, writing of Darnley, that Mary found it 'intolerable that he should be her husband and that there is no way in which she could be rid of him'. Already, at Craigmillar Castle before Christmas, Moray, Lethington, Bothwell, Huntly and Argyll had discussed with Mary the possibility of a divorce; and when she demurred at any step which might call her son's legitimacy in question, Lethington had reassured her that they would find a 'moyen' to rid her of Darnley and had assured her that Moray, although he was

25

'little less scrupulous for a Protestant than your Grace is for ane Papist', would 'look through his fingers thereto'. No decision was taken then; but in that same month Mary got Archbishop Hamilton's old consistorial jurisdiction restored to him, so that he had the power, without reference to Rome, to pronounce a decree of divorce by nullity, though whether it was her own divorce she had in mind, or Bothwell's from his newly-married wife, will never be known. At the same time there were reliable reports from the French government of a counter-plot by Lennox and Darnley to kidnap the baby prince from Stirling, so as to have a bargaining counter in the trial of strength which was clearly coming.

On January 14th Mary wrote to Darnley suggesting that she should come and see him at Glasgow. She got only a rude verbal answer. A letter which she wrote that week to Archbishop Beaton shows that she was in fact still preoccupied with countering Lennox's alleged kidnapping plot, and Prince James was brought to Edinburgh and lodged in the Castle. Nevertheless on January 21st she arrived at Glasgow and quite clearly easily re-established her old ascendancy over him. For two days later Darnley, though still only convalescent, not certainly free from infection and with his disfigured face still covered by a taffeta mask, against the strenuous advice of his father and friends allowed himself to be transported to Edinburgh in a litter which Mary had brought with her. There, on the grounds that he still might be infectious, she lodged him outside the walls 'in a solitair place at the outmost part of ye town', in a squalid, ruined neighbourhood approached by a street known as 'Thieves' Row', and in a quite unsuitable, small, four-roomed house known as the Kirk o'Field. There she had a bedroom magnificently fitted up for herself on the ground floor; and there she visited him for the last time, ostentatiously and by torchlight, on the night of Sunday, February 9th, when Bothwell and a few of his most trusted kinsmen and retainers were already carrying gunpowder into the cellars of the house. She left shortly before midnight to attend the masque given in honour of the wedding of her French Master of Ceremonies, Bastian, and at two o'clock the house was blown up. Darnley's body, with that of one of his pages, was afterwards found naked in the garden, unmarked by powder, though no sufficient examination was carried out for anyone, then or since, to be able to determine how he had met his death.

What is not known and can probably never be decided for certain is at what stage Mary fell in love with Bothwell and how far she was implicated in her husband's murder. That she did fall in love with him is beyond dispute. That she wrote him a series of sonnets and appallingly self-revealing love-letters at some stage before she ran off with him is almost beyond dispute. Certainly she handled the situation after the murder so ineptly that public opinion in Scotland and the diplomatic world of Europe, Catholic and Protestant alike, firmly believed that she had connived at her husband's murder. Protagonists on both sides have tried to make too much out of the inconclusive evidence that survives on all these points. What does remain clearly fixed is that Mary, inexcusably or not, made the great mistake which Elizabeth had so narrowly avoided in her relationship with Leicester: compromised her fair name in a sordid story of murder and divorce, and thereby threw away not only every political asset that she had, but her throne itself.

So, with Edinburgh placarded nightly with denunciations of Bothwell and his kinsmen as Darnley's murderers, bombarded with the reproaches and remonstrances of every court in Europe, amidst the abuse of the preachers and the murmurings of the Edinburgh populace, Mary and her lover moved almost briskly to their final disaster. On March 19th, escorted by the Earls of Huntly and Argyll, Prince James was moved out of the way again to Stirling and handed over to the safe keeping of the Earl and Countess of Mar. A fortnight later Moray gave Mary what should have been a final warning that she was headed for disaster and, 'because of the great trouble seeming to come to the realm', left for England. So far Moray had 'looked through his fingers' very well. He had prudently withdrawn to Fife for the actual night of Darnley's murder, but he returned to Edinburgh on perfectly amicable terms with Bothwell, and in the will he drew up before he finally left he made Bothwell and Mary his executors. But he was not to be involved in a ruin which he now saw to be inevitable. On April 12th, unable to resist any longer the pressure from abroad which backed Lennox's clamour for revenge on his son's murderer, Mary brought Bothwell to trial in Edinburgh. But since the city was policed by six thousand of Bothwell's Borderers and Lennox himself dared not appear to support his accusations, he was easily and unconvincingly acquitted. On the 17th, as a culminating insult to the whole of Scotland, Bothwell was selected to carry the Crown and Sceptre before the Queen at the opening of Parliament; and on the night that the Parliament ended, lest there should be any further doubt of his intentions, Bothwell gave his celebrated supper party at Ainslie's Tavern when, under the influence of drink and the fact that the house had been surrounded by armed men, almost the entire nobility of Scotland signed a bond pledging themselves to belief in his innocence and to support for a 'marriage betwixt her Highness and the said noble lord'.

On April 21st the Queen rode to Stirling to pay what was to be her last visit to her son. Mar, claiming that he held his trust not from her, but from the Estates of Scotland, not only would not surrender the child, but would only allow her to bring two of her ladies with her into the castle. Nothing shows more clearly the universality of the hostility Mary had aroused than the refusal of this most loyal of servants to trust a queen who had abandoned her whole will and future to a shameless political adventurer, even with the custody of her own son. For Darnley's death and Mary's misconduct had brought the infant James even more prominently into the centre of the political stage. The whole future of England and Scotland was bound up with his survival.

Mary stayed at Stirling for two days, and only garbled accounts survive of what happened there. It was said, rather improbably, that she tried to coax the child to stop screaming with an apple, which he indignantly rejected; and still more improbably that the rejected apple was subsequently eaten by a greyhound bitch, which swelled up and died. Whatever her object may have been and whatever may really have happened there, Mary left Stirling without the Prince, and at Linlithgow was kidnapped by Bothwell with farcically suspicious ease and carried off to Dunbar. He seems to have thought that the bond signed in Ainslie's Tavern would really prevent the bulk of the nobility from opposing his seizure of the throne, and Mary was too besotted to count the cost of what she was doing. Neither, certainly, was prepared for the instant upheaval of Scottish opinion, high and low, Protestant and Catholic, against conduct which, even by the standard of Scottish history and politics, was indefensible. Mary had a remarkable ability to win people over to her side and probably, even at this late stage, had she emerged from Dunbar and called for support as a genuine victim of Bothwell's rape, she would have found folk to fight for her. As it was the two played their comedy through to the end with the utmost ineptitude. During the three weeks that Mary remained at Dunbar Archbishop Hamilton rushed through an annulment of Bothwell's marriage to Janet Gordon who, poor girl, had never wanted to marry him in the first place, but was probably the only woman he ever really loved. So Mary could argue that, having been irretrievably compromised at Dunbar, she had now no alternative but to marry her captor, and she seems to have been genuinely surprised that nobody found the argument convincing. So completely had she fallen into Bothwell's power, she even allowed the ceremony to be performed according to Protestant rites.

It was the Protestant nobility, the Lords of the Congregation, who took the initiative in putting an end to this disastrous farce, and though they had all been implicated more or less in Bothwell's band against Darnley, they had the brazen effrontery to march out under a banner depicting his naked body crying for revenge. Since not even Bothwell's moss troopers would show any real fight in so indefensible a cause, the end was swift and bloodless. Bothwell, created Duke of Orkney for the occasion, was married to the Queen on May 12th. They had a brief, unhappy, three-week honeymoon at Holyrood, during which Bothwell wrote regularly to the wife he had treated so badly, Janet Gordon, while the hostile combination gathered swiftly together. In the first days of June Lethington slipped away— the last rat to leave; and as the situation in the capital grew more menacing Mary and Bothwell slipped away too, first to Borthwick, and then to Dunbar. On June 15th they moved out again to confront their enemies at Carberry Hill where, for most of the day, the two armies faced each other, both very reluctant to fight. Du Croc, who had always loved Mary, made a last attempt to mediate, but the only acceptable condition was that she should leave Bothwell, and that she utterly refused. Bothwell, true to form to the end, offered to fight the issue out in single combat with any one of the opposition Lords, but that, too, Mary would not allow. While she argued her army melted away, and in the end she could only surrender herself to enable Bothwell to escape with his life.

Only then was Mary brought to realize the hatred and resentment she had stirred up against herself. Kirkcaldy of Grange, who had negotiated her final surrender, had promised her that she should be treated properly and respectfully, but he was powerless to keep his promise and, indeed, did well to preserve her alive from his soldiers, and from the Edinburgh crowd which longed to lynch 'the adulteress'. Surrounded by the Protestant lords, whom she continually cursed and threatened, she rode into her capital for the last time through an uncontrollable, vindictive mob which howled its desire to 'burn the whore'. Obsessed with her passion for Bothwell, she had remained deaf and blind to all opposition and utterly unaware of the feeling she was arousing. In the shock of being brought brutally face-to-face with it, and then of having further to face the fact that her reign had come to an end, she almost lost her reason. There was another terrible scene at the Provost's lodging in the High Street, where she was temporarily lodged, when she was confronted with the terms on which her enemies would allow her to live, and appeared at a window with her hair loosened and her clothes indecently torn and disordered to clamour to the people for a rescue.

She was only 26 and the best of her life had seemed to lie in front of her. But with the hourly danger that the mob might be moved to pity and change sides, with Huntly in arms in the north and the Hamiltons in the west, her enemies dared leave her no future that was acceptable at all. The very next night she was removed to the island castle of Lochleven, still hysterical and utterly unprepared, if it meant giving up Bothwell, to accept any compromise by which she might have retained some shreds of dignity and position. At that stage a compromise would certainly have been possible, for the nobles were still very unsure of their ground. Theoretically they were in arms against Bothwell only, and they stated carefully that Mary was not being imprisoned at Lochleven, but merely 'secluded'. Open rebellion against the Queen would raise a majority in Scotland against them. Elizabeth, though she wrote privately to

Mary in the sharpest terms condemning her behaviour over Darnley's murder and her second marriage, told the victors of Carberry Hill that she would declare war if they attempted to depose their Queen. Thus Mary still had cards in her hand, but within a week her chance had gone. The discovery of the silver casket which Bothwell had left behind for safety in Edinburgh, in which he had kept her letters and sonnets and her promise to marry him, destroyed her. However much they may have been tampered with, the Casket Letters had a devastating effect on public opinion. Henceforth the rebel lords could leave it to a returned Knox and his fellow preachers to inflame feeling and to drive them along the road which they wished to follow. Under the impact of that attack, Mary, who had defied lords and soldiers and Edinburgh mob, gave way at last to fear. An old law in Scotland had just been brought back into use under which adultery was not only a capital offence, but punishable in women by burning, and she seems to have been genuinely afraid that her enemies would have her condemned under it and burnt. That she should abdicate in favour of her son and allow a regency to take over the government was indeed now the only possible solution for Scotland. She had forfeited too much good will ever to recover the ground she had lost. All sober, moderate opinion in Scotland agreed with the preachers that 'a Queen hath no more liberty or privilege to commit adultery or murder than any other private person, either by God's laws, or the laws of the realm', and Elizabeth's protests on her behalf were becoming half-hearted and undependable. So, when the deputation from the lords waited on her on July 24th and threatened openly to bring her to trial and execution, she gave way and signed the abdication they demanded. Her reign in Scotland came formally to an end, and on July 29th they brought the new King down from the castle to the parish church of Stirling to be crowned.

CHAPTER II

The Education of a King

*

It was a very maimed ceremony that inaugurated the new reign, designed only to throw a cloak of legality over the seizure of power by a faction of Protestant nobles. Naturally enough it was an aggressively Protestant reaction against the candles and incense and copes which had adorned the child's christening six months before. Only seven lords turned up for it. There were no trumpets and heralds to proclaim the new King, but only a bleak little service conducted by the Bishop of Orkney, who had last appeared in public when he married Mary to Bothwell, and an immense sermon by Knox on the theme of the coronation of the child King Joash, whose mother, Queen Athaliah, had rent her clothes and cried, 'Treason, treason,' and then been taken out and slain by the sword. It was the red-headed Douglas, Earl of Morton, the most crooked and treacherous of the whole shifty throng who had brought Mary to her ruin, who had held Holyrood for Rizzio's murderers, had signed Bothwell's bond against Darnley, and had now got himself nominated Chancellor in the new Regency Council, who read aloud on James's behalf a severely Protestant coronation oath which pledged the King not only in ancient form to maintain 'the lovable laws and constitutions received in this realm', but also to 'root out all heretics and enemies to the true worship of God that shall be convicted by the true Kirk of God of the aforesaid crimes'. The preachers, in fact, meant the new régime to subordinate the whole government of Scotland, civil and ecclesiastical, to themselves. The nobles were determined merely to keep power and wealth exclusively in their own hands or those of their friends. The child whom they were crowning was to spend half his life freeing himself from these two threatened tyrannies.

But it would be more than a dozen years before James would

32

be able to exercise the slightest influence over his own life, and in the meantime the Kirk and the Protestant faction among the nobility had their way. Mary's stupidity and shamelessness had alienated the whole effective public opinion of Scotland. The massive support of all decent, middle-minded, unprejudiced folk had been forced to unite behind the extremists of the Kirk and a gang of unprincipled ruffians among the nobles only to avoid the worser evil of Bothwell. But it was not a triumph of national interest. The causes for which Mary had stood—independence abroad and a balance of religions and parties at home —perished with her. The victory of her enemies was inevitably the victory of turbulence over good order and government, however much her own misconduct might have obscured the issue, and the dominance of an extremist Protestant minority which had been helped to power by English intrigues and often by English subsidies inevitably produced a dependence on England such as most thinking Scotsmen had long been trying to avoid. So, while James grew up behind the walls of Stirling Castle under the careful guardianship of the Earl and Countess of Mar, Scottish history became what it had so often been before, a prolonged faction fight without even the feeblest royal authority to restrain the factiousness. 'Nourishers of theft and raisers of rebellion', George Buchanan called the men who appointed him to supervise the King's education, 'for the most part of insatiable greediness, intolerable arrogance, without faith in promises, pity to the inferior, obedience to the superior, in peace desirous of trouble, in war thirsty of blood'. But the power and independence of the Kirk depended on these men; both were driven to an unavoidable and equally distasteful dependence on England.

There were four Regents during these twelve troubled years, and the first of them was Moray. In August of 1567 he made one of his well-timed returns to Scotland and brilliantly exploited the situation which he found there. The rebels had already asked him to become Regent, but he would not accept until he had visited his sister at Lochleven. Playing on her fears, he made it seem that he alone could save her from the trial and 'fiery death' which she had been brought to believe would inevitably follow the publication of her letters. Probably he promised too to suppress them if given the power to do so.

Thus he was able to assume the Regency at the urgent request of both sides, with apparent reluctance, and without forcing Elizabeth into opposition. 'That bastard,' as James called him later, 'who unnaturally rebelled and procured the ruin of his owne sovran and sister,' even stole Mary's jewels, which she gave him for safe keeping, selling her famous pearls cheap to Elizabeth and giving most of the rest to his wife. And one of his first acts as Regent was to have the Casket Letters and sonnets read aloud to the Scottish Parliament and their handwriting authenticated so that there should be no question of a restoration. How precarious his situation still was was shown the following spring, when Mary escaped and instantly found Gordons, Hamiltons, and Setons eager to take up arms for her. Moray moved swiftly, cornered her in the south-west before her forces could gather in overwhelming strength, and defeated her at Langside on May 13th; and, rather than face another humiliation like that of Carberry Hill, Mary fled for sanctuary to England.

So the pattern was set for the next eighteen years of Scottish history—the whole of James's youth and adolescence. Internally it presented a picture of pure gangsterism: on the surface of politics a naked struggle for power between men almost all of whom held some sort of blackmailing hold on each other. Of Moray's friends who joined with him in producing the Casket Letters before Elizabeth's perfunctory courts of inquiry at York and Westminster as proof of Mary's 'foirknawledge, counsal, devise, persuadar and commandar' of Darnley's murder, three had certainly been involved in it themselves. Mary held a bond signed by Lethington that proved him guilty; and Morton, years later, was to be tried and executed for it. Elizabeth of England had a blackmailer's hold over them all, since the threat to release Mary would always bring them to heel, and few of those who clamoured to bring the Queen of Scots to trial could actually have faced a proper sifting of the facts in public. Perhaps the most typical of the unprincipled transactions which made up most of the history of this period was Elizabeth's offer of 1572 to hand Mary over to Morton if he would guarantee that she would be tried and executed, which Morton refused only because Elizabeth would not accept in writing any share of responsibility. Meanwhile in the background Mary's cause

slowly declined and perished. In England the rising of the
Catholic northern earls on her behalf in 1569 and the plot of
1572 to marry her to the Duke of Norfolk and place her on
both English and Scottish thrones both ended in disaster. In
Scotland her friends were one by one caught or driven into exile.
In 1573 Huntly and the Hamiltons gave in at last, and only
Edinburgh Castle still held out for her under Kirkcaldy of
Grange, one of the few honest men in Scotland, who had been
horrified by the results of his own actions at Carberry Hill, and
Lethington who had been forced at last to come down on her
side because she held the only absolute proof that he had been
'art and part of Darnley's murder'. That same year the walls of
Edinburgh Castle were at last breached with guns borrowed
from England, Morton managed to poison the wells, and the
garrison had to surrender. Grange was hanged and Lethington,
already a very sick man, probably killed himself rather than
face a trial.

As far as maintaining law and order went, Moray governed
Scotland well. But his Regency lasted only until 1570, when he
was shot dead as he rode through the streets of Linlithgow by
an aggrieved Hamilton whose lands he had stolen after Langside. Six months of utter confusion, of civil war and large-scale
Border raids by both sides, ended in a compromise which
pleased nobody: the Regency of the King's grandfather, Lennox,
who had fought his way in with English troops. He was old,
ineffectual and a Catholic. The Protestant leaders mistrusted
him because most of them had been implicated in his son's
murder; the Catholics because he was sided against Mary. The
'sillie Regent' they called him; and he provided little more than
a figurehead to the prevailing anarchy. In 1572 he, too, was shot,
in a wild night raid on Stirling by Kirkcaldy of Grange, who had
hoped to profit by the confusion of a Parliament and kidnap the
young King. His successor, Mar, an honest, peaceable man, did
not even last for a year before he died, probably of exhaustion
and despair, though he may have been poisoned by Morton. It
was Morton, at any rate, the most blackguardly of all Mary's
enemies, who followed him as Regent, and who managed to
maintain himself in power for six years—the most important
formative years of James's life.

In theory James was supposed to be growing up closely protected from all these disturbances in the remote security of Stirling Castle. In practice they could not be excluded, even in the physical sense, and they exercised a powerful distorting effect on his education and on the development of his character. He was too important a political entity, as the only counter-weight the Protestant lords had to the sovereignty still pro-claimed by Mary and her Catholic supporters, to be allowed to remain wholly secluded, and by the age of five he was already being thrust into the forefront of politics. In 1571, with the Queen's friends gathering in Edinburgh and herself loudly protesting from her exile that 'a demission forced in prison' was of 'little import', the Protestant lords sought to bolster up the tottering authority of their Catholic Regent, Lennox, by holding at Stirling a Parliament which should show the world where sovereignty in Scotland really lay. There, before all the Protes-tant nobles and the more influential leaders of the Kirk, James was carried in with the Crown and Sceptre and Sword of State before him and set in the throne, gowned in purple and gold and ermine, to make a little prepared speech confirming his grand-father's authority. Too much has been made of his remark afterwards, as he sat gazing at a tear in the canopy over the throne—'This Parliament has ane hole in it'. But the fact re-mains that this tempestuous wrangling among Scottish nobles was his first experience of what men called a parliament, and that the whole ceremony was calculated to force on his mind the consciousness of his kingship before he was much conscious of anything else.

Before that Parliament ended he was to experience another and harsher intrusion of the outside world: Kirkcaldy of Grange's wild night raid from Edinburgh, which caught his enemies carelessly billeted about the town and in the first rush of surprise made prisoners of a dozen Protestant nobles, includ-ing Lennox, and with a little more luck might have snatched the King, too, and so put all the cards in his hand. As it was, a quick sally by Mar at the head of the castle garrison rescued all but Lennox and Wilmestoun, who were shot as they broke away. The memory of that night of shouting confusion, of the clatter of arms, and the shooting down in the town, and of his grandfather carried back mortally wounded, was another early and indelible impression on the mind of an already timorous and delicate child, reinforced as it was in the years that followed by the bars which went up over the windows of his apartments and the elaborate precautions which had to surround him whenever he rode out into the park. It is not necessary to look back to the pre-natal shock of the night of Rizzio's murder to account for James's horror all his life of naked steel, of violence, and men of war. Inevitably he was brought up in an atmosphere of fear of what 'the lords of the Queen, his mother,' might do, and taught to expect physical danger round every corner.

The six peaceful years of carefully planned academic education which followed could do nothing to eradicate these first, decisive lessons, and later experience was to confirm them still more strongly. George Buchanan did his best to produce a king of a very different sort from what James eventually became. The iron self-discipline of scholarship and the equally rigid spiritual discipline of Calvinism were to mould a hard-working, careful, conscientious ruler who wielded power as a trust from the people and in due subordination to the will of God as interpreted by the ministers of His Kirk. On the academic side and theologically Buchanan and his chief assistant, Mr. Peter Young, did very well. They produced a paragon of learning and precocity whose religious beliefs were firmly based on Calvinist dogma and logic. But they never made him really conscientious or, except under compulsion, hard-working. They could not eliminate the devious, secretive twists which were given to his mind by his early fears and shocks; and on the nature of kingship and on the proper relations between Church and State they failed altogether.

Buchanan was a great teacher of classics, but not a great pedagogue. In his day he had been one of the more celebrated European humanists, a lecturer at Paris and the teacher of Montaigne, tutor to some of the best families in France and Scotland, a master of all the Renaissance elegancies, and finally Mary Stuart's one great, courtly friend in Scotland. In the first two years of her reign, when she was still buoyed up with hope and ambition and he had not yet forsaken the Church of Rome, he had been the only really civilized contact she had made outside her own imported French court, and they had read Livy together. But in 1563 he had gone over to the Church of

Scotland, she had embarked on the course which led through Darnley and Bothwell to Lochleven, and their relationship was destroyed. A bitter hostility supplanted the elegiacs and the exchange of polished complimentary Latin poems. She, who had been for Buchanan of a 'nobility rarer than all her kindred' when he dedicated his paraphrase of the Songs of David to her, became the 'bludy woman and poysoning witch' of the *Detectio Mariae Reginae Scotorum*, the work to which he sacrificed all the early years of James's life, and into which he packed the accumulated venom of a lifetime and every filthy story about the Queen that could be gleaned from the Edinburgh gutters. It was he who swore to Mary's handwriting in the Casket Letters before the Scottish Parliament and to Elizabeth's court at Westminster. Her wickedness, her 'immeasurable but mad' love for Bothwell, her viciousness and greedy coveting of 'intemperate authority' became an obsession with him. The worst denunciation he could find for James in later years was to call him 'a true bird of that bludy nest'. By the time that he took James's education over seriously in 1570 he was a gouty, crabbed, ill-tempered old man with only the classical polish of his Latin left to recall the grace and charm of his youth. When he was 53 and nearing death James would still have nightmares about him and turn pale at the thought of him.

Peter Young, Buchanan's assistant, was a very different character, scholarly indeed, and fresh from the hothouse of Geneva, but gentle and lovable. He was probably James's first real friend and remained about his person to the end of his reign through a long series of unexacting ecclesiastical preferments which left him at the last Master of the Hospital of St Cross. He must have added a note of humanity to James's upbringing, but it was Buchanan who set the tone and between them they made the King into an infant prodigy. 'They gar me speik Latin,' he was to say later, 'ar I could speik Scottis'. From the age of four onwards he was subjected to a terrifying scholastic régime, morning and afternoon, of Bible reading and exposition, Latin and Greek, geography and astronomy, dialectic and modern languages. Already at the age of six Sir Henry Killigrew, visiting Stirling to report to Elizabeth on the progress of the child whom she would never admit to be her heir, found him 'a very toward Prince of his age both in wit and person'. Two years later, in 1574, Killigrew came again and wrote the celebrated description which, considering how distasteful it must have been to Elizabeth to hear the child praised, can scarcely have been exaggerated: of how James 'was able, extempore (which he did before me) to read a chapter of the Bible out of Latin into French and out of French into English as well as few men could have added anything to his translation'. Killigrew even found praise for James's physique and gracefulness, which is more surprising, since the King's face was to remain slightly pitted all his life from an early attack of smallpox, and inept treatment to rickets had left him permanently weak in the legs and incapable of graceful or dignified movement.

James certainly absorbed with ease as much formal learning as Buchanan cared to teach him. He was to grow not merely into the most learned sovereign, but one of the most learned men in Europe. King Henry IV of France might gibe later, with a backhanded allusion to the rumours about Rizzio, at 'Solomon, the son of David', and laugh over James as 'the wisest fool in Christendom'. But the learning was genuine enough and salted with a sour, crabbed kind of wit which, also, he probably owed to Buchanan. Dialectically, and especially in Latin, he could hold his own with any man. He could write competent verse in English, French, or Latin, and good, homely, pithy prose. To Peter Young he probably owed the wider mass of his unorganized knowledge of history and mythology, geography and medicine, which was so typical of the age in which he lived. Strange new worlds were still opening up to the sixteenth-century European; fiction was no stranger than fact, and a miscellaneous jumble of undifferentiated knowledge, true and false, of birds and reptiles and monsters in the New World, of strange foreign customs and foreign history, of ancient history and biblical history, herbalism and witchcraft, formed part of the intellectual equipment of any educated man of the period. James, having a better mind and memory than most, accumulated more than most. Peter Young was busy building up a library at Stirling round the nucleus of books left behind by Queen Mary; and *Aesop's Fables* in English, the *History of Ingland, Scotland and Ireland* 'in twa faire volumes', and the *Songs of Pantagruel* agreeably diversified the more solid reading favoured by Buchanan.

This, then, was one legacy of the upbringing at Stirling: an immense learning and a brain trained to think clearly and commonsensically, but in strictly academic terms. James was equipped to profess several different subjects at any university. On paper and in theory he could seldom go astray. But there was no room left in his mind for assessing the irrationalities of human behaviour or the necessary compromises of politics. Furthermore, his physical ineptitude led him to place an exaggerated value on these academic virtues in which alone he could really excel. The education designed for him by the Estates of Scotland in 1569 was not entirely bookish. He was given companions near his own age to share his outdoor amusements as well as his studies: John, son of the Regent, Mar, who succeeded his father in the Earldom at the age of eleven; John Murray, a nephew of Lady Mar; and a distant kinsman, Walter Stuart. In the ordinary garden games of the castle, in wrestling and martial exercises, he could not stand up to them, and that probably accounts for his early and life-long passion for hunting. On a horse he was fearless and could hold his own with anybody, in spite of a loose seat in the saddle and poor hands; and almost every early portrait of him that exists shows him with a hawk on his wrist.

With the twin passions for book-learning and hunting there went a number of psychological complications harder to analyse and in the long run of even more decisive importance in the history of his life. At the root of these lay a direct and painful conflict of feeling about his mother. The true facts of his mother's behaviour during her last year on the throne were not easy for a child to swallow. He was instructed not only in them, but in every lying slander her enemies had been able to invent about her as well. Buchanan was busy in those early years assembling them all for publication in his *Detectio* and naturally enough he passed them on. As soon as he could understand anything, James understood that his mother was an adulteress and a murderess; and it was not long before he grasped that it was because she was so that he was King. Any attempt that Mary made to bridge the gulf from her imprisonment—as she put it to Elizabeth, 'to remind him of his afflicted mother'—was ruthlessly suppressed. She had sent him in the first year of her exile an ABC and a pony complete with saddle and bridle, but because the loving letter that went with them was addressed to 'my dear son, James Charles, Prince of Scotland', and not to the King, they were never given to him. Two years later the Parliament at Stirling decreed formally that there should be no contact between the King and his mother save through the Council, and that was that. No feeling of tenderness, of pity, or regret was ever allowed to penetrate to the boy in his artificial orphanhood to modify his feelings about his mother.

On the other hand James was very soon old enough and shrewd enough to see that vilification of his mother pushed too far dishonoured him too. The slanderous rumours and bawdy songs about Mary and Rizzio still haunted the taverns of Scotland. James would have had to be much more insensitive than he was not to be aware that doubts about his paternity were one of the stock private jokes of the European Courts, and as late as 1600 he was to hear an angry Perth mob shouting up at the windows of Ruthven House: 'Come down, thou son of Seigneur Davie, come down.' So, alongside with the desire to believe about his mother everything that justified her exile and so kept him a King, there grew up in his mind an almost equally strong desire to have her vindicated. So long as Mary remained alive in England, a constant threat on the one hand to his hopes of the English succession and even to his sovereignty in Scotland, and on the other a standing reproach to his manhood and filial duty, this painful conflict continued. Only when her head was off could she become 'that poor lady, my mother'; and then he would grasp at any fact which suggested that the Casket Letters were forged and welcome eagerly any man who set out to prove Mary guiltless of Darnley's murder. He could afford sympathy then without injuring himself or his precious kingship.

This feeling about his own kingship was perhaps the most important of all the elements in James's make-up and lay at the core of all his thinking and feeling from the moment that he could think at all. He was, after all, a very lonely, loveless little boy. The affection and mild cosseting of Lady Mar could not make up for the absent mother or compensate the harshness of Buchanan's remorseless syllabus, and he had none of the easy, athletic success of a boy among boys which might have focused his interests and affections outside himself. Inevitably he was driven secretively in upon himself, and everything which hap-

41

pened to him intensified the process. The passionate pursuit of the learning at which alone he could excel was one compensation for his awkward, ungraceful sense of physical shortcoming. A great preoccupation with athletic beauty and strength in other young men was another, less healthy one. But the supreme consolation for everything he lacked lay in his kingship. The intense self-centredness which was to become his most dominating characteristic had its root in the importance which everybody else attached to his person and the kingship which it embodied. He was never really given the chance to love anybody better than himself. Even at the age of four his presence could add something of authority to the Parliament of loud-voiced, frightening, swashbuckling lords. Without him they would find it difficult to keep out his mother and her friends. It was to protect him that the castle was guarded and the windows barred. It was his person that raiders wished to kidnap.

Buchanan was one of the earliest believers in a theory of constitutional monarchy, and in his book, *De Jure Regni apud Scotos*, dedicated to his pupil, King James, he developed a surprisingly modern conception of the duties and responsibilities of a king whose power was held as a trust from the people he governed. On one occasion at least he was goaded into a more practical demonstration of the limitations of sovereignty, and when Lady Mar reproached him for flogging 'the Lord's Anointed' he retorted brutally: 'Madam, I have whipped his arse. You can kiss it if you like.' But all his theories conflicted with the facts of life as James could observe them around him. Kingship was the mysterious quality which made his person so important to everybody; and that was not the doing of the people, but of God. The preservation of himself and of that kingship by fair means or foul, became the first object of his life, too. Helpless in the grip of forces which he only gradually came to understand, the object of bewildering, frightening raids and plots, he learned to trust nobody entirely, to keep his thoughts deeply and darkly to himself, and to preserve his skin at all costs and by guile, since God had denied him the physical qualities to outface the savage, unruly men whom he was called upon to govern.

The peaceful days of unbroken education at Stirling which followed the death of Mar came to an abrupt end in 1578. For six years Morton had maintained himself in power, amassing lands and private wealth, annexing the properties of defeated enemies and pillaging the remaining endowments of the old Church on a scale unprecedented even in Scotland. On the whole he governed well; and it was this, rather than his predatory greed, which started his sometime friends combining against him. As his authority as Regent weakened he decided that he could only retain power if he could get possession of the 12-year-old King, formally resign the Regency, and rule directly in James's name. But his plot miscarried. Alexander Erskine, the Master of Mar, who had succeeded his brother as the King's guardian, refused to allow Morton's armed followers into the castle, and he had to see James alone; and when he dangled before the awkward, fidgety boy the suggestion that he should come to Edinburgh and take over the power which the weary Regent was longing to resign, James was noncommittal. His tacit refusal of Morton's invitation and the fact that he immediately passed on to Erskine and the Earls of Argyll and Atholl the news that Morton wished to retire are the first hint of independent thought and action on James's part. Certainly, if he really intended to supplant Morton, he was for the moment brilliantly successful. A formidable body of discontented nobles gathered round the two Earls and called on Morton to keep his word and lay down the Regency; and since Erskine was on their side, it was they who could now speak in the King's name. So important was the propaganda value of that, even in that land of nebulous authority, Morton dared not make a fight of it, gave in, and retired to Lochleven to take up landscape gardening. The 12-year-old boy became officially the ruler of his own country, and was formally installed at the head of his Council table on March 8th, 1578.

But the triumph of the new gang was short-lived. Since possession of the King's person was now the clue to power, Morton set himself to secure it. He worked skilfully on the hurt vanity of the young Earl of Mar, James's old playmate, to persuade him that it was he who should, as head of the family, have the custody of Stirling Castle and of the person of the King. It was easy for Mar to install himself in the castle and then to stage a *coup de main*. Once again James was woken in the small hours by the clash of arms and a shouting and trampling in the castle courtyard and, hearing that Erskine, whom he loved, was being attacked, rushed down shouting to know who had killed the Master. The Master, in fact, was not killed, though his son was trampled to death in the confusion, and he was shut out of his own castle. Morton rode over at once to take possession of the trump card Mar had snatched for him from his enemies' hand and in the King's name resumed the government of Scotland. There was a brief flurry of threatened civil war. The malcontents turned out the Edinburgh citizens under a banner depicting a boy behind bars, with the motto, 'Liberty I crave and cannot have it'; and Morton began to raise an army. But Elizabeth's ambassador, Sir Robert Bowes, intervened with offers of mediation and some substantial bribes, and a solution was patched up which left Morton still effectually in power and James relegated once again to the background and a resumption of his education.

So yet again circumstance had offered James the same dangerous set of lessons: that royalty carried some magical authority within itself; that no man was wholly trustworthy; that secrecy and double-dealing were the only means of self-preservation. Unfortunately in sixteenth-century Scotland they were valid lessons. Even George Buchanan figured, to the tune of £100, on Lord Burleigh's list of Scottish nobles and gentlemen to be bribed in the English interest; and the only one of James's entourage to refuse Burleigh's money was the last on the list, Mr. Peter Young, schoolmaster, who rejected £30. These sudden obtrusions of violence into James's life, undermining his self-confidence and shattering his nerves, were to recur with almost monotonous regularity over the next twenty years, accentuating his timorousness, the deviousness of his mental processes, and, as he gradually established his authority in the teeth of his nobles, his vanity. Only a very clever king, he would think, could have survived it all.

But before the next political upheaval occurred there arrived in Scotland a man who was radically to alter the whole situation and to transform James's whole life, Esmé Stuart, Sieur d'Aubigny. The Lennox Stuarts had for nearly two centuries held lands and titles on both sides of the Channel and as soldiers and diplomats had given rather more distinguished service to the Kings of France than to Scotland. Esmé was a nephew of the old Regent, Lennox, brought up wholly in France, but now by Darnley's death, save for a childless and ineffectual uncle, the last male representative of his line in both countries. His arrival in Scotland in September of 1579 may have been partly to re-establish the family's Scottish position. But it was also something politically far more important—a last attempt to restore the old French influence in Scotland and to save Scottish Catholicism before it was too late. For the past ten years a handful of noisy and assertive ministers of the Kirk, allied with a body of powerful and unscrupulous nobles, had maintained a delusively easy ecclesiastical supremacy in a Scotland in which they in fact commanded the support of only a minority of the population. A number of causes—the remoteness of the centres of Catholic power in north and west, the difficulty of supporting even a Catholic queen who had put herself so far beyond the pale by marrying Bothwell, and, since Mary's exile, the lack of any rallying point—had contributed to the eclipse of Scottish Catholicism. Most important of all, Elizabeth of England, to whom the emergence of an independent, Protestant Scotland was a vital national interest, had intervened constantly and effectively with money and troops to paralyse all Mary's efforts towards national unity and to maintain her enemies in their precarious power. France, meanwhile, to whom the other party would traditionally have looked for support, had herself been helpless in the throes of intermittent religious civil war.

Catholicism in Scotland had thus gone, as it were, by default. The lands of the old Church had been seized and four-fifths of her revenues impropriated by the Lords of the Congregation, and a Presbyterian settlement, pushed through by Knox and his powerful friends, had made the Kirk the established religion of Scotland when it could not command the support of even a majority of Scottish Protestants, who would have preferred a Church more on the lines of Elizabethan Anglicanism. Furthermore the dependence of this minority on England, though politically useful, was dangerous, since it ran counter to all Scottish nationalist tradition and even Protestant Scotsmen might be moved to resent the imprisonment of their Queen in England. The alliance with ruffians like Morton still further weakened the new Kirk's moral authority. It could find no more than 289 ministers for Scotland's thousand parishes, and there was just a chance still for the Counter Reformation in Scotland and for a revival of the 'auld alliance' with France. If James himself could be won back to the faith in which he had been baptized there was even the remoter possibility of rallying English Catholicism round an heir to the throne who would look for support to France rather than Spain.

The move was well timed, at a moment when James, at the age of 13, was just moving out into the foreground of politics. Stuart kings had always matured early, and James was preternaturally precocious. He had asserted no will of his own as yet, but Morton and the rest were finding it no longer possible to treat him merely as a chattel. At that juncture any influence established over him might be decisive—even permanent; and Esmé Stuart was perfectly equipped for the task. In his middle thirties, tall and red-bearded, good looking and well made as any man had to be to establish himself at all seriously in James's affections, he and his train of twenty gentlemen brought with them what proved far more important—the atmosphere and all the glamour of a high and courtly civilization. The cultured amenities of Stirling were few. Four fiddlers had been appointed to the establishment by the Estates as a pathetic remnant of Mary's efforts to soften the grimness of her northern kingdom; and there had been echoes of a fine Renaissance civilization even in Buchanan's bleak instruction. But Esmé Stuart and his friends were the thing itself, and James, temperamentally so remote from the stark and Spartan realism which satisfied most of his Scottish nobles, grasped it with both hands. A natural uncouthness of body and speech was to debar him all his life from looking and behaving as he would have wished. It was that, above all, which made him enjoy it so keenly, and even adore it, in others. He fell upon d'Aubigny in a passion of hero worship which transformed his entire life. In return he was treated with a courtly respect, a charm and deference in sharp contrast to the gruff, more than half contemptuous minimum of good manners shown him by Morton and his friends. For the first time he was made to feel that he really was a King, not merely as a sort of talisman to be produced when needed to checkmate the designs of rebellious or hostile nobles, but as a person whose wishes and tastes and ideas were matters of importance to all. From the moment of his arrival there was no doubt of the success of the first part of d'Aubigny's task: the captivation of the young King was instantaneous and complete.

By trying to make use of James for their own ends Morton and his friends had released a force which already they could not entirely control. They had taught him that he had power and authority of his own and it was now impossible, without a major political crisis, to prevent him from using them. Step by step they had to acquiesce in d'Aubigny's rapid advancement, distasteful though it was to them. He was provided with a solid endowment from the Hamilton lands forfeited after Mary's final downfall. He was given the Earldom of Lennox in 1580, his uncle Robert being induced to stand down from it in exchange for that of March. He became Governor of Dumbarton, the gateway to France and strategically the most important castle in Scotland; and eventually he was to become a Duke—apart from Bothwell, the first Scotland had ever had outside the Princes of the Blood. But these were only belated recognitions of a triumph long since secure. Within a fortnight of his arrival James made a state entry into Edinburgh and d'Aubigny rode at his bridle, an acknowledged favourite. The boy continually hung upon his arm or leant on his shoulder, fiddled with his rich clothes and jewels and listened open-mouthed to the worldly wisdom and wit of the Court of France. New worlds were opened up for him. For the first time in his life he was being treated really like a King and encouraged to behave like one, and he discovered the pleasure of giving, which was to remain his greatest pleasure throughout his life and the best compensation for his secret sense of his own inadequacy.

Though the preachers were from the start suspicious of 'Papistes with great ruffs and side bellies' so close about the King, Morton seems at first to have been unaware of the political threat behind this apparently purely social visit, and to have regarded James's obsession as a boyish enthusiasm which would soon pass off; a result, merely, of 'the flexible nature of the King in these tender years'. For a year Morton had been managing James easily. He had been, as a contemporary put it, 'always starkest about the King'. He under-estimated the devastating effect of the contrast between his uncouthness and d'Aubigny's polish, and he misunderstood James's nature which was in some respects not flexible at all. In any case Morton was launched on a policy from which he could not draw back. He had pushed the King into the forefront as the figurehead for his own power and policies; it was too late now to cancel the state entry into Edinburgh and all the celebrations and restore a Regency. The Privy Council had ordered a whole new wardrobe for the King: velvet breeches and doublets laced with gold and silver, red nightgowns of figured velvet, and a complete set of linen. The craft guilds of Edinburgh had prepared their displays and rehearsed their rather crude pageants. Mr Lawson was polishing up the sermon he was to preach before the King in St Giles's on the text, 'Be wise now therefore, O ye kings; be instructed, ye judges of the earth', and the city fathers had had a set of silver keys made and a cupboard of plate worth 6,000 marks. So James must be allowed now to ride from Stirling through Linlithgow and round Edinburgh to Holyrood, attended by 2,000 horsemen and almost every nobleman in Scotland and to enter Edinburgh on October 17th for his first visit since he was a baby. The climax of all was a Parliament at which all the world could see the King on his throne, formally responsible henceforth for the government of his kingdom.

Throughout 1580 the holiday atmosphere continued. James stayed for a little at Holyrood, blissfully happy trying to convert the new Earl of Lennox to his own Calvinism, and Lennox was clever enough to allow himself some formal instruction in Protestant belief and so temporarily still the clamour of the preachers. In the summer they went on a Progress round Scotland together and then returned to Stirling. Meanwhile the situation between Morton and Lennox slowly came to a head. Elizabeth and Burleigh were the first to take alarm at the thought of Scotland drifting back into the French camp. The Queen wrote to James hinting for the first time at the possibility of his succeeding her in England, and advising him 'rather to fear for his ambition than to comfort and delight his affection'. She wrote to Morton, too, suggesting that he should 'lay violent hands' on Lennox, and she sent Bowes north again to galvanize the Protestant lords into some effective action. But Morton was very slow to realize the urgency of his danger. In a secret midnight interview he confided to Bowes that the King was beginning 'to commend and be contented to hear the praises of France', and no longer confided in himself and his friends. In a letter redolent of the conspiratorial atmosphere which pervaded all Scottish politics Bowes passed on the further suggestion that it might be well to have a guard about the King and a hint that the English government might pay for it. By delaying a little longer Morton hoped to panic Elizabeth into paying for his protective measures, and that meanness was his undoing. He was still haggling when Lennox struck. While he talked Lennox had already provided the King with a hand-picked guard of gentlemen pensioners captained by James Stuart of Ochiltree, an attractive, unscrupulous careerist whom the King had already marked down for advancement. It was he who, on December 31st, 1580, 'belled the cat', breaking in upon a Council meeting to denounce Morton on the old charge which so many had found impossible to answer, of being 'art and part' of Darnley's murder. After a furious scene a majority of the Council voted Morton's imprisonment, and to make assurance double sure they transferred him to Dumbarton.

Too late Elizabeth began to spend the money she had re-fused. She sent Lord Hunsdon to the Border with 2,000 men and Randolph as special ambassador to denounce Lennox to the Scottish Estates. But in his new-found strength and inde-pendence James outfaced her. He, too, sent troops to the Bor-der. He promoted Ochiltree Earl of Arran; and on June 1st, 1581, Morton was tried and condemned in Edinburgh and executed the next day. His Douglas kinsmen under the Earl of Angus had plotted half-heartedly to save him and he was mourned by a few ministers of the Kirk. But a lifetime of treachery and brutality had left him with few friends and there were not many who shared his own confidently expressed belief as he mounted the scaffold that he was 'entering into the felicity of Almighty God'.

There followed a curious year of highly unreal politics which was for James probably the happiest of his life. All power was concentrated in the hands of Lennox and Arran, while he hunted and amused himself and left what he called 'auld men's cummer' to them. He began to write poetry and he had long theological arguments with Lennox, each seeking to convert the other. Lennox meanwhile launched simultaneously all the large schemes he had brought over from France, as though, by a few strokes of the pen, he could reverse the whole trend of Scottish

49   D

history. The Duke of Guise was to land a French army in England. Lennox himself would lead the Scottish Catholic Earls south and the English Catholics would rise. Mary would be set free, James would turn Catholic, and would agree to reign jointly with his mother. Even the Spaniards were to co-operate by landing some troops in Scotland. Meanwhile, as a step in the right direction, bishops were to be introduced into the Kirk to supplant the Presbyterian system of government. Amidst such dangerous nonsense as this any real chance there might have been for a Catholic revival in Scotland disappeared. Lennox's plans took no account of the European rivalry of France and Spain. They assumed that his own power was now absolute and permanent, though it was based on nothing more dependable than the doting favour of a sixteen-year-old King, and he ignored the forces which had broken Mary Stuart and would much more easily break him. There was not even the slightest chance that James would change his religion or, if he really understood the issue, consent to share his throne with his mother.

The end came abruptly in the summer of 1582. The Kirk had never really ceased its rumbling complaints of Catholic influences about the King. It now came thunderously into the open, and in July presented to James a set of articles denouncing his neglect of the true Church, his traffic with France, and his reliance on 'bloody murtherers and persecutors'. Meanwhile, as the effective mechanism of the revolt behind the propaganda of the pulpit, there was the usual 'band' of discontented nobles grouped round Morton's nephew, Angus, and held together largely by English bribes. Like Morton a year before, Lennox seems to have miscalculated the strength and pace of the mounting opposition, and foolishly he let go of the only card in his hand—his actual possession of the person of the King. James, contemptuous of the rumours of plots, deluded by the ease of his triumph at Christmas and overconfident in the efficacy of his newfound royalty, went off on his own to hunt with the Earl of Gowrie at Huntingtower. There on the morning of August 22nd he found himself a prisoner, and in the bitterly humiliating scene which followed his education really was completed. Mar and Gowrie took the lead, presenting a list of grievances which James tried to ignore. But when he tried to make his way out of the castle the Master of Glamis put his leg across the doorstep and told him roughly to stay where he was. In the crisis his kingship failed him and he burst into tears. 'Better bairns greet than bearded men,' Glamis said contemptuously. But it was in fact the last time that James would behave like a child, and his vow to be revenged should have warned them that it was rage, not fear, that inspired the tears.

So the King's three-year idyll with Esmé Stuart came to an end. Arran riding foolishly and alone to the King's rescue was captured the same morning, and without him or the King Lennox was powerless. He had no party; his attempts at a counter-kidnapping of the King failed; and all his grandiose plans were shown up for the flimsy, paper daydreams they were. Sitting in an Edinburgh window he had to watch a great procession of ministers and citizens welcoming back the preacher, John Durie, whom he had induced James to banish three months before; and as the words of the 124th Psalm—'If the Lord himself had not been on our side when men rose up against us, they had swallowed us up quick'—floated up to him it is recorded that he 'rave his beard for anger'. There was little else he could do, and in December, at the urgent request of the King who feared, quite rightly, for his life, he went back to France. James never forgot him. But he never saw him again.

CHAPTER III

James VI of Scotland

*

The Raid of Ruthven left James in what Sir Robert Bowes rather inadequately described as 'a ticklish situation'. He was once again powerless in the hands of a Protestant, pro-English faction of lords, treated indeed with reasonable respect, but trailed round with them and so closely watched and guarded that when Henry Gibbe of his Bedchamber had a secret message from Lennox to deliver it was only in the privacy of the close stool that he could do so; and all that James dared answer to Lennox was to tell him to send no more dangerous messages. But a curious—to the modern mind almost incomprehensible —set of conventions governed this kidnapping of the person of the King. It was, in the minds of the kidnappers at least, very far from being a rebellion. Almost it was a legitimate method of securing the theoretical source of authority and excluding rivals from power. But if it was to be effective it demanded some measure of co-operation between kidnappers and kidnapped. The illusion, at least, had to be created that the King had voluntarily accepted what had been imposed upon him. Unless he lent them something of his authority they could make no use of it; and to get it they had perforce to allow him some liberty of action.

Once woken from the daydream world which Lennox had created for him, James quickly learnt the basic conditions which governed all political action in sixteenth-century Scotland and saw how they could gradually be turned to his advantage. At sixteen he was intellectually mature, and his intellect was first class. For the next twenty years he was to apply it consistently and industriously to the single task of emancipating himself and his kingly authority from the forces which sought to control them. The central fact which he had to face was that he had

almost no real power of his own. The Crown, as such, had
neither the money nor the established administrative institutions to attempt an independent, centralized autocracy. Its
authority at any given moment depended on the allegiance it
could command. On the other hand, all the forces which would
dispute control with the Crown were curiously well balanced:
wherever he looked, James saw alternative forms of the same
tyranny. Every faction among his nobles inevitably provoked
a counter-faction anxious to substitute their own control for
that of the party in power. Two Churches claimed his allegiance,
each of which asserted a spiritual authority which could ultimately override all temporal power. Closely tied to the religious and political groupings within Scotland were two alternative foreign policies. The Protestant nobles and the Kirk
would tie Scotland to an English alliance and subordinate all
Scottish interests to the necessities of England's almost solitary
struggle with Counter-Reformation Europe. The Catholic
Earls offered equally dangerous entanglements with France or
Spain and a strong possibility of war with England. And for
James all these dilemmas were personally and poignantly fused in
the rival claims of the two queens whose heir he was: Mary who
commanded more and more the loyalty of Catholic Scotland as
the memory of her actual mismanagement receded, who would
involve him in the web of her ceaseless plotting with France
and Spain and Rome, and who would offer no more in the event
of her emancipation than an 'association' with her on the Scottish throne in which, clearly, he would be the junior and ineffectual partner; or Elizabeth whose ambassador was an active
partner in every Scottish Protestant plot, who intransigently
demanded his collaboration in all her Continental policy with a
root and branch Reformation in Scotland which might well provoke civil war, and offered in return a half promise of the
English succession.

In assessing James's handling of the problems thus presented
to him it is difficult for the historian to remember that these
were all still doubtful issues. In 1582 it was very far from clear
that the Presbyterianism of the Kirk was to establish itself
overwhelmingly in Scotland. There was no knowing that the
flood tide of the Counter-Reformation would be halted in
Northern Europe, that the Dutch would keep Philip II out, that

English Catholicism was a spent force, and that a combination of courage, seamanship, and luck with the weather would destroy the Great Armada. James never wavered in his personal adherence to Protestant belief. But he had to frame his policy if he could so that he would not be irretrievably ruined if one of his mother's many plots succeeded; if Elizabeth were assassinated, or if Philip II successfully invaded England. He needed to retain the loyalty of Catholic Scotland and a claim on the support of the English Catholics, whose real numbers nobody could accurately guess, without losing that of the more obvious Protestant allies. Furthermore, only by committing himself to neither side and by holding all the various opposed forces in some sort of precarious balance could he retain any freedom of action for himself. To him two objects only were of paramount importance. One was to establish his authority in Scotland independently of all parties, all religions, and all foreign pressure. The other was to ensure that, whatever happened, he should succeed to the throne of England. To these ends he would sacrifice every principle and use every means that came to hand, Catholic or Protestant. He had, if possible, to use everybody and be used by none.

It was a remarkable achievement for a boy of sixteen in the situation in which James found himself after the Raid of Ruthven to formulate in one year of semi-captivity principles on which he was able to base his actions with increasing success for the next twenty. Nevertheless the total effect of that year on his whole character and his future development was disastrous. In the first place it accentuated his always latent inferiority complex. He revealed his bitter sense of humiliation at the armed guard of Gowrie supporters who accompanied him everywhere to old Sir James Melville in a diatribe against his 'hard estate and mishandling by his own subjects', which must make his neighbour princes 'think him but a beast for suffering so many indignities'. He would never forget, he told Bowes later, how 'greatly wounded' his honour had been. By nature he was a gentle, peace-loving, friendly soul. But thenceforward any threat to his kingship, any calling in question of his sovereignty or attempt to impose on him an alien will would bring out in him not only an irrational self-assertiveness, but also at times a streak of vindictive cruelty which were beyond his own control.

It accentuated, too, his natural secretiveness. He learnt to trust nobody, to keep his thoughts and intentions wholly to himself, to speak most fair when he meant to act with a tigerish malignancy, to match double-dealing with double-dealing, and to move always obliquely and tortuously towards an objective. Policy, which demanded a foot always in both camps, brought out this habit of crooked dealing even more, until it became settled and instinctive. He ceased to be capable of straightforward thought or action, and concealed his inmost thoughts so skilfully that in many cases they have remained an enigma ever since.

He perceived and exploited the weaknesses of the Gowrie raiders so cleverly that he was free of them within a year. In the first place the ceaseless accompanying and guarding of the King was exacting, tedious, and very expensive. In spite of Bowes's pleas to her, Elizabeth refused to pay for it all, and inevitably, with James apparently so docile and resigned, the watching slackened off. The King was thus able to get in touch with the remnants of his mother's partisans: young Huntly, of whom he became extremely fond, Montrose and Seton, and his elderly, ineffectual uncle, the Earl of March. Gowrie and his friends made the same mistake as Lennox had before them: in June of 1583 they let James go off hunting on his own. A message from March that he had some fresh meat for a banquet which would not keep in the summer weather gave the King an excuse to ride suddenly to St Andrews to eat it, and though Gowrie followed hard, he was too late to stop him getting among his friends. There were a day and a night of tension typical of so many incidents in Scottish history, with St Andrews Castle full of the armed supporters of both sides, and both ready for a murderous riot, though neither anxious to take the blame for starting one. Then Gowrie's nerve broke. He reconciled himself to the King on condition that all should be forgotten and forgiven, and on the morning of June 28th James was able to announce to his assembled nobles that he was now free of all faction and intended to rule henceforth as a 'universall king'. Already Sir Robert Bowes had ruefully to report that freedom from faction meant freedom also from English dictation at home or abroad. There was, he wrote, a 'great alteration both in his mind and also in his face and countenance'. He added resentfully that James now kept the key of the box containing his private papers himself, so that he could not 'get any certainty of the contents'. All Elizabeth's pungent letters and a special embassy led by her ailing Secretary of State, Sir Francis Walsingham, would not alter the fact that Scotland now had an independent King with a mind of his own, 'a dissembling King,' Walsingham wrote angrily, 'both with God and man'. But he was wrong when he added that James would not last long.

That is not to say that James had sailed into calm water. In the next ten years he was to face two separate and major crises, one at home, the other abroad: the one a threat to his Scottish sovereignty; the other to his chances of the English inheritance. The major Scottish crisis was precipitated by the claim to a universal sovereignty in temporal as well as spiritual matters by the Kirk, under the leadership of Andrew Melville, on whom the mantle and a double portion of the spirit of Knox had descended. The external crisis would centre round his mother. Burleigh and Walsingham were determined at last to induce Elizabeth to put an end to the perpetual danger which Mary represented as the focus of every plot at home and abroad. When it came to acquiescing or not in his mother's execution it would no longer be possible for James to avoid taking a side, dearly though he would have liked to run with the hare and hunt with the hounds a little longer. Meanwhile, as the permanent background to these major issues, there were still the factions and rivalries of the undisciplined nobility threatening to engulf once more the precious freedom of action won at St Andrews.

Lennox was dead and all that James could do for him was to fetch his 10-year-old son, Ludovick, over from France to be brought up in high favour at his own Court. For the rest he recalled Arran, for whom he had not the same fondness, but who was a tough soldier and a capable administrator, and had most of the qualities the King admired but himself lacked. Arran also had a capable, if greedy, wife, who was accused of witchcraft and deeply hated by the preachers, and to the pair of them James left the government of Scotland, while he hunted and wrote poetry. In 1584 his first published work appeared anonymously in Edinburgh: *The Essayes of a Prentice in the Divine Art of Poesie*. The poetry itself was allegorical, classical, and uninspired, with an occasional vivid line; and the attached treatise on

The Reulis and Cautchis to be observit and eschewit in Scottis Poesie was an interesting foretaste of so many of James's later writings and speeches: a mixture of pedantry and platitude with flashes of homely and devastating common sense. What made the whole a lot more tolerable than most of his later work was a youthful diffidence which admitted that his was a 'dull Muse', and rather engagingly in one sonnet begged the reader:

> *'These, my first fruits, despise them not at all.*
> *Who wots, but these may able be indeed*
> *Of finer Poems the beginnings small.'*

But inevitably this peaceable interlude was short. No man could exercise the sort of power Arran had in Scotland undisturbed for long. There was an attempt to repeat the Raid of Ruthven in April, 1584, by some of the same men, which the competent and soldierly Arran easily frustrated. Gowrie this time was executed. Angus, Mar, and the Master of Glamis had to fly to England, and even some of the more outspoken ministers took refuge in Berwick. But the attempt was repeated again in the autumn of 1585 with powerful English backing. Arran was too tainted with the Catholicizing, French traditions of the Lennox régime to be acceptable to Elizabeth; and with the affairs of Mary Stuart moving to their inevitable crisis she was determined to get James for once out into the open and on her side. 'Who seeketh two strings to one bow,' she wrote to him, 'they may shoot strong, but never straight.' As a more effective method than writing critical letters she 'let slip' Angus, Mar, and Glamis across the Border at a moment when Arran's power was already shaken by the rise of a new young man to influence —Patrick, Master of Gray. There was the usual bewildering scene, this time in Stirling Castle, where Gray and Arran and their rival gangs confronted each other in the King's presence, but neither dared to strike because each 'suspected falsehood in friendship' and feared to trust his own side. The issue was settled by the arrival in the town of the exiles from England with the powerful support of the new Earl of Bothwell, nephew of Mary's lover and already, with his ramifying Border power, one of Scotland's major problems. Arran's nerve broke and he fled to the west to live and die in obscurity, leaving the King apparently once again the prisoner of the old Gowrie faction.

But it was not the same. For one thing there is some reason to suppose that James was himself alarmed by Arran's over-mighty position and had secretly encouraged Gray. For another he had already shown his teeth over Gowrie's execution, and the exiled Earls were thankful enough to get back their lands with a free pardon for the past. The King emerged still more or less his own master and with one added advantage: Arran's withdrawal left the way clear for the promotion of John Maitland of Thirlstane to the vacant Chancellorship, and for the first time James was provided with a competent statesman to manage his affairs.

All the statesmanship in the world would not, however, enable James to avoid the choice which he had to make in 1586. The start of the year found him still negotiating with both sides: writing desultorily to Mary of the terms on which an 'association' might be acceptable, and hanging out feelers in London with a view to a pension and some formal recognition of his position as 'second person' in regard to the English Crown. But the English government was forcing the pace. The assassination of William the Silent, the leader of the Dutch Protestant revolt, had shown that Catholic plots were something more than just paper games with which Mary might keep herself amused in captivity. Open war between England and Spain had taken the place of the unofficial hostilities of the past fifteen years; and Walsingham, with his hands already on the threads of the Babington Conspiracy, was only waiting to get written proof of Mary's approval of the plan to murder Elizabeth to make his final effort to bring her to trial and execution. In the looming crisis a hostile Scotland would be an intolerable complication. 'Scotland,' Walsingham wrote to Leicester a little later, 'is altogether neglected, whence all our mischief is like to come, where the employment of 2,000 men by the enemy with some portion of treasure may more annoy us than 30,000 men landed in any part of this realm.' And James had already, by implication, made up his mind. As John Colville said, though he seemed 'not to have lost all affection to his Mother . . . yet (as those about him will speak) hee had rather have hir as shee is, then him self to give hir place'. Moreover the English Parliament's Act of Association of 1584 had explicitly disqualified from the English succession anybody who took armed action in

Mary's favour; and anyway, under the semi-compulsion of the faction which had with English help just ousted Arran from power, James, if he chose at all, could only choose the Protestant cause.

So the preliminaries of the treaty which Sir William Knollys and Thomas Randolph came north to negotiate were signed with surprising speed on April 1st. There were some valuable commercial concessions to the Scots, a pension of £4,000 a year for James, and a promise from Elizabeth not to prejudice his claim to the English throne without due cause. Further than that she would not go, but it was far enough. James abruptly broke off all correspondence with his mother, telling her he was now compelled to refuse 'to associate her with himself in the sovereignty of Scotland', and that he could not in future 'treat with her otherwise than as Queen-Mother'. Mary, who had vowed to 'die a Queen of Scotland', was driven by this dissipation of her last daydream into just the state of despair that Walsingham needed. Her 'ungrateful son', if he persevered in 'the heresy of Calvin', was to be cut out of all rights in her succession, which were to pass to Philip of Spain, who was at least prepared to take active steps to set her free. By this act she precipitated the European crisis, since Philip could now push boldly on with the building of the Armada without feeling that he would be merely feathering the nest for a Calvinist Scot whose hereditary allegiance would be to France rather than to Spain. At the same time she sealed her own doom by furnishing Walsingham with all the proofs he needed that she had sanctioned Babington's assassination plans. In August he gathered in the conspirators, arrested Mary's secretaries, and sequestered her papers. On October 11th she was brought to trial at Fotheringay, and at the end of that month James heard the almost incredible and highly unwelcome news that his mother had been condemned to death.

There seems no doubt that the situation which burst upon James in the autumn of 1586 came as a severe shock. He had no idea in the spring that he was signing away his mother's life for a pension of £4,000 a year. As late as October he was assuring the French Ambassador that his mother was 'in no danger'. He added that 'as for the conspiracy, she must be content to drink the ale she has brewed'. He still could not believe at Christmas that Elizabeth seriously meant to cut off Mary's head. But there

was no impulse of pity or generosity or pride in the pitiable protests and entreaties which he sent south to Elizabeth and to the
ambassadors who were trying to save Mary's life. There was
acute misery that he should be forced to appear in public in his
true colours as a son who would acquiesce in his mother's
execution rather than risk his own inheritance; acute fear that
the rising tide of anger in Scotland, even among his Protestant
nobles, would either endanger his position there or force him
to some action which would cut him out of the English succession; and anxiety lest Mary, by forfeiting her own rights,
might have already compromised his 'title'. All that he really
did was to beg Elizabeth to spare Mary because she would
otherwise place him in an intolerable position.

The first formal protest he addressed to Elizabeth was dignified and straightforward enough, remarking how strange it
seemed to him that 'the nobility and counsellors of England
should take upon them to sentence a Queen of Scotland'. 'I
desire you to consider,' he ended up, 'how my honour stands
engaged, that is her son and a King, to suffer my mother an
absolute Princess to be put to an infamous death'. But when he
talked of his honour James meant only that he wanted his face
saved for him. 'Guess ye,' he wrote to Archibald Douglas, one
of the men who had helped Bothwell to murder his father, and
now his representative in London, 'in what state my honour
will be in, this unhap being perfected; since before God I already
scarcely dare go abroad for crying out of the whole people.
And what is spoken by them of the Queen of England it grieves
me to hear, and yet dare not find fault with it except I would
dethrone myself, so is the whole of Scotland incensed with this
matter.' Douglas was told to show that letter to Elizabeth;
and James's letter of December 15th to the Earl of Leicester
was even more explicit: 'How fonde and inconstant I were if I
should preferre my mother to the title let all men judge'.

There were two Scottish delegations in London working
nominally to save Mary's life from December, 1586, until the
following February. The special, more formal one, consisting
of the Master of Gray and Sir Robert Melville, almost certainly
worked quite honestly to that end. Gray was one of the problem figures of the period: handsome, intelligent, and elegant,
and treacherous in the manner rather of the Italian high Renais-

sance than of the cruder Scottish feudatory. He fascinated James and he betrayed at different times everybody who trusted him. But he had a redeeming charm and a debonair courage which had also captivated Sir Philip Sidney, and on this occasion at least he seems to have put up an honest fight for Mary's life. But he and Melville could move Elizabeth by none of their arguments and pleas. At the end of a long interview Gray pleaded for a fifteen-day respite and was refused. Then, he wrote in his own despatch, 'Sir Robert craved for only eight days; she said not for an hour; and so geid her away'. The two might have achieved a greater success if the ground had not been cut from under their feet by the other two, more private, emissaries, Archibald Douglas and Sir Alexander Stuart. It was they who reassured the Queen that James would 'with tyme digest the worst'. James was furious when he heard of this and vowed to hang Stuart before he put off his boots. But Stuart was right and Elizabeth knew it. James's protests never went further than asking Elizabeth to spare Mary as a piece of policy and a kindness to him. It was, he wrote, 'my freindlie advyce, but my earnest suite'. No fear of James but her own private misgivings made Elizabeth hesitate to sign Mary's death warrant until February, and then so contrive the matter that the blame could be thrown on Mr Secretary Davison and she could refer to the execution of the Queen of Scots as 'that miserable accident'.

By then James had known for a month what the end would be and had been fighting a dour battle with the ministers of the Kirk to induce them to pray for his mother. A Mr John Cowper actually defied him to his face from the pulpit and had to be pulled down, protesting that he spoke as the Spirit of God moved him, prophesying woe on all who lived in Edinburgh and that that day would be 'a witness against the King in the great day of the Lord'. In the end they agreed to pray for a limited objective only: that Mary Stuart 'should become a profitable member of Christ's Kirk'. The Scots nobility and the people at large reacted violently as to a national insult from a neighbour state which had plagued and harried Scotland for three hundred years. When James announced his intention of mourning in 'dule weid of purple', even Francis Bothwell, most unprincipled of Border magnates, answered that his only 'dule

JAMES VI OF SCOTLAND

weid' should be a suit of armour until the Queen of Scots was avenged. But it was all frothy talk. It started a process of romanticization from which the memory of Mary Stuart has never since been entirely free. But James had only really to save his face. Nobody in Scotland seriously expected a gallant gesture on behalf of his wounded honour.

There was, though, a brief pause in Anglo-Scottish relations. James refused to let Sir Robert Carey, who brought the official news, come beyond Berwick, where he was met by Peter Young; and he 'wes in great displeasour and went to bed without supper', retiring for the next few weeks to be 'solitar' at Dalkeith. Then the old relationship was renewed. Once clear of the entanglement of the 'uncouth, unkindly murder' of his mother—'yon unhappy fact' he called it—James could happily resume his old game of committing himself irretrievably to nobody. He kept an ambassador, the Archbishop of Glasgow, with the King of France and the Guises, but prudently refrained from signing or dating his appointment. At the same time he royally entertained the Huguenot poet, du Bartas, some of whose work he had translated, and he allowed Sir James Colville of Easter Wemyss to raise a Protestant company for service with Henry of Navarre.

As far as England went, his only fixed intention was to make friends with everybody there who could usefully support his claim to the succession, the payment of his pension, and his desire to recover the English lands of the Lennox family which Elizabeth had annexed. For the rest, he meant to keep in with Elizabeth, but not to let her dictate his policy nor for her sake to give up Catholic contacts which might yet prove valuable. On the whole he was throughout the 1590s successful in these limited objectives. His pension was very irregularly and unpunctually paid, but he got something most years and on average, from 1586 to 1603, about £3,000 a year. Walsingham and Burleigh favoured his claim as a matter of Protestant principle. Leicester was trickier, since he was tempted at times to support the Earl of Huntingdon's claim by descent from Edward IV; and after Leicester's death Essex, with his spectacular capacity for going splendidly astray, was trickier still. There was a very difficult year in 1588, when James thought it prudent to make secret and half-hearted arrangements for joint action with

Spain, though at the same time guaranteeing Elizabeth's northern frontier. He tried, naturally, to sell his friendship to her dearly, and screwed out of William Ashby, her special envoy, not only £2,000 in cash, but large promises of an augmented pension, an English dukedom, and formal recognition as Elizabeth's heir. But Elizabeth paid him in his own coin, and as soon as the Armada was safely dispersed repudiated Ashby's promises on the grounds that he had exceeded his instructions. But on the whole foreign affairs receded into the background after the crisis of 1586–8. The more immediate problem became the restoration of royal authority in Scotland on which all hope of the English inheritance would ultimately depend.

That is not to say that James was henceforward free of English interference in what he might have regarded as his private Scottish concerns. To earn his pension he had to submit to ceaseless interference, and Elizabeth considered that her grudging half-admission that he was her heir gave her the right to bombard him with letters of tart good advice, and to take offence when the advice was ignored. The humiliating thing was that he could not live at all reasonably without the pension, and that in certain cases he had to have additional sums to help him out, which also had to be earned. One such crisis occurred almost immediately after the Armada over his decision to get married. Tentative negotiations had been going on since 1585, both with the Danes for one of their two princesses, and with Henry of Navarre, who had an eligible sister, Catherine de Bourbon. For various reasons Elizabeth strongly backed Catherine, but by 1589 she had in fact dropped almost out of the running: her miniature had not proved alluring; there were rumours that she was 'old and crooked and somewhat worse if all were known', and that her dowry was already all spent; and there were riots against a French match in Edinburgh where the Danes had valuable trading contacts. So, after some show of hesitation, James plumped for Anne, the younger daughter of King Frederick of Denmark, and was married to her by proxy. Scottish resources would not run to a proper establishment for a young married king, and Elizabeth had to help out in a hurry at the last moment with plate. 'It is now time to give proof of affection,' James wrote to Burleigh. 'No hours nor days must be lost, for tempus deals most straitly with me'; and he got £2,000 worth of plate and £1,000 in cash.

Elizabeth was furious with him again in the autumn of 1589 when, his bride having been driven back by storms on the way over, James impetuously decided to go over himself to fetch her. It was in fact a rash thing to do, apart from the dangers of North Sea gales. Two years before he had made a strange and characteristic attempt to pacify his kingdom by healing all the feuds among the nobility. He invited all his lords to what was ostensibly a twenty-first birthday party at Holyrood. There, having made them all drink three pledges to eternal friendship, he delighted Edinburgh with a procession of the entire nobility of Scotland walking two by two, each man with his most notorious enemy, to take their dessert at tables laid out by the Mercat Cross amid fireworks and a lavish distribution of free wine. It was a grotesque and not unlovable gesture, but quite ineffectual in a country where private war was a settled habit, and its failure had already been amply demonstrated before James set sail for Denmark. There were two unsuccessful 'bands' to get Maitland out of office—always a popular objective—in 1588; and in the following spring there was almost a major rising. The Catholic Earls, Huntly and Errol and others, were caught in a treasonable correspondence planning to bring Parma over from the Netherlands with 6,000 men as a prelude to a joint invasion of England. James called out his feudal levies and dealt with them with surprising efficiency. He invaded the north in April before Bothwell, who was to have raised his Borderers as a distraction, could get going, and, after a surprising display of personal energy in the teeth of some very bad Highland weather, forced the Earls to come to terms with him at the Brig o' Dee, near Aberdeen. They were very lenient terms. James had a great weakness still for Huntly, and had not yet learnt to hate Bothwell. He also had no desire to quarrel irretrievably with his Catholic subjects whatever Elizabeth might say. But clearly they were none of them trustworthy subjects to leave, even for the twenty days which was all James was proposing to spend on his wooing, under the precarious authority of an improvised Regency.

Elizabeth made a great fuss, warned her Wardens of the Marches to stand by for trouble, and sent Bowes north again to

QUEEN ANNE OF DENMARK
From a miniature by Isaac Oliver

hold the Protestant interest together against a possible Catholic *coup de main*, but there was no need. Government was left in the hands of a Privy Council in which authority was so intricately shared out among the most dangerous nobles on both sides that they all acted as automatic checks on each other. Provided that no positive action was required, it was an admirable system and kept Scotland quiet very well. There was in addition a formal Declaration by the King addressed to all his subjects which showed how young and naïve he still really was in spite of his intellectual precocity. He set forth at length his reasons for going, insisting that it was himself and not Maitland who had made the decision, lest they should think him, as he put it, 'an irresolute ass who can do nothing for himself'. He told them to 'live a peaceable and quiet life without offending of any', and promised to be back within twenty days.

In point of fact he was away for the whole winter. He reached the Norwegian coast in five days and a fortnight later, after 200 miles of hard winter cross-country going, entered Oslo. Just a month after leaving Leith he was married to Anne by Mr David Lindsey, whom he had brought with him for the purpose lest there be any grumbling from the Kirk; and, having already overstayed his promised twenty days, should have sailed straight home. His Chancellor, Maitland, was already fidgety at the thought of what might be going on in Scotland in their absence and was anyway anxious to get the couple away before they started spending Anne's dowry in riotous living. But James was never able to make any sustained effort. His achievement in getting himself uprooted from Scotland and across the North Sea and now safely married had required from him an altogether unusual energy and pertinacity, and his instinct was to relax and leave the tiresome threads of Scottish government to be picked up later; so they went on to Copenhagen for the winter where his new brother-in-law, the twelve-year-old Christian IV, already set a tremendous pace in hospitality. They did a lot of hunting. There was entertaining company and more intelligent conversation than was normally to be had in Scotland; and James made one delightful and informative excursion to go over the observatory which King Frederick II had built at Uranienborg for the greatest astronomer of the day, Tycho Brahe—an occasion which he celebrated in three indifferent poems. But predominantly they ate and drank. Mr. David Lindsey summed up the whole three months' visit in his diary in one terse, disapproving sentence: 'Our King made good cheer and drank stoutly till the spring time'; and even James admitted in one of his letters home that they were 'as is our custom drinking and driving ower in the old manner'.

It is impossible to tell whether at this stage the marriage was proving the success of which James had dreamed. He had gone about the whole business very solemnly in the first place, retiring with the miniatures of the rival princesses for a fortnight of meditation and prayer before making up his mind, and working himself into an imaginary love-sick fever during the long waiting when Anne was hourly expected and never came. He wrote to her as 'his dearest love', and described himself in sonnets as frying 'in flames of that envenomed dart'.

> *'The fever hath infected every part*
> *My bones are dried, their marrow melts away,*
> *My sinnews feebles through my smoking smart,*
> *And all my blood as in a pan doth play,*
> *I only wish for ease of all my pain,*
> *That she might wit what sorrow I sustain.'*

These were, of course, but the imaginings of a young man who had never yet loved a woman and only knew the sort of love he wrote and dreamed of from books and poetry. The decision itself to go romantically off over the sea to fetch his bride sprang from romance poetry and smacked of Quixote rather than practical politics or serious passion. But all these show, with a certain pathos, what a dangerous amount of emotional stock James was investing in this so far untried relationship. There had been no women in his life save Lady Minny, the old Countess of Mar; and she, it was said, had been 'wise and sharp and held the King in great awe'. Worse still, there had been little or no love. He had lavished on Esmé Stuart and on his lesser friends—Gray, Huntly and Bothwell— a great store of pent-up affection which had been inadequately, if at all, returned. All the hunger for the comfort and love and cosseting and kindness which had been left out of his childhood and had failed to reach him in adolescence was packed into the demand he was making of marriage. Only a very exceptional girl could have met it, and something more than the ordinary disillusionment of high romance inevitably struck James when he descended from sonnets and daydreams to reality.

For Anne was in no way exceptional. She was fair, blue-eyed, and pretty, well educated, and with all the proper accomplishments of a princess. She liked hunting and dancing and dressing up and acting, was perhaps a little self-indulgent about food and drink, and was more than normally fond of gossip and intrigue. She was cheerful and affectionate and made, in fact, a perfectly good ordinary wife. But she had neither the character nor the intellect to deal with the special needs of James, who was very far from being an ordinary husband. She had not the wit to see where and how he needed buttressing against a mocking, hostile world, and she lacked the strength to do so if she had. She could not wrap him in the warmth of a great passion, and she could never become what he had dreamt of and needed so badly all his life, the one person with whom he could share his inmost secrets. On the other hand, in view of the mass of oddity which James landed on her, with his mixture of timidity and self-assertiveness, his physical awkwardness and his psychological twists, she did very well indeed to succeed in making him a good, ordinary wife. All things considered, they settled down remarkably well and, as Bishop Goodman was to say later, 'did live together as well as man and wife could do, not conversing together'. James never looked at any other woman, and though there were occasional whispers about Anne's behaviour, she seems in fact never to have gone further than the mildest of flirtations with the better-looking of her husband's courtiers. She tolerated, though not always patiently, his extraordinary relationships with good-looking young men, and even accepted his requirement later on that she should introduce them to him and intercede for their advancement.

How far James was aware of any personal disappointment it is impossible to tell. Certainly in the course of the next ten years there was to be a sad loss of spiritual vitality. But for the moment he derived great pleasure from bringing back to Scotland so presentable a bride to justify his winter escapade, and one who was already rumoured to be with child. They were received at Leith on May 1st, 1590, with the maximum pomp and circumstance Scotland was capable of, including, for the sake of the

Danes who loved them, some exceptionally loud discharges of artillery. The all-round political truce which had held Scotland in an unnatural calm all through the winter lasted for the ceremonial entry into Edinburgh and for Anne's coronation, which was also as ceremonial as James could make it. There was a brisk row with the Kirk over his determination that she should be anointed as Queen, but his threat to call in one of the few surviving Scottish Bishops to do it if the ministers refused, coupled with the argument that there were sound Old Testament precedents for holy oil, carried the day; and all was done as the King wished. The first and last great adventure of James's life was over, and he settled back to the old game of trying to establish his personal authority with wholly inadequate means; to playing off powerful nobles and rival Churches and foreign powers one against the other; and to the long, dreary wait for Elizabeth's death and the opportunities of a more glorious inheritance.

CHAPTER IV

Crisis and Final Triumph in Scotland

*

In the perspective of history it is easy to see that the defeat of the Armada was a turning point, not only in the fortunes of England, but for the whole of Northern Europe. To understand the behaviour of the rulers and statesmen in the following ten years, however, it is necessary to remember that it did not seem so at the time. For contemporaries the Armada was an episode: the beginning rather than the end of a long struggle in which the chances of the northern, Protestant powers often seemed to be getting not better, but worse. Try as they would, the Elizabethan seamen and soldiers could not reproduce the triumphs which had culminated in 1588. In 1596 Spain assembled a fleet every bit as formidable as the Invincible Armada which, but for its providential dispersal in a great storm, would have caught the English extremely disorganized and unprepared. All politics in the north had to be conducted under the shadow of this far from empty threat. It trebled Elizabeth's anxieties about her 'northern postern'. It made James's chance of securing the English succession, which was gradually obsessing his mind to the exclusion of all else, very much trickier and less of a certainty than it now appears to the historian; and it alone makes comprehensible the Catholic pipe-dreams: the serious canvassing of King Philip's own claim to the English throne by descent from Edward III; the alternative of transferring that claim to the Infanta Isabella and her Habsburg husband who ruled the Netherlands; the hopes entertained even by Pope Clement VIII that James might be frightened by these threats into becoming a Catholic himself. Inevitably it coloured all James's policy at home and abroad.

After the promising beginnings of the Armada period, when it had seemed that something like an independent royal power was again emerging in Scotland in spite of the Protestant lords, James's reign appeared, during the years from 1590 to 1596, likely to end after all in a fiasco. The surface of politics was dominated by a final climax of feudal disorder, in which the feuds and intrigues of the Catholic Earls, Huntly, Errol and Angus, played their part, but the centre of the stage was taken throughout by Francis Stuart-Hepburn, Earl of Bothwell. This remarkable young man, nephew both to Mary Stuart and her second husband, and also to the Regent Moray, would appear to have been quite unbalanced. He certainly had the family brains and charm. At one stage in his complicated and chaotic career, he found himself for a few nights the guest of the Bishop of Durham, the shrewd and entertaining Tobie Mathew, who wrote him an excellent testimonial. 'The noble man hath a wonderfull wit, and as wonderfull a volubilitie of tongue, as habilitie and agilitie of bodie on horse or foote; competently learned in the Latine, well languaged in the French and Italian; much delighted in poetrie, and of a very resolute disposition, both to do and to suffer; nothing daintie to discover his humour or anie good qualitie he hath'. These were the qualities which had at first captivated James and brought him into high favour during the period that followed the fall of Lennox. He was, moreover, officially a Protestant and therefore something of a hero to the Kirk, which could not afford to be over careful in its choice of political champions. But he was quite unprincipled and wholly irresponsible. He earned in the end the vindictive hatred of James by trampling ruthlessly on what little personal dignity he possessed; and there seems no doubt that he had sold himself to the devil and was one of the central figures in the witchcraft cult which hung always obscurely in the background of Reformation Scotland.

An implicit faith in the powers of evil and the efficacy of black magic, a real and abiding terror of witches, were an unexpected and not very easily explicable by-product of a religious upheaval which in all other respects was dedicated to the triumph of reason. The anomaly can be seen in its clearest form in James himself, whose well-trained, rational mind and clear common sense were accompanied and at times entirely overlaid by the crudest of superstitious fears. He regarded his book on Demonology, published in 1598, as one of his most important contributions to knowledge, and it makes clear that where the black arts were concerned there was a complete suspension of his intellect. On the subject of witchcraft he would believe anything, and its terrors continually haunted his mind, fusing and concentrating all his childhood fears and becoming at times almost an obsessional mania. Towards the end of his life he was to admit some doubts, but chiefly on the question of the actual prevalence of witchcraft, and on the grounds that the evidence for it always and unavoidably rested on confessions of unbalanced and deluded persons, generally wrung from them under torture or the threat of it. This last consideration still makes it extraordinarily difficult to decide how widespread the witch cult was. It seems certainly true that there was a considerable increase of it in Northern Europe towards the end of the sixteenth century and that it was worse in Scotland than elsewhere. It was not just a question of village gossip and weak-witted old women ill-wishing their neighbours' cows, but of an organized pagan cult, celebrated in midnight orgies by covens of men and women who believed that they had sold their souls to the devil. It penetrated every class. It seems indisputable that the Ruthven family dabbled in it for generations, and Bothwell was undoubtedly in it up to the neck, though how much and what he believed about it it is impossible to say.

Whatever may be said of the importance of this so-called 'Dianic Cult' in sixteenth- and seventeenth-century Scotland, its political consequences are undeniable and were sometimes important. It vitiated James's relations with the tainted Ruthvens, and it actually touched off his major troubles with Bothwell in 1591. That year was the climax of one of Scotland's major witch hunts. The Kirk, of course, was more or less continuously engaged in seeking out and persecuting the unclean thing. But soon after he got back from Denmark James was drawn to take a direct interest in the campaign by persistent rumours that the exceptional storms which had prevented his bride from crossing the North Sea in the autumn had been provoked by a widespread conspiracy of witchcraft with its centre in East Lothian. For nearly a year he worked at little else but 'the sifting out of them that were guilty', gripped in a sort of fascinated horror which drew him to attend some of the more important examinations in person, and to make one of the

71

self-confessed witches, a maidservant from Tranent called Geilie Duncan, play over to him the tunes she had piped for the Kirk-yard dances on All Hallows' Night at North Berwick. In all some thirty-nine people were involved, some of them educated and of some standing in the world, and it appeared that there had been three or more organized covens working against the King and his marriage with all the usual apparatus: a toad hanged and roasted to extract its venom and a cat flung into the sea with suitable incantations to raise the storm; magical practices upon the King's bed linen that he and it might waste away together; and finally, of course, the waxen image of James which should be melted slowly in the fire to consume him in agony.

Even when all allowance is made for the natural boastfulness which goes with the insanity of black magic and the distortions of confessions extracted by torture, there seems no doubt that something of the sort had actually been going on and that Bothwell himself was at the centre of it as the leader of one of the most important covens of witches at North Berwick, where there had been abominable ceremonies in and around the Kirk at nights. What is much more difficult to believe is that James, along with all the most intelligent Protestant ministers, not only believed in the facts, but in the efficacy of the charms. If James could seriously think that he and the Queen had been in real peril of their lives, it is quite easy to believe that Bothwell, all of whose behaviour was a little mad anyway, thought so too, and quite probable that the waxen image really was passed from hand to hand in North Berwick Kirk, each saying in turn, 'This is King James the Sixth, ordained to be consumed at the instance of a noble man, Francis, Earl of Bothwell.' It is true, of course, that James never lost his native shrewdness even in the grip of the wildest superstition and was conscious always of the entirely practical and seditious intentions which lay behind the imponderables of Bothwell's sorceries. One of those arrested as ringleaders, Barbara Napier, had the luck to be acquitted, and escaped being 'put into a great fire' with the rest of them, and James in fury had the jurors arrested and tried for a false verdict. The address which he delivered to them showed clearly the mixture in his mind of common sense and a mild insanity. 'We are taught,' he told them, 'by the laws both of God and man that this sin is most odious; called Maleficium or Veneficium, an ill deed or a poisonable deed; and punishable likewise by death. As for them who think these witchcrafts to be but fantasies, I remit them to be catechized and instructed in these most evident points.' But he went on to analyse quite plainly the legal and political evil that sprang from the corrupting of juries and witnesses by powerful men and from the fact that in Scotland all men would stand by their friends against the law. 'This corruption here bairns suck at the pap,' he said, and announced his intention of rooting it out, 'not because I am James Stuart and can command so many thousands of men, but because God hath made me a king and judge, to judge righteous judgements'.

He made a bad start, however, in his campaign to root out evil in high places by letting Bothwell escape from Edinburgh Castle in 1591, and for the next five years lived in continual danger from the raids of that impossible young man. Bothwell stood for no cause or principle, but merely wanted the King to pardon him and to drive the over-powerful and efficient Chancellor, Maitland, from office so that he might continue to behave as intolerably as he pleased in his Border semi-independence. Without a standing army and with few dependable friends, the King was extremely vulnerable. At Christmas, 1591, Bothwell broke into Holyrood one night at the head of a band of 'murderers and broken men' and all but seized the King in the first rush. But both James and Maitland found refuges in locked towers, the din turned the city out, and dawn showed eight of Bothwell's Borderers hanging in front of the Palace. But Bothwell was away, and the royal household was forced to move for safety into cramped lodgings at the top of the town, under the shelter of the Castle guns. In a sonnet written to commemorate his Master Stabler, John Shaw, who had been killed that night defending the Palace, James wrote that he minded 'with deeds, and not with words to pay'. But it was easier written than done. He went after Bothwell courageously enough—a bleak January chase through the Border country in the course of which he fell into the Tyne—and failed to catch him. Bothwell had too many friends on both sides of the Border and was anyway a tougher campaigner than James.

So the intolerable, humiliating situation continued. In June of the following year Bothwell tried again, in a midnight attack on Falkland, and James had to stand a seven-hour siege before help arrived. When Scotland became too hot to hold him, the Earl simply crossed the Border, certain of Elizabeth's tacit approval whatever her official instructions to her Wardens of the Marches, flaunting his independence quite openly, as James bitterly complained, at race meetings and football matches and accepting invitations to card parties with the English Border gentry. In the summer of 1593 he came again, and this time successfully. He had banded together almost all the leading Stuarts—Lennox, Atholl and Ochiltree—and Lady Atholl let them into Holyrood in the early morning of July 24th. James was trapped, half dressed, in his closet and found himself in the most humiliating situation of his entire life. He had to make terms, to pacify the citizens of Edinburgh, reassure the Danish ambassador, dismiss his friends from Court and pretend to the world that it was by his own wish that he moved about surrounded by a mob of Bothwell's armed ruffians. Bothwell was brought to trial for his witchcraft in August and, not surprisingly in the circumstances, acquitted. The outlawry three times proclaimed against him from the Mercat Cross was annulled. He assured Elizabeth, whom he addressed as 'Most Renowned Empress', that with her continued help he was confident that he could 'manage the estate about the King', and even talked of becoming Lord Lieutenant of Scotland.

It was the old kidnapping game, successfully played for the last time in Scottish history, and as always it suffered from its own essential limitations. Against Bothwell, England and the Kirk, James could play the Catholics and all Bothwell's personal enemies. Lennox and Mar were easily detached from the conspiracy, and in due course the King slipped away from a Parliament at Stirling to Lochleven, returned with an armed force sufficient to restore his authority, and banished Bothwell once again. Even then it was not the end, for Bothwell reappeared in April in an attempt to capture Edinburgh. But this time Elizabeth had limited her help to a mere £400 and his forces were inadequate. James was ready and waiting for him and was able in addition to turn out 1,000 of the Edinburgh citizens and three of the great cannons from the Castle. Against such a force Bothwell was helpless. After a short engagement which cost the King's forces but twelve men killed he disbanded his army and withdrew again to England, where he was promptly disavowed by Elizabeth.

While Bothwell and his Borderers thus mocked the King's authority in the south, he was in almost equal difficulties with Huntly and the Highland Catholics. It is true that Huntly did not harry him personally as Bothwell did and retained in consequence James's personal affection however badly he behaved. But there were other complications. Huntly and Errol were in close and continuous touch with Spain, even in 1590 when they had not yet been formally pardoned for their last escapade which had ended at the Brig o' Dee. Lord Worcester, when he came north that year, with a belated wedding present, to confer on James the Order of the Garter, also brought some of Huntly's intercepted treasonable correspondence. In spite of this, James formally pardoned him in December, 1590, and was very ill-rewarded for his generosity. For two months later Huntly, pursuing his family's vendetta against the Stuarts, staged one of Scotland's most celebrated and spectacular murders—that of the Earl of Moray at Donibristle Castle, just across the Forth from Edinburgh. Moray was a striking creature, the Bonny Earl of the famous ballad, 'comely, gentle, brave, and of a great stature and strength of body', a Protestant and something of a hero to the Kirk, and a friend of Bothwell's. He was probably privy to the unsuccessful Christmas raid on Holyrood and had concentrated on himself at that time a good deal of enmity. The King disliked him, as he disliked anybody who had anything to do with 'that bastard', his uncle the late Regent; and rumour and legend have given him another cause for dislike by coupling the Earl's name with that of the Queen, though there is no evidence to support this. There is some evidence that Maitland coveted some Moray lands and had procured a warrant for Huntly to arrest him as a Bothwell partisan. The main fact is at any rate clear. On February 7th, 1591, Huntly, with an escort of forty horsemen, accompanied the King out hunting. On the way he rode suddenly up to James and asked leave to pursue some accomplices of Bothwell's who were reported in the neighbourhood. Having got it he crossed to Queensferry and made for Donibristle. Moray and his clansmen held the castle against them all that day, but in the evening the Gordons piled corn stooks against the house and fired it. Moray left his sally too late, for as he came out behind the stream of survivors who poured from the castle the plume of his helmet and his hair caught fire and made him a certain mark as he fled to the river. Huntly himself struck the last blow at him with his dagger at his face, and earned from the dying man a sneer that has become immortal. 'Ye have spoilt,' Moray told him, 'a better face than your own.'

In itself this was but a typical episode in any one of a hundred Highland feuds of the past four centuries, and James would have preferred to shrug it off as such. He was a callous young man already when his affections were not directly involved. He did not care for Moray. He liked Huntly and he badly needed his northern strength to counterbalance both Bothwell and the Kirk. But this was not an incident which could be ignored or hushed up. The flames of Donibristle could be seen across the river, marking the spot where a popular hero of the Kirk was being martyred by Scotland's leading Papist. Moray and his dead friends lay in state in Leith Church and his bloodstained shirt went round the Highlands on a spear to start another clan war. His mother theatrically demanded vengeance, giving James a picture of her murdered son and a bullet taken from his body; and when Huntly voluntarily warded himself at Blackness and was almost immediately released untried a howl went up from the pulpits, the Edinburgh mob rioted, and Maitland was forced for a while to withdraw from Court altogether. 'Since your passing from here,' James wrote to Huntly, 'I have been in such danger and peril of my life as since I was born I was never in the like, partly by the grudging and tumults of the people, and partly by the exclamation of the Ministry whereby I was moved to dissemble.' Dissemble as he would, he could not avoid the suspicion that he himself had been privy to the murder, and dark stories circulated which have never been proved or disproved of how Ochiltree, riding to his kinsman's rescue, found the ferry barred by the King's order to all save the Earl of Huntly. Elizabeth of course wrote to point the moral, on which she had been harping ever since the Brig o' Dee, that no good ever came of clemency shown to Catholics, and one of the minor penalties James had to pay for tolerating Huntly as a counterpoise to Bothwell was a steady worsening of his relations with England. He wrote peevishly to Elizabeth about his pension, that she was not 'contente as frielie to pay it as frielie ye promisit it', and his protests about the unofficial help given to Bothwell were ignored. It was a further disadvantage that Bothwell, as a kinsman of Moray, was given a cause to fight for and the whole-hearted support of the Kirk in fighting for it. But worst of all was the surrender which James had to make to the Kirk. Under the leadership of Andrew Melville the extremist Presbyterians were now deliberately trying to set up a domination of the Church over the State. Hitherto they had been partially restrained by what they called the Black Acts of 1584 which prohibited 'treasonable, seditious, and contumelious speichis' from the pulpit, forbade Church Assemblies without the King's permission, and any challenge by the ministers to the 'dignitie and authoritie' of the three Estates. Thanks to the stampede of public opinion against him after Moray's murder, the King was obliged to let Parliament repeal these last safeguards of his own sovereignty and to pass the 'Golden Act' which established the annual General Assembly of the Kirk independently of the King as the governing body of the national church and abolished the ecclesiastical jurisdiction of bishops. This in the long run represented a much more serious threat to his kingship than Huntly and Bothwell together.

Even so James was not at the end of the price he had to pay for his lenience to Huntly. At the end of 1592 he was brought hurrying back from some wild Christmas festivities with Mar to deal with a more serious Catholic plot: the affair of the Spanish Blanks. It had been hatched by some of the wilder of the Jesuits, one Father James Gordon and a Father Crichton, and was just the sort of thing which Walsingham had always feared: a project to land 30,000 Spaniards from the Netherlands, of whom 4,000 were to stay to help establish Catholic control in Scotland, while the remainder marched south against England. Since it contained no arrangements for securing the Narrow Seas during the passage of the army from Belgium the immediate danger of such a plan was slight. But the Catholic messenger, one Kerr, who was captured with the plans had also blank papers signed by Huntly, Angus, Errol, and Sir Patrick Gordon of Auchindoun committing them to nobody knew what. Even worse, there was a paper in Kerr's packet in James's

77

handwriting in which he discussed the merits of such a project as an incidental means of getting his English throne and which, although it was quite in accord with his general policy of keeping a hold on all Catholic support possible inside Scotland and out, took some explaining away. In any case, to keep his pension and Elizabeth's good will he had to make some showing against the plotters once they were discovered, and there was another futile campaign in the north, in which James got as far as Aberdeen and hanged a few unimportant folk, but failed to catch any of the Earls, who went into hiding in Caithness.

By the winter of 1593–4 it really seemed as if James's policy of playing off the rival parties and religions had brought him to complete disaster. Shuttled to and fro by the openly Catholic plottings of Huntly and his friends and the so-called Protestant raids of Bothwell, his authority had been so diminished that it now seemed negligible. For Elizabeth the issues and dangers were as clear and straightforward as the critical dangers which she herself confronted. Spain was rearming. The Protestant champion in France, Henry of Navarre, had just joined the Catholic Church as the only means of reuniting his kingdom, and Ireland was in revolt. The only hope was for James to co-operate with her in stamping out the last remnants of a seditious Catholicism in Great Britain and so present a united front to the Spanish threat. It exasperated her beyond measure that James tolerated the barefaced plotting of Huntly and Angus and Errol, and when he wrote to her to tell her that by an Act of Abolition he had virtually pardoned the Catholic Earls on condition of their conforming outwardly to the Kirk, she wrote back that she doubted 'whether shame or sorrow have had the upper hand when I read your last lines to me'. Her treacherous subsidizing of Bothwell, and even her occasional intrigues with the Catholic Earls themselves, she would have justified by the absolute necessity of maintaining a pro-English party in Scotland. Bothwell, she told James, when she heard of the Spanish Blanks, was at least a better proposition than Huntly and his pro-Spanish friends.

For personal reasons alone James rejected this last suggestion out of hand. He would rather, he told Elizabeth, 'be a slave in the turkes galles' than make friends with Bothwell. In spite of all apparent failure he stuck doggedly to his policy of preserving the Catholic power as the only safeguard against the alliance of the Kirk and Bothwell, which would have obliterated him altogether. Lady Huntly and Lady Errol were allowed to administer the estates which their husbands had nominally forfeited and a Scottish Parliament decided that there was insufficient evidence to bring the Earls to trial for treason. Thus through the early months of 1594 James's situation looked very critical indeed, and it was weakened rather than strengthened by the birth at Stirling in February of his eldest son, Henry. Though the possession of an heir improved his eligibility for the throne of England, it opened up fresh possibilities to every plotter in Scotland: another objective for kidnapping plots, and an alternative source of authority which might be used against him as he in his babyhood had been used against his mother. It also seriously complicated his domestic life. So soon as she had settled down in her new home and accustomed herself to the astonishing vicissitudes of royal existence in the barbaric north, Queen Anne had developed an unexpected taste for political intrigue, and to James's extreme displeasure had been involved in all the recent combinations against Maitland. Now James's decision that his son should be brought up like himself by old Lady Minny in the comparative seclusion of Stirling Castle and under the guardianship of his old play-fellow, Mar, gave Anne a real grievance and a focus for all her plots.

Part of the Queen's grievance was genuine enough. Most mothers would find it intolerable to be separated from an only son and deprived of any say in his upbringing. But that was a hardship queens often had to accept, and in any case James believed, undoubtedly with truth, that Anne had an ulterior motive. She had looked forward to the custody of Prince Henry as an asset which would bring her into the centre of the political stage and give her the importance which James had so far firmly denied her. Apart from all other considerations, this was one thing James was quite determined to avoid. Anne had strong prejudices, no scruples, and very little intelligence, and the more remote she was kept from politics the better. As custodian of the Prince she might be tempted to all sorts of dangerous madness. So James stood firm against all her stormings and entreaties. He was curiously convinced that Mar, who had often enough shown himself undependable, would on this one important matter prove entirely trustworthy; and he gave him formal written instructions whose terms show clearly what dangers he had in mind: 'Otherwise for any charge or message that can come from me, you shall not deliver him. And in case God call me at any time, see that neither for the Queen nor the Estates their pleasure you deliver him till he be eighteen years of age, and that he command you himself.' In her rage Anne even made common cause with Maitland, who could see fine opportunities for himself if, through the Queen, he could also hold in his hand the heir of England and Scotland. But James never wavered. Maitland died, and Anne was left raging and plotting against Mar, which she continued to do for the next eight years.

Prince Henry's christening gave James one brief interlude in the political crisis in which he now lived almost continuously. First he had to silence Elizabeth who had the impertinence to write, at a moment when half his difficulties were of her making, deploring 'the evident spectacle of a reduced king, abusing council, and wry-guided kingdom'. For once James did exactly the right thing: retorted with 'a round plainness', nailing down in clear terms all her double dealing over Bothwell, and then asked her to stand godmother. It worked very well. Elizabeth, all smiles and graciousness, promised a rich present and at last sharply forbade Bothwell to 'show banner, blow trumpet, or in any way live or breathe in England'. That once settled, James plunged happily into an orgy of the sort of spending he most enjoyed, designed to make a splash with foreign visitors. There was to be jousting with a good deal of incidental pageantry, and a banquet accompanied by masque-like conceits which were to make artistic history. James supervised every detail himself, working away day after day in a way that he never did at affairs of state.

In the end the expected French ambassador never turned up, and Elizabeth was represented, owing to the illness of Lord Cumberland, only by the young and quite unsophisticated Earl of Sussex who was, perhaps, too easily impressed. But James gave the assembled nobility of Scotland and the citizens of Stirling a very good show. It was too much to expect that the unathletic King should take the prize for running at the ring and glove in the tournament yard, but the victory of Lennox,

JAMES VI OF SCOTLAND SHORTLY BEFORE HIS ACCESSION
TO THE THRONE OF ENGLAND
Artist unknown, probably German

Scotland's only duke, was the next best thing. The actual christening was scarcely less ceremonial and colourful than James's own twenty-eight years before, including to the fury of the ministers an anointing with holy oil by the Bishop of Aberdeen. And the stage machinery for the serving of dessert at the banquet that evening really does seem to have been remarkable. There was a great chariot, twelve feet long and seven feet broad, apparently drawn by a single Moor, from which Ceres, Fecundity, Faith, Concord, Liberality and Perseverance, in silver and crimson satin, dispensed fruit; and then, to symbolize James's journey oversea to claim 'like a new Jason, his Queen', a great ship eighteen feet long and with forty-foot masts, taffeta sails and silken rigging, which discharged a salute of thirty-six cannon into the great hall of Stirling Castle before handing out fish and all kinds of shell fish 'made of sugar and most lively represented in their own shape'. After which, not perhaps entirely appropriately, the choir sang a fourteen-part harmonized version of the 128th Psalm: 'For thou shalt eat the labours of thine hands: O well is thee, and happy shalt thou be'.

This slightly pathetic display of the sort of civilized kingship for which James hankered and which in Scotland was so very difficult to achieve, was not entirely without its political importance. For the incidental consequence was that Bothwell, deprived suddenly of Elizabeth's help, could see no way to the fulfilment of his ambitions but to make common cause with the discontented Catholics of the north. This unprincipled alliance ought on the face of it to have finished James altogether, since his whole precarious survival of the past five years had depended on exploiting the enmity of Huntly and Bothwell and playing one off against the other. In point of fact it gave him the opportunity to rid himself dramatically and simultaneously of both. Still more surprisingly, he seized it energetically and successfully. For the Kirk, which had been prepared to connive at Bothwell's lawlessness and even to wink at his traffic with sorcerers and black magic, was outraged by his alliance with the Scarlet Woman of Rome, and by turning against him deprived him of the only solid support he had. James immobilized his Border strength by parcelling out his lands among his more powerful neighbours, Hume, Buccleugh, and Cassford, and demanded the immediate collaboration of the Kirk, the Lords of the Congregation, and the citizens of the Lowland burghs in an all-out assault on the Catholic Earls which, in so good a cause, he for once got wholeheartedly.

The result within six months was a startling change in the King's situation. Hitherto he had barely survived by exploiting the only two solid assets Scottish kingship possessed: a sacrosanctity of the royal person which over and over again had prevented the kidnapping plots from being crowned by assassination; and the ability to call out a feudal army for a month or two which would at least contain the forces of his immediate enemies at any given moment. Now he was to show that these assets could be exploited aggressively. On Midsummer Eve the Catholic Earls, confident in Bothwell's alliance and promises of Spanish help, held a great feast with dancing and drinking and bonfires to celebrate their coming triumph; and when Argyll moved north in October with a Protestant force 6,000 strong Huntly did in fact defeat him at Glenlivet. But it was such a hard-fought victory that it left him practically without an army, and James, actually accompanied into the field by Mr Andrew Melville in so good a cause, was able to push with another force through Dundee and scatter what resistance remained. This time, moreover, there was no halting compromise as there had been at the Brig o' Dee. Huntly's fortified stronghold at Strathbogie and Errol's in Buchan and another half-dozen Catholic fortresses were blown up, and the north for once was really broken. Without allies Bothwell was suddenly powerless: merely a 'grand traytor' with a price on his head. So by the spring of 1596 Huntly and Errol were in France, Angus in hiding in Scotland, outcast and ruined, and Bothwell was soon to set out from Paris on the aimless, impoverished wanderings round Europe which were to last until his death nearly thirty years later. In a single campaign James had destroyed two of the three forces which had hitherto paralysed his power and made a mockery of his kingship.

There remained the Kirk which, because its claims cut at the mystical authority of that very kingship on which alone James depended, was the most dangerous enemy of all. Between James who was beginning, as Bowes put it, 'in severity to rule like a king', and ministers who claimed an absolute authority for whatever the Lord might move them to say in the pulpit, a showdown was bound to come soon. It came in fact in 1596 with the return of Huntly and Errol. James, with his eye always on the English succession and the possibility that he might one day have to arm and lead a united Scotland to claim it, was bound to want them back. He would only do so if, whatever their private convictions, they were formally received into the Kirk, and this with some difficulty he achieved in the teeth of the grudging suspicions of the leading ministers. Scenting some 'further dealing of the adversary', they tried to establish a permanent Commission of the General Assembly which with the Presbytery of Edinburgh was to exercise a general supervision over the government in the interest of Christ's Kirk. It was in the course of these negotiations that there occurred the famous scene between James and Andrew Melville in which both lost their tempers and raged against each other: 'The King used his authoritie in most craibed and cholerick manner, yitt Mr Andrew boore him doune'. James, Melville told him, was 'but God's sillie vassal'.

The issue in principle was clear enough already. But wisely James waited for a concrete case for a trial of strength, and in November of the following year he was offered it. One of the most troublesome of the preachers, Dr David Black of St Andrews, preached a sermon full of seditious matter, in which he denounced all kings as 'children of the devil' and Queen Elizabeth as an atheist. Then, when summoned before the Privy Council, he refused to come. In the pulpit, he said, he was only subject to Christ's word, and answerable for that to 'the prophets', or 'the ecclesiastick senat'. James had warned the ministers against just that when he summoned Black. 'Take heed, sirs,' he had said, 'that ye decline not my judicature; if ye do so it will be the worse.' The fight was forced on him, and he proceeded with Black's trial in his absence, while the Kirk fought back with inflammatory sermons and a sinister warning that, whatever happened, they were 'free of his Majesty's blood'. The blatant threat of mob rule, and a wild Edinburgh riot centred round the 'Little Kirk' and Tolbooth in December, in which he was himself involved, gave James his excuse. His counterstroke the next day was masterly. He and the Queen and the Court, and with them the judges and lawyers and the whole official world, removed themselves from Edinburgh to

Linlithgow, and a herald at the Mercat Cross proclaimed that this was to be for good, since the town was no longer fit to live in. Nobles were ordered at the same time to withdraw to their country seats. Faced with certain ruin the city abandoned its preachers and within a fortnight James was back on his own terms. A General Assembly of the Kirk called to Perth formally withdrew the extreme claims Melville had made so arrogantly and, by accepting representation in Parliament, accepted also the authority of the secular arm in its necessary sphere. James even had the wit to exploit his victory slowly and with careful moderation. Bishops, unconsecrated still, and unmitred, but charged with administrative functions and sitting as peers in Parliament, reappeared in the Church as the King's nominees. It was the beginning of a cautious move towards conservatism in religious affairs which for a time was to prosper very well.

Thus in the nine months which followed his son's christening James emerged simultaneously from all the major perils which had threatened to engulf his authority altogether, and for the next six years there was comparative peace in Scotland. Maitland was dead, and there was no single, dominating figure beside James. Instead a group known for a time as the Octavians got to work on what was always the essential problem, the provision of an adequate revenue. They could not do very much and they did not make James rich. But by economy and improved administration they made him solvent, and even occasionally provided out of Queen Anne's revenues more money than she needed. The King was left free to turn his mind to literature, and he quickly followed up his *Demonology* with a thousand-word pamphlet called *The Trew Law of Free Monarchies*, in which he expounded that doctrine of the divine right of kings which, as he saw it, had alone saved him from the many enemies, Catholic and Presbyterian, who had been threatening his sovereignty. Finally there was the *Basilikon Doron*, the book dedicated to his infant son, into which he tried to pack all the wisdom and the understanding of the art of being a king, at any rate in Scotland, that he had acquired in sixteen complicated years; and since it really was written for the Prince and only accidentally fell into the hands of a wider public, it was much less self-conscious, more honest, and pleasanter to read than any other of James's published works. But even these were

only distractions from what was now the all-absorbing preoccupation of James's life: the worrying and scheming to make sure
of the English throne.

If James had only had the wit to see it, the best thing he could
do about the English succession was to let well alone; for, however men might argue, he was really the only possible candidate.
None of the Englishmen whose Plantagenet or Tudor blood
gave them any claim to consideration, Beauchamp, Derby or
Huntingdon, had the prestige, character or ambition to make
them acceptable. Arabella Stuart had a clearly worse claim than
James through the same line of descent from Margaret Tudor,
and in any case only wanted to be fetched to Court to have a
good time and did not dream of being a queen. English Catholics abroad, nourishing the exaggerations and wild hopes on
which exiles have to live, and quite out of touch with realities
in England, made serious play with the pretensions of Philip III
of Spain, either by descent, or as Mary Stuart's nominated heir,
and it was tacitly agreed that these should be vested in practice
in Philip's sister, the Infanta Isabella, who was married to the
Archduke Albert and shared with him the government of the
Netherlands. Not even Father Parsons, the Jesuit responsible
for English affairs at Rome and a strong Spanish partisan, could
visualize another King of Spain actually on the English throne.
But all the premises on which they based their plans were false.
There were far fewer Catholics in England than they thought,
and patriotism would prevent many of them from supporting a
Spaniard. The Infanta and Archduke had no wish to exchange
the comfort and security of Brussels for a wild English gamble;
and Parsons' firm belief that Sir Robert Cecil, Burleigh's son and
successor, was favouring Spain against the Scottish claim was
pure moonshine. Unless James by some major foolishness alienated both Elizabeth and her leading ministers, his succession
was a certainty.

But on this issue, such was his fever of anxiety, James was
incapable of patience. He could not let well alone, but must
ceaselessly importune Elizabeth to make a definite statement to
put him out of his misery. He revolved quite absurd schemes:
sent embassies round the Protestant courts of northern Europe
asking for armed support for his claim to 'be declared and
acknowledged the certain and undoubted successor to the

Crown'; bought war materials and asked the Scottish Parliament for money in 1600 so that he might have an army ready to enforce his claim if necessary; plagued Elizabeth, long after she had clearly made up her mind against it, to grant him the Lennox lands in England, so that he might not be debarred from inheriting as an alien. He only succeeded in provoking the English Ambassador to wonder whether he was meaning 'not to tarry upon her Majesty's death', and in making Elizabeth very angry. 'He hasteth well,' she warned him, 'that wisely can abide'; and she was prepared to assure him that she would favour his claim 'as long as he shall give no just cause of exception'. The one thing she would not do was nominate him officially and suffer the miseries of seeing her courtiers and ministers turning to the 'sun rising', as she remembered them turning to her in the last months of her sister's life.

All things considered, it is surprising that Elizabeth put up with as much as she did without taking 'just cause of exception'. James's ludicrous embassies abroad, his dabblings with Papal and Spanish agents, and his attempts to make a party for himself at her own Court were all infuriating. Still more so were his toleration of trade between her rebels in Ireland and South-west Scotland, the fact that he allowed the arch-rebel, Tyrone, to recruit Scottish troops, and that she actually caught him out exchanging letters with Tyrone. But it was during her own crisis over the Earl of Essex that James came nearest to burning his fingers fatally. The long rivalry between the Cecils and Essex, the peace party and the war party, sober statesmanship and spectacular adventure, dominated the English political world throughout the 1590s. From 1592 onwards, largely because he thought Burleigh had been responsible for holding up his pension, James had got into the habit of dealing through Essex whenever he had a cause to further at the English Court, and he counted on Essex and his friends to see him safely on to the throne when Elizabeth died. By 1599, however, the boot was on the other leg. Essex was toying with plans to oust his rivals from power by force and play against Elizabeth a version of the old Scots kidnapping game, and it was he who wanted James's support: an army, he suggested, to be prepared 'at a convenient time'. What James promised in the end nobody knows. Essex was said to wear his letter in a black bag on a string round his neck, and to have destroyed it with his other papers before surrendering, when he made his bid for power in 1601 and failed. A good deal of evidence that James had been closely in touch with Essex did in fact come to light at the examinations of Southampton and others of his friends, but Elizabeth generously suppressed it.

Then, suddenly, with the death of Essex, James found that he was in calm water over this matter of the English succession too. Inevitably he had to turn to Sir Robert Cecil, who had now no rival, and Cecil's urbane assumption that there never had been and could not be any other successor had at last the sedative effect which James so badly needed. Mar and Kinloss, the ambassadors he sent south in 1601, had instructions to be very wary of Cecil; but he penetrated their reserve and initiated with Lord Henry Howard a secret correspondence with James designed to make sure of all their futures. Only those three and the two Scots ambassadors knew of it, and it had at all costs to be kept from the Queen. It was a very tedious correspondence, packed with long-winded assurances of goodwill, but Cecil and Howard managed to slip in a good deal of sound instruction on the English political situation and how to handle it. Inevitably in that cut-throat world they spent a good deal of time and ink in discrediting their enemies with the future King: what Howard called the 'diabolical triplicity that meet every day at Durham House'—Lord Cobham, the Earl of Northumberland and Sir Walter Raleigh. But there was much sound advice too, and James was at last able, at Cecil's bidding, to stop fussing Elizabeth, 'to whose sexe and qualitye nothing is soe improper as ether needles expostulations or over much curiositye in her owne actions'. He followed 'clear and temperate courses', left it to the local experts to do what was necessary 'to prepare the vulgar beforehand', and waited quietly, if very impatiently, for the moment which now seemed inevitable.

Only one sudden, violent episode disturbed the peace which had so miraculously descended on the closing years of James's direct rule in Scotland: the Gowrie conspiracy, last of all the many kidnapping plots, and the most impenetrable of all the baffling mysteries in James's life. James's own account of the matter was that on the morning of April 2nd, 1600, as he was riding out from Falkland to hunt, Alexander, Master of

Ruthven, drew him aside with a tale of a strange, muffled man whom he and his brother, the 22-year-old Earl of Gowrie, had captured in the fields the day before with a pot of gold, and both man and gold were now locked in a room in their house at Perth and at the King's disposal. For the moment the King ignored the matter, suggesting that it was the business of the ordinary Perth magistrates, and going on with his hunt. Ruthven, however, at once sent his servant, one Henderson, back to Perth to warn Gowrie that he might expect the King and Lennox; and at eleven, when he had killed his stag, the King did in fact ride off to Perth with Lennox and Mar and a few of their gentlemen. There, in spite of the warning, no preparations had been made and there was a long pause before a very bad dinner was set before the company, while the King went off with Alexander Ruthven to a remote turret chamber, where they found Henderson already posted and wearing his armour.

All accounts of what happened after that are very confused, but it seems that Ruthven slammed the door and drew Henderson's dagger from his belt to kill the King in revenge for his father's death sixteen years before; that James argued with him so successfully that he went off to consult his brother; and that he then returned with a garter to bind the King's hands, and, crying, 'By God, sir, there is no remedy', fell upon him. Gowrie meanwhile was trying to persuade the attendant nobles that the King had already ridden away and that they must follow, and they were still arguing the matter down below when James managed to thrust his head from the turret window and shout for help. In the still wilder confusion which followed Sir John Ramsay alone was able to find a back way into the turret, stab Ruthven, and rescue the King. But the danger was not over then. Gowrie had rallied some of his servants; the Perth mob was turning out, mostly on Gowrie's behalf; there were ugly shouts of, 'Come down, thou son of Seigneur Davie, come down'; and James's friends were still entirely confused as to what was happening. Then Gowrie, too, was stabbed by Ramsay, and James and his party, having thanked God on their knees, went off to pacify the mob.

On the known facts it is impossible to determine whether what happened that day was what James made it seem; a desperate, if very clumsy attempt by the Ruthvens, tainted for generations with treason and witchcraft, to revenge their father by killing the King, or a very subtle and successful plot by James to rid himself of the Ruthvens. The first doubts of the King's version were sown by the Edinburgh ministers when they were asked to give public thanks in church for the King's merciful escape and refused, accepting the King's account of the matter as a matter of good manners only. This alone would probably account for the touchy care with which James elaborated and published his story and the fact that he insisted on a public celebration of the anniversary of the conspiracy for the rest of his life. A furious partisanship has obscured the whole issue ever since and no version of the story as it has come down seems wholly credible. As an event in history it was isolated and meaningless, without visible cause or consequence; an episode only too typical of that phase of Scottish history which was then coming to an end.

On March 24th, 1603, it did in fact end. After fighting death off for more than a week, Elizabeth died at last, and late at night on the 27th Sir Robert Carey, who had brought the news of Mary Stuart's death north sixteen years before, staggered muddied and 'be-blooded with great falls and bruises' into James's antechamber to gasp out the news. The King's ship, in Cecil's expressive phrase, 'had come into the right harbours without cross of wave or tide that could overturn a cockboat', and the problems and trials of governing Scotland receded abruptly into comparative insignificance. On April 6th a great thunder of cannon greeted James's arrival at Berwick, and it would be fourteen years before he returned for a brief visit to the land of his birth.

CHAPTER V

The English Inheritance

*

There is little evidence that James ever seriously considered or properly understood the complex problems of which his new inheritance was compounded. For him the English Succession had taken on all the qualities of fantasy, and the King of England was to be all that the King of Scots had longed in vain to be. Even the parsimonious Court of the ageing Elizabeth glittered like Eldorado when contemplated from the draughty, curtailed splendours of Holyrood and Stirling. James saw no deeper than the young Venetian nobleman who in 1596 had found the English country 'the most lovely to be seen in the world, so opulent, fat, and rich in all things, that you may say with truth poverty is banished'—and that in a year of widespread agricultural distress, a trade slump, and a hot dispute between the Queen and the impoverished south coast ports over the levy of Ship Money contributions. Not unnaturally he drew the same fallacious conclusion as the young Venetian: that 'of the Queen's riches there is no need to speak, for with such wealthy subjects she, of course, is no less'. So there it was. Elizabeth was rich where James was poor; could command where he could only contrive and manœuvre; was listened to with respect and watched with almost superstitious awe by European great powers which scarcely bothered their heads over the intrigues and counterplots which were the fabric of Scottish politics. He did not, either in 1603 or later, really grasp the system of delicate balances and compromises upon which Tudor government had rested; the extent to which Elizabeth's power had been the achievement of her own political genius; the subtle, almost ju-jitsu trickery which for a century had used the expanding strength and wealth of the gentry and merchants to consolidate the power of Tudor monarchy. All

James knew in 1603 was that henceforth he would be rich and generous instead of poor; free from the perpetual fear of kidnapping and assassination, from the necessity of playing off against each other the clan feuds and individual jealousies of Scottish noblemen, from the maddening pretensions of the Kirk and the galling sense of the unimportance, in the great world of European politics, of the kingship which he so greatly prized. Twenty years of governing England were scarcely to teach him any more.

For James knew all about kingship, but little of the history of English monarchy. His academic passion for clear definitions was to be a positive danger in a country where political success would always depend on compromise and the avoidance of definition, and his clear-cut conceptions of law and justice could not contain the jumble of usage and precedent, statute and common law so dear to the tortuous minds of men like Lord Chief Justice Coke. There was very little in the political, social, religious, or economic structure of Elizabeth's England which was capable of logical analysis or simple explanation. The habit of mind which makes the Englishman normally prefer an immediately practical working solution to any theoretical ideal had already by 1600 produced a history and a system of government widely different from those of any other European nation. Haphazard, almost defiant of political theory, it forces the historian who would describe it accurately into paradox and contrast. The ferocious patriotism which made it the rule for English seamen to blow up a beaten ship themselves rather than surrender it to the Spaniard has to be set against the selfishness and greed of officers and men alike which had prevented Essex from exploiting his success in 1596 lest the booty taken at Cadiz should be lost again. The same men who, when the Queen could or would not find money, spent their private fortunes in the public interest would recoup themselves from the public purse by graft and bribery. For Elizabethan government was a highly inefficient system run by highly efficient men; and this unselfconscious mixture of patriotism and personal ambition, of selflessness and greed characterized both Elizabethan heroes and Elizabethan statesmen: Drake had dropped out of the fight against the Armada at a critical moment to secure the flagship of Don Pedro de Valdes as his personal prize, and the two Howards who won honour

91

and glory in the sea fighting, Howard of Effingham and his cousin, 'honest Thomas', were to provide between them the greatest bribery and corruption scandals of the Jacobean age.

The central fact in the England of 1603 was the dominance in every department of the national life of the gentry: that land-owning, trading class which had during a century of Tudor rule engrossed most of the power and wealth in the country. It was a class very diversely recruited, containing as it did all that sur-vived of the ancient feudal and hereditary governing class along with the descendants of the merchants who had made fortunes from the wool and cloth trades, and of the farmers who had raised themselves by clever sheep farming on the Dorset hills or by judicious enclosure and drainage of common lands. The endless litigation provoked by the sudden and large changes in land ownership and values in the sixteenth century had added another stream of recruits from among the successful lawyers, and there were those who had enriched themselves by careers in government service. The redistribution of monastery lands by Henry VIII and the shameless profiteering and land-grabbing of the Reformation era had further immensely streng-thened these same men, and by the turn of the century the whole was settling down into what was recognizably a govern-ing class.

At the top of this the nobility had itself taken on a fairly uni-form pattern in which intermarriage and the all-important factor of wealth had quite obscured the social distinctions. While a faint aura of medieval glamour still hung about names like Vere and Percy and Talbot, there were many who, like the Howards, could reach back through the female line to the vanished splendours of Mowbray and Fitzalan; and Plantagenet blood flowed in the veins of families essentially upstart like the Seymours and Greys. Almost a majority of the families which formed the Elizabethan Court circle—Sackvilles and Careys, Howards, Dudleys, Sidneys, Devereux and Knollys—could call the Queen cousin. With the heraldic and antiquarian self-consciousness, which was another characteristic of the age, those families without long pedigrees were busily getting them forged; and in general the Tudor nobility formed a block solid enough to stand deliberately a little apart from the very numerous new creations which James was to begin making from the moment of his accession. But, though they would resent an upstart Stuart peerage, no very clear line divided the nobility from as yet un-ennobled familes of great distinction, wealth, and antiquity like the Arundells of Wardour; and at Montacute and Hinchinbrooke and Temple Newsam the richest squires maintained on their hereditary wealth or India Company dividends, or on the profits of successful financial jugglery, a state as great as that of many peers. Thus the gradations which divided the gentry were at all stages blurred, and a certain solidarity of outlook characterized the whole class from the richest nobleman to the poorest squire; a consciousness that at their different levels, in their different spheres, one way or another they dominated every important activity in the country.

Solid though it was, however, this block never settled into anything like a rigid caste. There was always recruitment of new fortunes and a falling away of the incompetent, the unlucky, or the spendthrift. For the whole tendency of the age was lavish and showy. Public opinion demanded from those with social pretensions or political ambitions a magnificence of background—of architecture and dress and careless, open-handed spending—which easily became ruinous. The richest of the great families could stand the racket; and the splendour which enshrined Sackvilles and Herberts among 'the marble pillars of Knole and Wilton', and which Bess of Hardwick was to bequeath with her great mansions in Derbyshire, was to root itself in English life and history for three centuries. But even the prosperity of the richest peers was founded, partly at least, on the ruin in bad times of their poorer land-owning neighbours; and the very scale of their operations often left them with a margin of spare capital which could profitably be used in merchant adventuring. For most the intake of new land, by enclosure and otherwise, improved drainage and better methods of farming, and the raising of rents wherever possible, did little more than balance the steady rise in prices of the past half century, and their world was as full of spectacular crashes as of spectacular fortunes: the collapse of the Radcliffes' attempt to maintain an earldom on an inadequate rent roll, or the failure of the Cromwells to keep up the Hinchinbrooke tradition of over-lavish hospitality.

But, in spite of the kaleidoscopic changes which were going

on all the time within the social fabric, the gentry as a class remained astonishingly stable. The general tendency was to settlement and consolidation: the rounding off of estates and the beginnings of the large ramifications of family interests and properties which were to give an almost dynastic quality to the Whig oligarchy a century later. The whole was ballasted by those, probably a large majority, who resisted the fashion for ostentation and reckless extravagance, and were content with a restrained dignity and an unforced hospitality suited to their incomes and their position in the county, who passed down their lands and houses from generation to generation, finding at Court or in the City employment for their younger sons and suitable husbands for their daughters. These men were, in the Victorian phrase, the backbone of the country, the poorer of them distinguished from the richer yeomen by a Manor Hall and the habit of hunting all day while their neighbours farmed, the better-off—the Shallows and Silences so remorselessly guyed by Shakespeare—Justices of the Peace wholly absorbed by county administration and the price of beeves at Stamford Fair. They lived remote from Court and City, their last contact with the great world a dimming memory of the chimes at midnight and the smattering of law left from the two years at Clement's Inn which had rounded off their education. For nearly a century, from Elizabeth's accession to the outbreak of the Civil War, their existence was singularly static. Politics touched them vividly only with the Armada beacons and on occasional crises like the Gunpowder Plot. Their political attitudes were negative: a dislike of taxation which unbalanced their precarious yearly accountings; an intense insularity, and a conservatism which found its outward political expression in the silent mass of back-benchers in the House of Commons.

But if the direct impact of the gentry on politics and national affairs was remote and often somewhat negative, indirectly it dominated them too. Not only did the county hierarchies of noblemen and squires, of Lords Lieutenant and Deputy Lieutenants and Justices of the Peace control all local government in an age when it constituted nine-tenths of the effective administration. Though the gentry represented in the House of Commons what was beginning to be called the 'Country Interest'—an interest normally in opposition to Court and government—

Court and government were themselves staffed by the same class: 'We be the Gentry', the Solicitor-General started his speech to the Commons in 1610. At the higher levels not only was a direct share in the government of the country part of the inherited obligation of a nobleman. It was an essential for survival to those who wished to keep up successfully a state greater than their acreage in the country would by itself support. The rich suits, the underhand profits, perquisites and salaries, the wardships and reversions, could only be got by those on the spot and holding office. It was from the incidental profits of the London Customs and Alum contracts and the like that Sir Arthur Ingram kept up his magnificence at Temple Newsam; and Audley End, the palace which Thomas Howard, first Earl of Suffolk, built for himself in Essex, was paid for out of his perquisites as Lord Treasurer. Only the richest families could afford to abstain from this scramble for office and profit, and in practice even they, for reasons of prestige, frequently became involved in it too.

Furthermore, apart from this competition at the higher levels, it was only in London, in the City or at Whitehall, that the younger sons could hope to find any opportunity for advancement. Apart from the fact that the gentry were continually reinforced from among those who had made fortunes in the City, there was a reverse traffic of young men from the manor houses eagerly seeking openings in commerce. Many of the more able would enter the public service, and most of the secretaries and diplomats and minor officials who made up the bulk of what the Country Interest lumped together as 'the Court' were drawn from this class. Many of the more able and ambitious went for the law. The more learned might seek preferment and advancement in the Church, which would again largely depend on the patronage which flowed from the throne and the great men who surrounded it. Thus the ramifications of family and territorial interest extended into every department of the official world. All those who stood for divergent interests, religions, politics, or economic policies, shared to some extent the same background and often some of the same interests in different contexts—a fact which blurred and confused every issue and dispute. Only the main fact was clear: that in one way or another, in the situation bequeathed to James by Elizabeth, the government of England depended on the support of the gentry. It was a fact against which no theory of monarchy, however logical, could hope to prevail.

The England of Elizabeth was in fact in 1603 a very deceptive inheritance. In one sense it was true that what is often called the new Tudor aristocracy was the creation of the Tudor monarchy. By ceaselessly strengthening the gentry and by welding together into a solid mass of support gentry, lawyers, and merchants, Tudor sovereigns had broken the disruptive power of the old feudal nobility, destroyed the power and wealth of the medieval Church, restored order and the rule of the common law, and fought off the European Counter Reformation. But for all this a twofold price had to be paid. To make this support worth having the Crown had not merely to tolerate, but to encourage the influence and self-reliance of the classes on which it depended; and the spirit of independence thus fostered had already begun in Elizabeth's reign to present serious problems when it took the form of opposition in Parliament to the Queen's religious or commercial policies. The other part of the price was paid by the common people of England who, in a world of rising prices, saw their standard of living cut by perhaps as much as two-thirds in return for a century free from foreign invasion or religious civil war.

Under Elizabeth, moreover, these two aspects of the problem tended to coalesce. During the middle period of the century, when there had been no strong, restraining power at the centre, the propertied classes had shown themselves to be predatory and conscienceless, without any sense of national duty or responsibility. They reduced England to a frightening state of weakness abroad, and at home of disunity, discontent and near starvation. Thus the survival both of England and of Tudor monarchy depended not only on mobilizing the effort of the gentry, but also on restraining its greed and canalizing its thirst for power into more responsible channels. And for Elizabeth there was more at stake than a coldly calculated political need. She had a deep, personal sense of her duty to govern England well, and her determination to give the mass of her subjects a fair deal was just as likely to provoke opposition in the House of Commons as any attempt at despotic or arbitrary government subversive of the nation's liberties. She herself was well aware of the dual nature of the opposition she sometimes encountered. 'I am not so simple as to suppose,' she had remarked in her reply to the clamour against Monopolies in 1601, 'but that there be some of the Lower House whom these grievances never touched; and for them I think that they speak out of zeal for their countries, and not out of spleen or malevolent affection as being parties grieved.' This realistic awareness of the self-interest which lay behind much of the clamour that sounded so public-spirited, this mixture of praise and rebuke, were wholly characteristic of her and a very large part of her successful technique of government. The same note of carefulness for the welfare of the ordinary subject is struck in Burleigh's note of 1584 protesting to the Archbishop of Canterbury against the arbitrary proceedings of some ecclesiastical courts. 'I think,' he wrote, 'the inquisitors of Spain use not so many questions to comprehend and trap their preys. I know your canonists can defend these with all their particles, but surely, under your Grace's correction, this judicial and canonical sifting of poor ministers is not to edify or reform.'

To some extent Elizabeth had succeeded in inspiring her statesmen with her own conception of government not as the exercise of arbitrary power, but as a paternal and infinitely painstaking care for 'the generality of the people'. Some of it permeated the Members of Parliament who left Westminster with the rebukes and adjurations of her parting speech still ringing in their ears, and percolated to the county magistrates who were from time to time hauled up for a failure to keep wage levels and bread prices in proper balance. But in general her soldiers and sailors, magistrates and politicians, remained a very difficult team to drive; and a large part of her trick of government lay in diverting to the national service their intense individualism, and even their greed. So she made valuable and devoted servants, as well as national heroes, out of pirates like Drake and Hawkins, and by a careful control turned predatory and potentially corrupt noblemen like Howard of Effingham and Thomas Sackville, Lord Buckhurst, into useful and conscientious public servants. By the end of her reign time and success had completed the building up of her romantic legend, and long practice had taught her to handle the passions and ambitions with which she was surrounded with effortless and deceptive ease. But no successor, however able, would find her easy to imitate. 'Let the army know,' she had written to her generals on the first news of the success at Cadiz in 1596, 'I care not so much for being a Queen, as that I am sovereign of such subjects'; and so in a single phrase dissolved in ecstatic loyalty all the grievances and criticisms provoked by her parsimony and indecision. It was the same trick as she used in 1601 to turn what was, in fact, a humiliating surrender into a resounding personal triumph.

Elizabeth's very success was in many ways to make James's problems even more difficult. She used her personal prestige to maintain unchanged a religious settlement which had ceased to command the loyalty of a substantial body of her subjects. By exploiting the greed and adventurousness of volunteers she concealed the fact that the Royal Navy was so dangerously short of ships that it would prove incapable in peace time of protecting commerce from piracy, even round the coasts of England and Ireland. All through her reign the Crown was getting poorer, thanks to the steady rise in prices, while every year the needs of government became more complicated and more expensive. But rather than court unpopularity by asking Parliament either for more regular subsidies or for alternative sources of permanent revenue, she sold Crown lands, which still further impoverished the Crown, and she rewarded deserving servants by expedients such as the grants of Monopolies which must ultimately create more problems than they solved. She had no standing army—a fact which made the reality of her power almost incomprehensible to her European contemporaries—and her administrative machine was rapidly becoming out of date. It was still in 1603 a system which could be made to work reasonably well so long as it was closely and continuously controlled at the centre. But it was headed certainly towards insolvency; and insolvency would equally certainly mean trouble with a House of Commons which had been deliberately encouraged to participate intelligently in the business of government.

All these things were remediable by a young and vigorous sovereign who understood the elements with which he was dealing. But certain tendencies, leading England along a path different from that of any other European nation, had already gone so far that they were probably irrevocable. Almost everywhere else, the breakdown of the feudal order under the successive impact of Renaissance and Reformation had created problems similar to those the Tudors had dealt with. Continental monarchs had solved, or were solving, these problems by accumulating more and more power in themselves: by a centralized state resting on military strength. They used Machiavelli's doctrines of *raison d'état* to justify the destruction of all established privileges and liberties which impeded them, overrode the law where necessary, and, because they found that the forces they were fighting only too often took refuge in the surviving representative institutions—Estates General, Cortes, Parlements, and the like—destroyed or by-passed those institutions themselves. The Tudors, pursuing precisely the same practical objectives—the restoration of law and order—had made Parliament co-operate at every stage, and, instead of costly military forces, had mobilized all the public opinion which could be politically effective. In practice this meant that in any crisis Henry VIII and Elizabeth were every bit as powerful as any of their continental rivals. It also meant that Englishmen got reasonably good government much more cheaply than any other nation, with no standing army to pay for and the administration largely supplied by the unpaid labour of the county landowners. But, as the experience and knowledge of the Parliamentary classes increased session by session, and as the hold of the nobility and gentry tightened on every department of government whether central or local, it became increasingly difficult for the monarchy to go back on its tracks. By 1600 the centralized, efficient, bureaucratic state of which Strafford was to dream, and which Cardinal Richelieu was to found in France, was probably in England already unattainable.

History was to show that the haphazard, chaotic English system had in the long run a greater survival value than superficially more efficient systems elsewhere. But it made the problems which James had to face from the moment of his accession very much harder to solve. Reform and reorganization were possible, but only on the condition of collaboration with the governing class in and out of Parliament, which would demand from a ruler not only great skill and tact, but also endless patience. For, though the leaders of public opinion in the City and country had often knowledge and experience enough to criticize governmental incompetence effectively, they had rarely any practical alternative to offer. Above all they would constantly demand more than they were prepared to pay for. In this respect they had been spoilt by Elizabeth. Her great skill and her good fortune had enabled her to achieve remarkable—at times spectacular—results with very amateurish means and on an inadequate income. It was difficult for her subjects to understand that she could not have done so for much longer, though for ten years before she died all the signs had been pointing that way. For if James was coming to rule a nation which was in the flood tide of a great literary and architectural renaissance and was commercially prosperous as never before, on its political side Elizabeth's reign had ended on a note of decline—even of failure.

On the surface there was much to justify James's feeling, as he listened to Carey's gasped-out news, that he was coming at last into the promised land. For the England which he was taking over was Shakespeare's England, and much of what is thought of today as the Elizabethan age in fact fell within his reign. Shakespeare himself was only just entering his greatest period: *Hamlet, Othello, King Lear, Macbeth, Antony and Cleopatra* and *Coriolanus* were all still to come, before the sublime fairy story of *The Tempest* and his retirement to a well-earned prosperity at Stratford in 1610. And though there is little evidence that James either patronized Shakespeare or appreciated the greatest poetic and dramatic genius of his, or indeed any modern age, there were many lesser men whose talent he could exploit to fulfil his dream of presiding over a Court so brilliant that it should be the envy of all those polished Europeans who might have sneered at the somewhat clumsy and inept gaieties of Stirling and Edinburgh. There was about James an uncouthness, a lack of dignity or of a sense of occasion, which would in fact always prevent him from cashing in on the success he really had. It would be Louis XIV, much less intelligent and in many ways a less admirable man, who would scoop the spectacular and cultural laurels of the century in which they both lived. But if Louis had Racine and Molière to write plays for him, James had masques by Jonson and Campion staged, as often as not by Inigo Jones; and the funeral sermons of Dean Donne, though every bit as fine as Bossuet's, were by no means his chief claim to fame. Inigo Jones was to leave at Greenwich and Whitehall, and in the notebooks which laid the foundations of English Palladian architecture, more enduring monuments than his elaborate stage machinery. Lancelot Andrewes was to crown the theological work of the Elizabethan divines; and Elizabethan prose was to reach its splendid climax in the Authorised Version of 1612.

But James had a mind much more mundane and materialist than he liked to think, and his patronage of the arts sprang less from good taste than from a desire to make a splash. It was the spectacular lavishness of the great English country houses and the solid, cautious advance of the City of London which offered the best guarantee that the humiliating Scottish poverty was a thing of the past. English shipping, it is true, already lagged behind that of Holland; most of the foreign goods that reached London and almost all the foreign trade of the Irish ports were carried by the Dutch, and the Dutch were ahead, too, in the race to acquire the trading stations and the riches of the decaying Portuguese Empire in the Far East. But the English rivalry was already declared. The East India Company had been granted its charter in 1600 and had begun to add its argosies to the immense wealth which already flowed into London from the Muscovy and Turkey Companies and the Levant merchants, and from the new markets still being opened up for English cloth by the Merchant Adventurers. Soon there would begin a great diversion of surplus wealth, population, and enterprise westwards; for the exploitation of the riches of Hudson's Bay and the colonization of Virginia and Bermuda. Here, round the board tables, the worlds of Court and City overlapped, and the great merchants like Sir Thomas Smith and Sir Edwin Sandys sat together with the more enterprising landowners such as Sir Walter Cope, who owned Kensington, and the rich peers—Suffolk, Warwick or Southampton—to capitalize and organize and tidy up the large, haphazard gains of Elizabethan adventuring.

England was indeed a rich and splendid inheritance and was fast getting richer. Only the Crown was impoverished; and it was in the political situation that James might have found some cause for misgiving. Ever since the crowning mercy of the

Armada in 1588 Elizabeth's world had been moving towards anti-climax. The truth was that the Spaniards learnt more from their defeat than the English government did from its victory. Better ships and better tactics, and a well-organized convoy system, made the Plate fleets hard to intercept, and ill luck dogged all the great naval expeditions of the 'nineties. Lord Thomas Howard's attempt on the Azores in 1592 achieved nothing to counterbalance the loss of the *Revenge*; Drake's last voyage to the West Indies three years later was a costly failure; and neither of Essex's ventures, to Cadiz in 1596, and the Islands' Voyage of 1597, paid their way in prizes and plunder. The old Elizabethan mood of high courage and the certainty of victory was fading into disillusionment. To Drake, as he lay dying in Nombre de Dios Bay, it seemed as if the Indies which he had known in his youth as 'a delicious and pleasant arbor' had now become 'a vast and desert wilderness'. The career of Essex, which had seemed at the moment when he stormed Cadiz likely to eclipse them all, came to a dreary end in ruin and treason. Only bad weather saved England from another serious Spanish attack in 1598, and all the energies of the closing years of the reign were absorbed in the long, unrewarding and costly struggle to conquer Ireland, which ought to have been undertaken years before.

James knew clearly enough before he left Edinburgh what he intended to do about the Spanish war. He hated fighting, and Elizabethan heroics struck no answering chord in him. He understood European politics much better than he did the internal situation in England. In the Spanish monarchy he saw much to admire and nothing to fear and he was quite cut off from the English feeling which made hatred of Spain and all things Spanish a patriotic duty, even among those whose world was entirely remote from that of Raleigh and Essex. *Beati Pacifici* was to be his motto. His mere accession in England would put an end to centuries of warfare on the Scottish border. He intended that this should immediately be followed by an effective union of the two nations. With the great added strength of such a union behind him, the costly, useless Spanish war at an end, and Ireland at last pacified, he believed that he could become the peacemaker of Europe. All his life he was to exaggerate in his mind his own international importance. The position taken up by the Church of England half-way, as it seemed to him, between Rome and Geneva, even suggested the possibility that he might heal the religious as well as the secular feuds of Europe, reconcile the Pope and the King of Spain to the Anglican Settlement, and bring a Great Britain united on a basis of religious toleration to accept the spiritual primacy of the Bishop of Rome. All his life he was to be haunted by this dazzling daydream, even long after Anglo-Scottish union had broken down and the Pope and the King of Spain had made it clear that they were uninterested and Englishmen that they would not tolerate each other, let alone Spaniards. For James could never bring himself to face as political facts invincible prejudices which his reason told him were unfounded. He was quite right on all his three basic points. Anglo-Scottish union, religious toleration among all Christian sects, and peace with Spain were all common sense. But only the peace with Spain was practical politics.

Some of the more superficial aspects of the English political situation James also understood pretty well, and he had some sound commonsensical ideas about them, too. On the administrative side there had been in Elizabeth's latter years the same signs of decline as had affected the conduct of the Spanish war. Walsingham had died in 1590 and Burleigh in 1598; and the death of Burleigh in particular had necessitated a certain decentralization of functions, so many of the threads of government had the old statesman kept under his own gouty hand. The main burden of government fell, however, on his crook-backed younger son, Sir Robert Cecil, Secretary of State since 1598, who had served a long apprenticeship under his father and who stood for all that was most conservative and stable in the Elizabethan régime. Burleigh had always represented the element of caution and restraint in Elizabeth's Council: long-headed elder statesmanship was his line, resisting and curtailing the more wild-cat schemes of Leicester and Drake, Raleigh and Essex. This tradition Robert Cecil had inherited, adding to it the caution and mistrust of high-flying adventurers natural in a cripple who had to make his way in the world by his intellect alone. Moreover he came to high responsibility too young, and so presented all his life a closed and rigid mind to new problems and alien points of view. With Cecil, and also representing the older Elizabethan school, was the Treasurer, Lord Buckhurst, head of the wealthy Sackville clan, competent, reliable, and unadventurous. Francis Bacon was to tell James that Cecil was 'no fit counsellor to make your affairs better', though 'fit to have kept them from growing worse'. He might have included Buckhurst in the same judgement. Both men moved with a solid certainty through a world which they had thoroughly mastered, undesirous of reforming or improving it, unshocked by abuses which time and long usage had seemed to sanction; though in Cecil's case it is probable that this lethargy was partly due to the exhaustion of a frail constitution, and also to the disproportionate amount of energy he had to expend merely to keep himself in office and to side-track the unending plots of enemies and rivals. To these two Howard of Effingham, the Lord High Admiral, now Earl of Nottingham, made a suitable appendage. Never one of the adventurous school of Drake and Hawkins and his own cousin, Thomas, he had served his distinguished turn in command of the fleet against the Armada and at Cadiz and now, idle and careless rather than corrupt, was fairly launched on the twenty-year process of his decline into senility.

It was characteristic of the age that such a political combine should tend also to become a family combine, and Cecil was cautiously engaged in extending his own power and influence by alliance with the Howards. His motherless daughter was brought up in the household of Lord Thomas Howard, and he was to find a Howard wife for his eldest son. It was a great weakness of Elizabeth's method of government that by trusting all real power to a few old friends and new favourites she automatically created round the fringes of Court and Council a band of dispossessed or disappointed men often as closely allied by ties of family, dependency, or territorial interest as the group in power. There were those like Lord Henry Howard, uncle to that Duke of Norfolk who had been beheaded for treason in 1572, whose loyalty had become suspect during the difficult years of Mary Stuart's imprisonment. There were men whom the Queen simply disliked and distrusted: like Francis Bacon, whose ceaseless, over-fulsome efforts to gain advancement defeated their own ends and made him a life-long personal enemy of his cousin, Cecil. There was the great band of Essex's friends, relations, and dependants, many of whom, though personally innocent, saw their whole fortunes and careers jeopardized by his rash conspiracy. There were the men who stood for unpopular or outworn policies, like Raleigh, whose Captaincy of the Guard entrenched him securely in the Household, but whom Cecil jealously excluded from any share in the making of policy. James was reasonably well informed of all this. It was not only Cecil who had been sending him coded secret letters for the past few years, and he had already had cause to complain of the 'Asiatic and endless volumes' of political information and advice inflicted on him by Lord Henry Howard.

With politics in this form James was perfectly able to cope. He knew little of English law or history, and he would never to the end of his days learn to adapt his political theories to the realities of the delicate relationship built up between Elizabeth and her Parliaments. But he knew all about family and personal rivalries and the struggle for power and profit in Court and government. It is doubtful if he ever considered displacing the existing government in England. Whatever he might decide in the future, he would be lost in the first few months without Cecil to guide him. But he had already formed the idea of enlarging the basis on which that government rested: of bringing into office and into the orbit of his favour all those who had found themselves in opposition to Elizabeth. He saw no inherent reason to mistrust the loyalty of Catholics; and he had furthermore formed the sentimental and not very logical notion that he owed a debt of gratitude to all those who had championed at any time the cause of his mother. That meant in practice that all Essex's disgraced friends might hold up their heads again. The only *bloc* whose hopes were from the start doomed to disappointment was the war party. James had no use for the heroics of Raleigh and his friends, and in any case he wanted peace.

But this was all for the future. While James collected the train which would enable him to cut a suitably impressive figure when he came south to take over his new kingdom, he had no alternative but to leave the existing Council in office. The complete orderliness of this brief interregnum, the sureness and ease with which Cecil handled the situation, are the best commentary on the massive solidity of the power built up by the English governing class in the previous century. There were those who expected a renewal of the Wars of the Roses; and there were indeed plenty of people who had a good enough claim to the throne on paper to make trouble. The Tudor title had never been a very good one; and James's was not even a perfect Tudor claim, since it was specifically invalidated by Henry VIII's will, which had been the basis of the succession of Edward VI, Mary and Elizabeth. Moreover, the figure of the old Queen had bulked so large at the centre of things for forty years that to the man in the street it seemed inevitable that her death should create an emergency.

But the leading politicians had made up their minds long since to the Scottish succession, and there was nobody powerful and at the same time irresponsible enough to challenge their decision. Cecil and his friends had handled real power for long enough, often behind the Queen's back and in the teeth of her wishes, and they felt no difficulty in continuing to do so. The draft of the Proclamation of the new King was already in existence in a form approved in advance by James, and within six hours of Elizabeth's death the Heralds were reading it out in London. As the news spread, city after city and town after town followed the capital's lead and there was no sign of a disturbance. A few mild precautionary measures were taken, such as the closing of the Cinque Ports and the round-up of some known Papists whose loyalty was not certain; and a stream of courtiers and place-hunters began to move north to get their claims in early. Chamberlain's letters to Dudley Carleton written from London during April record some of the more important figures 'posting that way . . . as yf it were nothing els but first come first served, or that preferment were a goale to be got by footmanship'. Unfortunately James's impulsive, indiscriminate generosity only too often justified such hopes, and John Peyton, son of the Lieutenant of the Tower, who was one of the first Chamberlain noted on the road north, achieved the distinction of being dubbed by James in Scotland as 'his first knight'. But it was only the comparatively small official world which was disturbed, and the folk who lived near enough to the Great North Road to have a chance of seeing James on his progress south. Mostly England went about her business and peacefully awaited the arrival of her new King.

CHAPTER VI

Taking Over a New Kingdom

*

The arrival of James at Berwick on April 6th was perhaps historically more significant than any other incident of the accession of the new King. For, if 1603 marked no great turning-point in English history, on the Anglo-Scottish border it ended an era. A frontier which had been in dispute for five centuries was abruptly obliterated; and to those accustomed to the more or less continuous sporadic fighting of the Marches it seemed hard to believe that the mere peaceful proclamation of a single King of England and Scotland had destroyed the whole fabric of their lives. To watch a King of Scotland, attended by the Wardens of the Marches from both sides of the border, greeted at Berwick with a salute only from the loudest peal of ordnance in any soldier's memory, offered the keys of the city, and loudly cheered by citizens and garrison with shouts of 'Welcome', and 'God save King James', was to see history being made; and no achievement of James's kingcraft was to be one-tenth as important as this, which he owed merely to the accident of his birth.

Right from the start of this journey south a holiday tone was set. There had been no time for the citizens of Berwick to prepare the elaborate greeting, the masques and spectacles and addresses which were proper to such an occasion, and they presented instead what was much more welcome—a purse of gold. James spent a day wandering round the walls inspecting the garrison and fortifications, chattered with the soldiers and fired off one of the big cannons for fun. Everywhere there was a warm and spontaneous welcome such as he had never known before, and he was still young enough to respond gratefully to it. In such an atmosphere his lack of dignity became an asset, and his natural talkativeness and familiarity, his approachable-

107

ness and his easy, impulsive generosity surrounded him with a haze of goodwill. For a brief fortnight all his day-dreams came true as he moved on into what seemed indeed, to eyes accustomed to the bleaker landscapes of Scotland, a promised land. From Berwick he rode to Widdrington, where Sir Robert Carey had had more time to make adequate preparations for a proper reception by a Warden of the Middle March. It would not be long before Carey sadly lamented that James had 'deceived my expectation and adhered to those that sought my ruin'; and he had in fact to wait twenty-three years for the peerage which ultimately rewarded his desperate ride. For the moment, however, a Gentleman of the new King's Bedchamber and the envy of all 'the Great Ones of the Court', he was out to back his good fortune, and he provided not only a prodigious banquet, but also one of those small, contrived effects which helped to make Elizabethan England so much pleasanter and more urbane than the dour matter-of-factness of Scotland. For as the King after a short rest was strolling in the park he was allowed to see, as though by accident, a number of deer grazing and 'the game being so fair before him, he could not forbear; but according to his wonted manner, forth he went, and slew two of them'; and before leaving for Newcastle the next morning he made four more knights from among the local gentry.

So the tone was set for the whole of that long, leisurely journey: prolonged and princely civic entertainments alternated with hunting and feasting in the great country houses, amidst a continual shower of gifts and knighthoods. Newcastle shouldered the whole charge of the growing royal household for three days; York for two more. Dr Tobie Mathew, the Bishop of Durham, received them at his palace with a hundred gentlemen in tawny liveries and, at dinner, so well exploited with the King a common taste for theology and scholarship that he not only secured a number of immediate benefits, but laid sound foundations for his own future. In James's Scottish background learning combined with humour had been rare indeed, and there had been few to laugh at his choicer witticisms. At Durham he made his first contact with the urbane, serene world of the Anglican Bishops, which so happily combined theological soundness with a proper deference for royalty, and he responded to it even more expansively than to the hunting and the gigantic

dinners of the great houses. Before he left the next morning
the Bishopric had recovered much alienated property, including Durham House in the Strand, which had been granted
to Sir Walter Raleigh. Three years later Dr Mathew would
find himself Archbishop of York and Lord President of the
Council of the North. Of all his English subjects it would be the
great churchmen of this second generation of Anglicanism
who would make the most genuine contact with the new King.
'Learning, humanity and gravity,' combined with a judicious
worldly wisdom, were a wonderful relief after the asperities
of the ministers of the Kirk.

But by the time that the royal progress reached York it had
almost become unmanageable. James had set out with a representative selection of Scottish nobles and a not unreasonably
large train of courtiers and officials, English and Scottish. But
the two streams, of north-bound English place hunters, and
impoverished Scots hurrying south for fear of missing the pick-
ings, had swollen the train to a disorderly rabble of over a
thousand which gave the King no peace and placed an intolerable burden on hosts, who, like Sir Edward Stanhope at Grimstone Hall, extended 'most bountiful entertainment' to 'all
comers, every man without check eating and drinking at
pleasure'. Proclamations ordering home all Scots not in immediate attendance on the King, and restraining 'the concourse of
ydle and unnecessary posters' north were largely ineffectual,
since James's own careless, miscellaneous gifts and grants and
favours made it seem that first come, first served might after all
be the rule. The honour of knighthood, so jealously husbanded
by Elizabeth, James bestowed uncritically on almost every
eligible English gentleman who came his way, so that by the
time he reached London he had already made over three
hundred new knights; and the landlord of the Bear at Doncaster
got the reversion of the lease of a valuable royal manor as the
reward of one good night's entertainment. So the train continued to swell, putting an intolerable strain on such great
households as Lord Shrewsbury's at Worksop, Lord Rutland's
at Belvoir, and on the notoriously princely hospitality of Sir
Oliver Cromwell at Hinchinbrooke.

But, if, in the eyes of the English official classes, the pre-
dominant function of Monarchy was that of dispensing patron-

age—a function in which the old Queen had sadly failed in her closing years—there was also an atmosphere of genuine welcome such as James had never known in Scotland. It was not only that these English noblemen could afford to entertain so much more lavishly than the Scots. They took trouble to please their new King, and especially to gratify his overmastering passion for hunting. In the park before he got to Worksop 'there appeared a number of huntsmen all in green; the chief of which, with a woodman's speech, did welcome him, offering his Majesty to shew him some game; which he gladly condescended to see; and with a train set he hunted a good space, very much delighted'; and all the way from Sir John Harington's house to Stamford 'Sir John's best hounds with good mouths followed the game. the King taking great leisure and pleasure in the same'. At Hinchinbrooke the entertainment was more varied. Not only did the Court get the best dinner of the whole journey, 'such plenty and variety of meats, such diversity of wines, and those not riffe ruffe, but ever the best of their kind; and the cellars open at any man's pleasure'. The Vice-Chancellor and Heads of the Colleges of Cambridge waited on him there, too, with speeches and poems of welcome and a present of books; and just beyond, at Godmanchester, there were seventy ploughing teams drawn up to ram home the lesson of the prosperity of his new kingdom.

Probably at no time in his whole life did James feel so entirely and satisfactorily a King as during the three weeks of this journey. The real problems he would have to face were still remote. Until he was forced to nominate his ministers and so long as no financial stringency limited the flow of small grants and favours there would be no body of hostile, disappointed men to shake his serene confidence in his conception of kingship and his own ability to fulfil it. He would be the beneficent, affable, patriarchal dispenser of favours and justice, responsible only to God for the welfare of his subjects, who were palpably loyal and grateful. It was so simple to assure the mayor and aldermen of Hull that they should be 'relieved and succoured against the daily spoils done to them by those of Dunkirk' without having to stop to consider the naval expenditure involved in the proper policing of the coasts, or to earn an easy popularity by promising 'their hearts' desire' to the Huntingdonshire commoners who waited on him to complain of the enclosure of their land by Sir John Spencer, when he knew nothing of the intricacies and economic forces involved. He could promise still more confidently to consider and redress the grievances presented by some Puritan clergy who claimed to represent the views of a thousand of their brethren, since in matters of theology he felt himself to be on safe ground, and he had yet to discover that what he called English 'Purinisme' could be, in its different way, as intractable and difficult as Scottish Presbytery. The enlargement of all prisoners save Papists and wilful murderers from the gaols of every town he passed through ministered further to this large illusion of power, as did the famous episode of the 'silken base thief' caught red-handed picking pockets at Newark and hanged out of hand by the King's Warrant to the Recorder without charge or trial. Historians have rightly seen in this a dangerous misconception of the English law and his own prerogative under it; and in fact the English preoccupation with forms and precedents was constantly to come into conflict later with James's robust, common-sensical view that forms did not matter if justice were done, and was to be a major cause of misunderstanding. But it does not appear that any loud voices were raised in protest at Newark at the time, since the man was clearly guilty and nobody wished to spoil the party. So that episode, too, went to swell James's sense of himself as a second Solomon.

All this brought out the best and the worst in James. The genuine warmth of his welcome everywhere drew from him an answering ease and friendliness which went far to compensate for his lack of dignity, disappointing physique, coarse manners, and Scottish accent. 'Nor shall it ever be blotted out of my mind,' he was to tell his first Parliament with the ring of sincerity, 'how at my first entry into this kingdom the people of all sorts rid and ran, nay rather flew to meet me.' Aware for the first time in his life of general popularity, he made a good impression himself. But it brought out, too, the tendency, which was to grow on him fast, to substitute irresponsible day-dreaming for carefully thought-out policy: a disposition to treat genuine obstacles as irritating and unnecessary difficulties raised by factious people to plague and thwart him, and to ignore opposition once he had satisfied his own logical mind

111

that he was in the right. He may have entered upon his new in-heritance with some trepidation: there is evidence that he found Cecil and Dorset and some of the Elizabethan grandees some-what awesome when he finally met them. But there was no humility, and in consequence he learnt very little that was fun-damental in the first precious, irresponsible weeks, when the old Privy Council governed England under his Proclamation, and he could as yet make no important mistakes.

Fortunately, when serious politics first impinged on this slightly unreal, daydream interlude, they did so in the form that James was best fitted to understand. The art of governing in Scotland had largely consisted of balancing powerful factions one against the other; of penetrating and exploiting the private intrigues of public men. On a superficial analysis the govern-ment of England might seem to consist of much the same pro-cess, though expressed in less violent terms. James knew little or nothing of English law and Parliamentary precedents. But he was perfectly equipped to grasp the elements of the struggle for power at Whitehall: the enmities, less noisy than those of Ruthven and Gowrie, but no less deadly, between Burleigh and Essex, Raleigh and Cecil; and the delicate balance of forces by which Elizabeth had maintained an outward harmony round her Council table. The letters of Cecil and Henry Howard had kept him closely in touch, and he was quite capable of accurately assessing the suggestions of Lord Cobham, who had posted hot-foot northwards to get the opposition word in first, without help from Howard, whom the Council sent hastily after Cobham to countermine his intrigues. His opening moves were wisely non-committal. He provisionally confirmed the existing Council in office, but at the same time released Lord Southampton and Sir Henry Neville from the Tower, where they had been ex-piating their share in the Essex conspiracy, and announced his intention of bringing up the young Essex, restored in blood and title, in his own household as the companion of Prince Henry. Henry Howard, whom Elizabeth had always kept at arm's length since he had been canvassed as a possible husband for Mary Stuart after Norfolk's execution in 1572, was reasonably sure of coming at last into royal favour by dint of his alliance with Cecil and his long, boring, helpful letters of the past two years. All this was only following out the general intention he had already formulated to bring back into favour all who had in any way identified themselves with his mother's cause, and in so doing to bind to the new dynasty not only the supporters, but also the enemies of the old. The consequence for the first few weeks was a wild uncertainty, 'inasmuch that not only protestants, but papists and puritaynes, and the very poets with theyre ydle pamphlets' flattered themselves with extravagant hopes, while the Council, blandly ignoring James's summons north, gathered at Cecil's house at Theobalds in Hertfordshire for the meeting which must force a final decision.

This meeting took place on May 3rd, when Cecil found himself the host not only of the old Council and most of Elizabeth's principal household officers, but of a vast concourse of hangers-on and sightseers, all of whom were regaled with 'beef, veal, mutton, bread and beer'. It proved a good investment. For after the formal speeches of welcome and an interlude during which the cheers of the people forced him to appear repeatedly at his chamber window, James withdrew with Sir Robert to a 'labyrinth-like garden, compact of bays, rosemary, and the like'; and there in an hour's intimate conversation, the immediate future of England's government was settled. As was almost inevitable the upshot was a triumph for the Cecil–Howard grouping. From James's point of view it would have been the act of a madman to displace a body of men whose level-headed competence had just been so strikingly demonstrated in his peaceful accession, and who embodied almost all that remained of Elizabethan wisdom and prestige. Inevitably a number of Scots—Lennox, Mar, Home, and one or two others—joined the reconstituted Council; but it was the English additions which were significant: Henry Howard, shortly to become Earl of Northampton; his sailor nephew, Thomas, likewise promoted to the Earldom of Suffolk; and Mountjoy, who had just successfully completed the conquest of Ireland. For Raleigh and his friends, against whom Cecil and Howard had been so long and so successfully poisoning the King's mind, there was no crumb of comfort. Indeed James almost immediately set about displacing Raleigh, against financial compensation, from his Captaincy of the Guard in favour of an old friend and contemporary, Sir Thomas Erskine of Gogar.

For Cecil it was perhaps even more important that he had

H

laid in that first hour the foundation of an acceptable personal relationship with his new sovereign. There was in fact very little that they had in common. Cecil stood for the calculated dignity, the restrained decorum, with which the Tudor aristocracy were buttressing and securing their hold on power and wealth. Everything about him was grave and serious-minded; a matured and careful judgement was brought to bear on his lightest decision. Occasionally he would be able genuinely to share a recondite academic joke with the King; the rest of their relationship would inevitably be largely artificial. But since a large part of the art of politics in any age consists of getting and keeping rather than exercising power, Cecil was prepared in reason to adapt himself to whatever tone the King cared to set. If James liked to banter him clumsily on his puny figure and address him as his 'little beagle', it was a small price to pay for keeping the reality of power in his hands, and he would play up urbanely to James's moods and jests. For James the relationship was based on gratitude and a certain awe. He owed his peaceful, unchallenged succession to Cecil as much as to any man, and without his guidance he could not easily have mastered the complicated politics of Whitehall. But there was a self-confidence—an assurance of civilization—about the Elizabethan elder statesman which made even a King from Scotland something of a provincial, and almost certainly the somewhat boisterous, patronizing tone James adopted with his new grandees was a defence against that knowledge. As the years went on and he felt himself more securely established on the English throne both gratitude and awe would tend to evaporate; and in the end Cecil's death would bring a sense of relief and emancipation which are in themselves the best proof of the extent to which this influence in the early days held in check the King's disastrous political impulsiveness. So for once, and almost for the last time, James was compelled to live up to his own precept that 'evidence of a King is chiefly seen in the election of his officers, as in places which require a peculiar sufficiency, not to choose them that he affects most, but to use every one according to his proper fitness'. In consequence the new reign began with what was probably the best available government in power.

After the heady triumphs which culminated in this meeting at

Theobalds there crept in a note of anticlimax. They left, after a short day's hunting in Enfield Chase, in the old manner, with the Lord Mayor and the Heralds and the great Officers of State to greet them with speeches of welcome at Stamford Hill amidst a throng so dense that a man could charge eight groats for the use of his cart as a grandstand for only a quarter of an hour. And from there to the Charterhouse a cunningly contrived drag hunt kept hounds running in view beside the road all the way. The chain of events should have continued with a state entry into the City of London, the arrival of the Queen and her children, and a coronation designed to eclipse in glory and ostentation anything that England had ever seen before. The old Queen had been given her splendid funeral on April 28th, with the Lady Arabella Stuart as chief mourner, and James was longing to take the stage himself. Unfortunately, however, the death rate from the Plague in London had risen to twenty a day and the programme was brought to a standstill. James could only skirt the City in a closed coach to Whitehall and inspect his new capital from the river on his way down to the Tower. There followed a maddening two months of delay while the weekly Plague death rate rose in London to seven or eight hundred, and James moved uneasily round outside, to Greenwich and back to Whitehall, to Windsor, where he presided over a chapter of the Order of the Garter, and on a tour of some of the better-stocked deer parks of the home counties. In the end the state entry into the City had to be postponed to the following spring. But the coronation could not be much longer put off. Queen Anne was summoned from Scotland, where she had been taking advantage of James's absence to stage a major quarrel with Mar over the guardianship of her children, and on July 25th the ceremony took place in a sadly empty Abbey. Any concourse of the people had been forbidden, and nobles and gentry were severely limited in the numbers of attendants they brought; an earl, whose dignity would normally have required a following of at least a hundred and fifty for a London visit, being allowed only sixteen, and lesser folk in proportion.

Once safely crowned James and Anne set off on a wider tour of the southern counties with yet more hunting and banqueting, masques and pageants. But the honeymoon period of James's reign was now really over. The fulfilled daydream was merging into reality. Little though James liked business, there were political and financial reckonings to be faced, and occasional discordant notes of complaint and criticism had begun to penetrate the chorus of welcome and praise through which he had hitherto been moving. Royal progresses, as Elizabeth had well understood, were an essential method of keeping in touch with the people and popularizing the monarchy. But they were exceedingly expensive, not only to the Exchequer and to the wealthy landlords who did the entertaining, but to the whole districts through which they passed. No great house in England was large enough to accommodate both James and Anne and the vast trains of courtiers and attendants which moved with them. Country life was disrupted and provisions inevitably ran short wherever they went. Only the ancient royal right to requisition horses and carts and fix low maximum prices for the purchase of local produce made these lavish and ill-organized journeyings possible at all, and already by the time James first reached London there were murmurs against the 'general, extreme, unjust, and crying oppression' of 'cart takers and purveyors' who, as Parliament was sharply to inform him a month or two later, 'have rummaged and ransacked since your Majesty's coming in far more than under any your royal progenitors'.

Furthermore, in spite of these devices and of all the lavish hospitality he had received, James had spent over £10,000 on his journey south alone and had given away in his careless, openhanded way another £14,000. Elizabeth's funeral had cost the Exchequer another £17,000, and there was a debt of £400,000 left over from the last Irish campaign. The illusion that money worries and financial expedients were things of the past was thus all too quickly dispelled. Within two months of the coronation Cecil was writing to Shrewsbury: 'Our Sovereign spends £100,000 yearly on his house, which was wont to be but £50,000. Now think what the country feels, and so much for that.' An Order in Council requiring all gentlemen with lands of £40 a year or more to come to Court to be knighted or compound with the King's Commissioners brought in a small sum in knights' fees for immediate expenses, but only at the cost of starting fresh grievances, and the City made difficulties about a loan. Amid these mounting irritations what finally put an end to the halcyon period and forced the King rather testily to face facts was, as John Chamberlain had prophesied in a letter to Carleton months before, the diverse hopes, religious and political, of which the new reign had raised so many 'that to satisfie or please all would be more than a man's work'. By the time that James reached London there were already two actively disappointed bodies of men in the country: the Catholic community as a whole, and all those on the fringe of official life who found themselves excluded from office by a Cecil–Howard administration.

For the Catholics there was some excuse. Pursuing his dream of healing the religious feuds of Europe James had already resumed diplomatic relations with the Papacy and had reached in his own mind a clear definition of the limits within which toleration would be possible for English Catholics. He drew a careful distinction between those who would loyally accept their duty of allegiance to the King as lying outside the scope of their religion, and those who followed what was the official doctrine, which required all Catholics to rebel and if possible to assassinate a heretical sovereign. To the loyal he was prepared to allow the free exercise of their religion in private, provided that they made no attempt to increase their numbers; and in the face of all the facts he clung to the belief that the Pope must be able to appreciate his difficulties and be brought to see that such a solution would immensely benefit both sides. But, however impeccably commonsensical and enlightened, the very idea of toleration was ambiguous and suspect to the seventeenth-century mind, whether Protestant or Catholic; and James made his position even more ambiguous and liable to misunderstanding whenever he tried further to define and explain it. To say publicly that he acknowledged 'the Roman Church to be our Mother Church', however he qualified the statement, was inevitably to rouse every dormant Protestant suspicion and prejudice and to encourage impossible Catholic hopes. The Scottish Jesuit, Robert Tempest, had boasted in 1599 that he could produce evidence 'in the King's own hand' that he was a Catholic; and among the English Catholics abroad such rumours were constantly bandied about. 'The King of Scots,' one wrote to another in Belgium in April, 1600, 'is growing wiser in these points, complying with the

Catholic Princes, and promising, when he has obtained the Crown of England, to be a Catholic, and to tolerate that religion in his country meanwhile. . . . The Pope told this to the Spanish ambassador, and he to me this day.' Even the Pope, moving along lines of argument equally logical to the conclusion that all means were justified which might save millions of Englishmen from eternal damnation, failed to understand: his last informal communication before James left Scotland had been an inquiry whether Prince Henry might not be brought up a Catholic. The English Catholics were convinced, though it was not strictly true, that James had pledged himself in effect to remit all fines for recusancy and tolerate their worshipping in private; and it was on this understanding that they joined in the welcoming throngs and accepted the Stuart succession. In Ireland the delusions were even wilder. It was there almost universally believed that the new King was himself a Catholic and it was taken for certain that Catholicism would become an officially tolerated religion. 'Jesuits, seminaries, and friars now come abroad in open show,' wrote a contemporary chronicler, 'bringing forth old rotten stocks and stones of images.' In Cork priests moved through the streets with 'the Cross carried like a standard before them', and Mountjoy had considerable difficulty in re-establishing the authority of the proper magistrates and in extracting the necessary oaths of allegiance from the corporate towns of the south.

The situation was further complicated by the fact that there were two parties among the English Catholics themselves. There were the seculars, survivors of the old English Catholic body, who longed to be able to remain loyal Englishmen without forfeiting their religious allegiance to the Pope— who would be perfectly satisfied in fact with the sort of toleration James was anxious to grant them; and there were the Jesuits and their following, children of the Counter-Reformation trained in the school of Douai, who would make no compromise of a spiritual allegiance to the Pope which overrode all the claims of King and country. Garnet, the Jesuit Provincial in England, had acquiesced with his party in James's accession merely because the King of Spain was not at that moment prepared to support opposition with armed force, and without any illusions of coming toleration. It was the seculars who were

118

bitterly disappointed when the recusancy fines continued to be
enforced in spite of all that had been said; and it was out of this
disappointment that Father Watson, a secular priest, hatched
the silly conspiracy known afterwards as the Bye Plot. Once
again, James was to be kidnapped, but no harm was to come to
him, and he was to be released as soon as he had agreed to keep
his promise of toleration. The plot was clumsily planned and
without hope of success, and it was in any case maliciously
revealed to the government by the Jesuit Father Gerard before
it had even matured. Its only importance lay in the revelation
of the extent to which James had already mismanaged the question of Catholicism, and the fact that it overlapped on the
fringes with another conspiracy—the only slightly more dangerous Main Plot—the link being provided by the Catholic
Sir Gervase Markham, who was involved in both.

The Main Plot sprang not from religious, but from purely
secular disappointments. It was hatched by men who, for wholly
diverse reasons, felt that their hopes and ambitions had been
frustrated by the continuance in office of Cecil and his friends.
Markham was a Catholic, Lord Grey of Wilton a leading Puritan. Lord Cobham, Warden of the Cinque Ports, an unstable,
nervous and unimpressive figure, seems to have hoped by his
wild dash north to meet the King to substitute a grouping of
himself and his friends for the Cecil-Howard combine; and his
brother, George Brooke, as Cecil's brother-in-law had felt himself entitled, one way or another, to some substantial advancement. Remotely in touch with these, though it is doubtful if he
even knew their plans, or did more than share their discontent,
was Sir Walter Raleigh. The last great figure of the Elizabethan
tradition of high adventure and the apostle of aggressive war to
the death against Spain, Raleigh can scarcely have hoped very
much from the change of dynasty. Only the personal favour of
the Queen had kept him in office in the teeth of the enmity of the
Cecils, father and son, and the new King was known to want
peace with Spain at almost any price. But to be deprived of his
Captaincy of the Guard and forbidden the Court could scarcely
fail to embitter him, and he may well have expressed himself
forcibly on the subject to Cobham, who was his cousin.

Precisely what projects these muddle-headed young men had
in mind neither the lawyers of the time nor historians since have

ever clearly fathomed. 'That the muddy waters were stirred was apparent,' one contemporary wrote, 'but with such a mixture that little could be visible in it.' Another thought that George Brooke started the whole plot in order to get the credit for revealing it to his brother-in-law, Cecil. Certainly they discussed the deposition of James in favour of his cousin, Arabella Stuart, who had the next best Tudor claim after James, with the advantage, which some lawyers thought essential, that she had been born and brought up in England; and George Brooke also certainly sounded Spanish agents on the possibility of military help for such an undertaking. There was no substance in it all, and the government could almost have afforded to ignore both these confused conspiracies. But James so handled the matter—and it was to be typical of so many episodes of his reign in England—as to extract from it the maximum of personal discredit. On Watson no pity need be wasted, nor on George Brooke, who was duly executed for treason. But there was clearly a strong case for clemency for the other three. Characteristically James argued himself into a logical impasse over it, and equally characteristically laid bare in public the processes of his own logic. It was to Englishmen one of the most surprising things about their new sovereign that, in his overmastering desire to be understood and approved of, he would constantly and at great length expose the inmost processes of his own thought, not only to his intimates or his Council, but often to a whole assembled Parliament. In this case he was tangled between his duty to make an example in a case of treason and his duty to be merciful. 'To execute Grey, who was a noble young spirited fellow,' so his argument ran, 'and save Cobham, who was base and unworthy, were a manner of injustice.' On the other hand, 'to save Grey, who was of a proud, insolent nature, and execute Cobham, who had showed great tokens of humility and repentance, were as great a solecism.' The surprised courtiers listened to this dilemma, endlessly prolonged and expounded 'in contrarieties', until it seemed that no conclusion was possible at all. Then at last James announced that he would spare all three.

It is easy to see what a puzzling exhibition of bad taste this must have seemed to many of his hearers. It is also clear that the dilemma in James's mind was a real one. What was really unforgivable was his method of putting his final decision into practice. For Markham, Grey and Cobham were brought each in turn to the scaffold to go through the grim ritual of a seventeenth-century execution, to bid their friends farewell and make their peace with God, and were then on a trivial excuse withdrawn. All three were then reassembled on the scaffold to stand in the rain while their crimes were again read over to them, and only at long last told of the reprieve. All this elaborate, long-drawn-out agony was of James's own private devising and can only have sprung from that recurrent streak of cruelty that was in his nature. Only Mr Gibbe of the King's Bedchamber was made privy to the plan; even the sheriff was in ignorance of it until Gibbe stepped dramatically on to the scaffold just as Markham was about to die. And even Cecil, though he was careful in the detailed account which he wrote for Winwood to extol 'the excellent Mixture of the King's Mercy with Justice', added pointedly on his credit and reputation that James had 'made no soul living privy, the messenger excepted'. The whole scene gives one glimpse into a character which James's subjects would never find wholly comprehensible.

For the treatment of Raleigh on this occasion, which did him infinitely more harm with public opinion in the long run, James was not so directly to blame. For Raleigh, most of whose life had been dedicated to fighting Spaniards, was brought to trial at Winchester for treasonably conspiring with the other three to bring Spanish troops into England. The evidence against him was pitiable; confessions of Cobham's at a moment when he had completely broken down, which even he had retracted when he had slightly recovered his nerve. The trial was conducted unfairly, even by the standards of the seventeenth-century treason laws, and Sir Edward Coke's handling of the prosecution as Attorney-General was unbelievably brutal. Cecil seems to have had no direct hand in it all, but he had done the real damage two years before when he wrote to James in Scotland that Northumberland, Cobham and Raleigh, 'in their prodigal humour of dissensions . . . would not stick to confess daily how contrary it is to their nature to resolve to be under your sovereignty'. One seed of suspicion was enough in James's mind, and probably accounted for the very wrong decision to bring Raleigh to trial at all on such flimsy evidence. Once that decision had been taken Cecil could well afford to sit smugly back. 'Always,' he wrote, 'he shall be left to the Law, which is the right all men are born to.' For he knew very well that in that age, once committed to a trial, the Crown could not risk an acquittal without a fearful loss of prestige.

But here again, not so much in allowing the trial, but in his subsequent treatment of Raleigh, James revealed a streak of that same unimaginative callousness. Raleigh was intolerably proud, a quick-tempered and violent man of action whom even his contemporary Elizabethans found an intolerable colleague. He stood for all the fierce, athletic, physical success which James most consciously lacked and envied, and for policies of war and piracy which it was James's mission in life to reverse. But to consign him to the Tower and leave him there for thirteen years with the suspended death sentence still hanging over him was to show a meanness of spirit which even James's own son would not be able to forgive. None but his father, Prince Henry was to say, would have found a cage for such a bird. In the days of his pride Raleigh had made enemies everywhere. In the Tower he became a national hero: the last great Elizabethan who stood for the vanished glories after which Englishmen sighed, even while they reaped the solid blessings of King James's peace. It is probable that the philosophic studies and the chemical experiments with which he beguiled the years, and above all the great *History of the World*, which was to be one of the major formative influences on the minds of the coming generation, were a more valuable contribution to English civilization than anything Raleigh's flaming, uneasy genius would have achieved at large in the world. But that does not excuse King James.

The total effect of these episodes was that by the Christmas of 1603 an atmosphere of disillusionment and anticlimax had begun to overlay the happy triumphs of the early summer. James himself was beginning to realize that governing England was to mean something more than hunting and feasting and watching masques by Jonson and Campion elaborately staged by Inigo Jones, and being free at last from the money worries, the intractable religious disputes, and the ceaseless intrigues for power which had made the pattern of his life in Scotland. For his Queen it was turning out to be just that. Without a spark of ambition, with hardly any interest in politics and the personalities which surrounded her, Anne was settling down to enjoy the rest of her life as luxuriously as possible. Buying clothes and jewels regardless of the state of the Exchequer, hunting, and touring round the great country houses on separate, and very expensive, progresses of her own, designing dances and masques in which she herself could act—these became the whole fabric of her existence, and she rapidly ceased to count for very much even in James's private life. In his heart James probably hankered after a more boisterous version of the same thing, with some intellectual and literary activity thrown in, since that was the field in which he could most easily excel. But it was not working out like that. The Exchequer was not after all inexhaustible. Neither English men nor English events would conform to the clear, sensible patterns laid down for them in his mind, and he was becoming aware of problems which might not yield so easily as he had assumed to his experienced, kingly wisdom.

On the part of his subjects, too, the first triumphant rapture of a peaceful succession was beginning to die away. It would be wrong to assume, as many historians have in the past, that the impact of James on a public accustomed to Elizabeth was wholly disastrous. For those whose duty or ambition brought them into direct contact with him he was in many ways an improvement. The Elizabethan grandees had never really liked taking orders from a woman, and Elizabeth's flaring temper, her eccentricities and her caprices had made life at Court and round the Council table a perpetual strain. A King who, for all his coarse manners and his Scottish accent, could be approached on terms, almost, of easy familiarity, who was generous and talkative, and whose rages very seldom went beyond testy irritability, restored the feeling of normality. A virgin queen of Elizabeth's calibre was a phenomenon to be proud of, but in many ways it was a comfort to have a man with a wife and young family and with the ordinary, obvious human weaknesses. It must be remembered, too, that for the first six years or so of his reign in England James was very much at his best. His relationship with Anne, though it could never, in view of her placid stupidity, be very complete, was for the moment satisfactory. He seemed to have outgrown the necessity for youthful favourites—for intense intimacies concentrated on one man— and there was no reason to suppose that he would relapse. Moreover, though his private life would never be really deco- rous, the formidable English social background did to some extent for a year or two force him on to his best behaviour, while the obvious irreplaceability of Cecil as the years went on removed the temptation to entrust power and policy to those who shared the intimacies of his leisure. Nothing would make James great; but there was much in those early years to make him, to the governing class at least, acceptable.

None the less the first excitement of a new reign with all its possibilities of fresh openings for men hitherto excluded from favour by accident or prejudice died down fast. The shower of gifts and favours and pensions gradually diminished as even James became aware of the limitations of his Treasury, leaving the voices of the disappointed and the envious to drown the chorus of approval. Without Elizabeth's parsimonious super- vision, the struggle for profit and pension was intensified, with the added bitterness of a general rivalry between English and Scots. Rumours of all this, spreading into circles outside the orbit of Court and government, were rousing, if not a hostile, at least a highly suspicious public opinion among the tax-paying classes. For the grants and pensions, though they never formed a very high proportion of the Crown's total indebtedness, bulked large in the gossip of St Paul's and were enlarged in the telling, and every letter-writer in the capital dwelt on the elaboration and expensiveness of the festivities planned by both King and Queen for their first Christmas in England. The granting of new honours similarly defeated its own ends by excess. The first gratifying knighthoods for the more distinguished gentle- men who rode in to greet the King at the borders of each new county had lost their value in the indiscriminate shower of titles which began with the King's arrival at Theobalds, and it was not long before the market in peerages, too, began to be cheapened. While Bacon could write sadly of 'this almost pros- tituted title of knighthood', a lampoon posted in St Paul's offered 'to help weak memories to a competent knowledge of the nobility'. A few months of prodigality, in fact, very quickly depressed spirits which had been so elevated by James's 'boun- tiful beginnings'.

Of James's impact on the still wider public which lined the main roads and thronged the streets of Islington to gape, and of its importance, it is harder to speak with precision. The London mob and the great, inarticulate, labouring population of the countryside were at all normal times unrepresented in Parliament and without direct political significance. But that did not mean, as the Tudors had well understood, that they were politically unimportant. It was not only during a crisis, when invasion threatened, or when economic mismanagement had put bread beyond the means of the very poor, that governments needed to reckon with the men who manned Drake's ships and on whose labour the whole structure of England's propериty was founded. They formed at all times an important element in the climate of public opinion which must powerfully, even if indirectly, affect the most self-centred gentleman or merchant who sat in the House of Commons; and the growing Puritan movement was rapidly making a portion of them at least into an articulate political force.

The trick of managing this sort of public opinion had been one of the greatest Tudor assets. Regular progresses had given the majority of Elizabeth's subjects a chance to see their already legendary Queen, and she had contrived exactly the right combination of pageantry and intimacy, of dignity and a cheerful, coarse amiability, to rouse and keep their devotion. So long as James remained on a horse he did not do too badly, in spite of his quilted clothing and his lack of any sense of occasion; and his passion for hunting appealed to all classes as kingly and manly. Afoot his shambling walk robbed him of all dignity and he had no feeling for ceremonial. What was worse, he had none of the ready tricks that keep crowds well-tempered: he could not, like Elizabeth, bandy words with draymen and fishwives, or find the right phrase to compliment a village schoolmaster on the singing and dancing of his pupils, or thank the actors for a much-rehearsed masque or pageant which had delayed an already belated and tedious procession. James found that he hated the masses. Close contact with crowds roused all his old fear of assassination, and even their enthusiasm was distasteful—smelly, disorderly and uncontrollable. This distaste grew on him very fast after he crossed the Border and realized what extremely large crowds England could produce. 'I will have no coach,' he said, when he started out for York Minster, 'for the people are desirous to see a King, and so they shall; for they shall as well see his body as his face'. This very right-minded attitude entirely disappeared under the impact of the jostling, undisciplined London crowds, and before long those in touch with the Court were urging the mob not 'in love so to press upon your Sovereign thereby to offend him'. James wanted the love; it was indeed his absolute right as an anointed King. But he wanted it on his own terms, at a decent distance, and without any interference with his own pleasures or convenience. The English public was not to be had on those terms, and in this attitude of mind lay the root of much of James's later failure. Furthermore, these three months of almost enforced idleness and luxury while he waited for the Plague to abate brought out all the worst of his tendency to laziness and self-indulgence. Henceforth he would increasingly expect both men and events—the London mob and the crowned heads of Europe alike—to conform to his wishes and convenience without any serious effort on his part, and would relapse into ineffectual, testy rages when they failed to do so. With a tenth of Elizabeth's ability as a ruler of men, James was about to attempt to govern both England and Scotland in his spare time.

CHAPTER VII

Puritans and Catholics. The First Failure

*

Among the many and idealized visions which James cherished of himself the most important, and the one to which he clung most persistently, was that of the wise mediator who, having united England and Scotland, would then intervene to bring peace to the warring nations of Europe, and finally between her warring religions. A peace treaty between England and Spain was the obvious first step towards this, which, indeed, James had already attempted to negotiate as early as 1590, sending ambassadors to the German princes to organize a joint threat of economic boycott to force Spain to come to terms. Though Elizabeth had given this premature attempt at international action and the application of sanctions her official approval, there was no chance of its succeeding so long as the Spaniards thought they had a real chance of conquering Ireland, or until the English were certain that the revolted Dutch provinces could fight off Philip's troops without direct foreign aid. It was only at the very end of Elizabeth's life that these two conditions were fulfilled, and James, therefore, succeeded to the throne at precisely the right moment. One of his first Proclamations ordered the cessation of all hostilities at sea on the doubtful grounds, which strained the theory of Divine Right to its limits, that he, personally, had never been at war with Spain and could not become so merely by inheriting the English Crown. But the Spaniards, too, were ready for peace, and by the end of September a Spanish Ambassador, Don Juan de Tassis, was presenting his credentials at Winchester with a view to opening preliminary negotiations.

Since the war had reached a deadlock in which neither side could hope for any positive success, the only sort of peace to be had was really a mere cessation of hostilities, and there was little ground for prolonged negotiation. Nevertheless there were endless delays, largely on account of what Sir Henry Wotton called 'Spanish gravity sake', and it was not until August of 1604 that the Constable of Castile at last crossed the Channel with full powers to sign the treaty. The Spaniards could not induce the English to denounce the Dutch as mere rebels and break off trading with them; nor could the English extract from Philip of Spain permission to trade with his American Empire. James, still resolutely pursuing his role as European mediator, announced that as long as Dutch and Spaniards went on fighting he 'was resolved always to carry an even hand betwixt them both;' and when the Spaniards demanded the disbandment of the English regiments serving with Sir Francis Vere in the Low Countries they were told firmly that these were volunteers in the service of the United Provinces, and that the Spaniards might come and recruit similar regiments in England if they pleased. This strong stand by Cecil for England's trading rights and her obligations towards the Dutch prevented James's treaty from being wildly unpopular, since trade with the Spanish European dominions alone opened up a tremendous market for London merchants. But in spite of the solid commercial advantages to be derived from trading with both sides while the Dutch and Spaniards remained at war, Englishmen never liked this treaty which was the one great triumph of James's statesmanship. They felt it as a betrayal of their own great past; and anti-Spanish and anti-Catholic feeling, fanned by inflammatory sermons from Puritan pulpits, ran so high that at any time in the next twenty years most of them would gladly have sacrificed the material profits of peace for the sake of another crusade against the ancient enemy.

Simultaneously with his Spanish negotiations, James boldly tackled the religious question, and in the same mediating spirit. For here he was planning to bring peace not only within his own dominions, but throughout the whole of Europe. To the end of his life James would never quite lose the illusion that it was possible to 'win all men's hearts'; and his own reasoning always seemed to him so clear, logical, and utterly convincing, that he could not believe that others could remain unconvinced by it except out of mere wilfulness. 'It should become you,'

128

THE SOMERSET HOUSE PEACE CONFERENCE OF 1604

The English delegation is on the right and, reading from the far end, consists of
the Earl of Dorset, the Earl of Nottingham, Lord Mountjoy,
the Earl of Northampton and Sir Robert Cecil

Believed to be painted by Marc Gheeraerts

he would write some years later to Archbishop Abbot, when they had differed on a theological issue, 'to have a kind of faith implicit in my judgement, as well in respect of some skill I have in divinity, as also that I hope no honest man doubts of the uprightness of my conscience; and the best thankfulness that you, that are so far my creature, can use towards me, is to reverence and follow my judgement, except where you may demonstrate unto me that I am mistaken or wrong-informed.' The crux lay in the last sentence. Nobody—not Abbot, not Cardinal Bellarmine, nor the Puritan Dr Reynolds—was ever able to demonstrate to James's own satisfaction that he was 'mistaken or wrong-informed' about anything whatever. Yet it remained a perpetual puzzle to him that they could not see how wrong-headed they themselves were.

This mediating approach involved James also in the idea that the Church of England was a sort of half-way house between Rome and Geneva: a little too Catholic in some of her ways and worship for the Puritans; a shade too Protestant in belief for the Pope. Since by such an arrangement he himself would not be asked to concede any point of doctrine to either, it seemed to him only too simple for Catholics and Calvinists to make the slight concessions which would enable them to meet in the middle, which would be found to be the position of the Church of England. He cannot really have thought that religious beliefs could be treated as bargaining counters, with one truth being exchanged for another. It was more the case that, since on all points of difference both sides were demonstrably mistaken, it would only be a matter of patience and time to make them realize the fact. It is in his religious controversies that James's inability ever to understand how another man's mind worked comes out most clearly; and at the root of his misunderstandings of Catholic and Puritan alike there lay a basic misunderstanding of the nature of the Church of England, which was not in fact a *via media* at all. Her predominantly Catholic ritual and worship were abhorrent to Puritans; her largely Calvinist theology was quite unacceptable to Roman Catholics. She thus represented a combination of extremes, some Catholic, some Protestant, which has always been acceptable to large numbers of Englishmen, but seldom to anyone else.

It had not been easy for Elizabeth and her Bishops to build a national Church out of the chaos left behind by Henry VIII, Edward VI and Mary. Elizabeth's own approach to the problem had been severely practical. In her Acts of Uniformity and Supremacy, and in her Book of Common Prayer, she had provided a decent and orderly form of worship designedly so Catholic in texture that it might coax into the fold of the Church the lukewarm and the merely conservative among her Catholic subjects, whose chief importance in her eyes was their potential value as a fifth column to a French or Spanish invader. If the question of Papal supremacy were set on one side, there was little in her Thirty-nine Articles of Religion which had not, at one time or another, been considered as possibly acceptable by the reforming group of Cardinals at the court of Clement VII; and she caught the English Catholics at a moment when the rigid and uncompromising statement of Catholic belief by the Council of Trent had scarcely launched the full force of the Counter Reformation, and had certainly not penetrated to the outer confines of Western Europe. She had in consequence largely succeeded in her main object of getting the majority of her subjects to come to church. The relentless pressure of the recusancy fines for non-attendance had been more effective than any dramatic persecution; and the Armada had helped by making Catholicism unpatriotic. The emphasis throughout had been secular; to shore up the nation's loyalty and solidarity with religious sanctions. The Church became one of the most important departments of state and the Bishops the royal officers appointed to administer it. Thus the Queen always insisted on the major importance of the act of weekly worship rather than of preaching, which she personally detested; and she deprecated all theological argument as tending to produce and exacerbate differences of opinion, rather than promote unity.

But Elizabeth's Bishops, working within the Erastian framework she had provided for them, had made of her Church something very much more than the department of state she had intended. While accepting the royal supremacy they clung fast to their own spiritual authority derived not from the Crown, but by the laying on of hands by Apostolic succession. Their insistence on the historic continuity of the Church in England and their acceptance of all Catholic teaching and theology that went back beyond the Papacy to the early fathers and the primitive Church created something far more deeply rooted and harder to remove than a mere reformed communion, and which contained much that was far removed from the logic of Calvinism. The difficulties they had to contend with were enormous. The dearth of clergy at the outset was very serious, and by the end of the century the ouput of trained, competent men from Oxford and Cambridge still fell far short of the demand. The depredations of profiteers and land grabbers, principally during the Protectorates of Somerset and Northumberland, had left a majority of parishes and many of the higher positions in the Church quite inadequately endowed, so that most parsons were wretchedly poor and it was impossible to prevent the evils of pluralism. Elizabeth, always at her wits' end for money and anxious to avoid unpopular taxation, had often sanctioned further raids on Church property to reward the services—Raleigh's notably, among others—which she was not prepared to pay for herself. As late as 1585 Archbishop Whitgift estimated that more than half the beneficed clergy of England had incomes between £8 and £10 a year, while less than half could be licensed to preach, since hardly any had university degrees. This situation only remedied itself very slowly and was still scandalous in 1603. Izaak Walton tells the story of Hooker, whose *Ecclesiastical Polity* gave the Church of England her first coherent statement of faith, that when two of his ex-pupils went to see him at Drayton Beauchamp, in the days before he was promoted to the Mastership of the Temple, they found him 'tending his small allotment of sheep in a common field' while he read the Odes of Horace; and though Walton, it is true, was out to show what a shrew and bully Mrs Hooker was, it is clear that conditions in that 'poor Parsonage' did not make it easy for the vicar to become either a great scholar or a spiritual force in his parish.

This was the situation which had laid the Church so dangerously open to Puritan attack, both in Parliament and outside, in the 1580s. But, thanks to Hooker as much as to anyone, that attack had by 1603 been temporarily beaten off, and before long Lancelot Andrewes, whom James found as Dean of Westminster and promoted first to the See of Ely and then to Winchester, was to complete the job of giving the Church an ordered system of belief. By the time that James came to the throne the clamour for a drastic revision of the Prayer Book and for the abolition of Bishops in favour of some more democratic form of Church government had largely died away. An overwhelming majority of English opinion still attributed to Monarchy that mystic authority which constituted Divine Right and saw the government of Church and State as inseparable aspects of the same problem. Thus the Puritan grievances embodied in the Millenary Petition were not very radical, and many of them would have been endorsed by the Bishops, and indeed by anyone with the interests of the Church at heart. Everybody agreed that pluralism should be abolished, that stipends must be raised, and that a 'preaching, Godly ministry' must somehow be established. For the rest, they asked mainly for small modifications of ceremonial which might be applied at the discretion of each individual parson.

In analysing later to his first Parliament the religious situation in England as he found it in 1603, James distinguished three elements: the religion 'publicly allowed and by the law maintained', and 'another sort of religion, besides a private sect, lurking within the bowels of this nation'. The other religion was, of course, 'what is falsely called Catholics, but truly Papists', whom, in spite of the Bye Plot, he still proposed to conciliate by toleration. The sect consisted of 'Puritans and Novelists, who do not so far differ from us in points of religion as in their confused form of polity and parity, being ever discontented with the present government and impatient to suffer any superiority, which maketh their sect unable to be suffered in any well governed commonwealth'. In so describing 'Purinisme' he was allowing bitter Scottish experience to warp and over-simplify his judgement, and like so many who have used the word then and since was lumping together a strikingly varied body of opinions. It included, of course, the real Calvinists, whose democratic theory of Church government and ultimate subordination of State to Church were alike anathema to him: the men who would force him back into the position of 'God's sillie vassall'. But there were already in England men who went further than that, rejecting with Henry Barrow the authority of even an autonomous Church, and preaching the 'independency' in matters of belief of each separate congregation. At the other end of the scale there were those who would broadly accept the Church of England as constituted by Elizabeth, but with various modifications. Some desired a compromise with Presbyterianism which would join a Council of Elders with the Bishop in the administration of diocesan discipline. Others wanted the use of ceremonial and vestments to be left to the discretion of the incumbent in each parish and there was a strong body of opinion which wished to see the Communion Table removed from the altar's old position at the east end of the church, where they feared it might be worshipped as a 'graven image', and placed firmly in the body of the building. Some would have forbidden altogether the practices of bowing at the name of Jesus and of 'knocking', or beating the breast. There were objections to the use of the sign of the cross in baptism, to the ring in marriage, and the rite of Confirmation; and there were the purely doctrinal objectors who demanded the exclusion from the Thirty-nine Articles of everything for which there was no direct scriptural warrant. By the end of James's reign the word Puritan would be used for all those whose lives were strict and orderly and sober, and who disapproved of the profligacy and extravagance of the Court.

Broadly speaking, when purged of irrelevant detail, there were three basic points in dispute between the Bishops and their Puritan opponents. One was the question of sermons. The Puritans clamoured for 'a preaching ministry' and denounced the 'dumb mouths' who held so many country livings, while the official doctrine of the Church laid all its stress on ordered liturgical worship. The dispute over the position of the Communion Table, whether it should be 'altar-wise' or 'table-wise', involving as it did so many other points of belief, became another fundamental issue. Finally there was the Sabbatarian controversy which has echoed from Elizabeth I's day to this, which also involved a great deal more than the mere question of how the people might suitably amuse themselves on Sunday. For those who claimed for an Anglican Sunday all the traditions, observances, and restrictions which had surrounded the Jewish Sabbath, it raised the real and fundamental issue which lay behind all these controversies; between the Puritan view that only that was permissible for which direct Scriptural authority could be found, and that of the Bishops that usages and ceremonies sanctioned by the Church's own tradition or by the early Fathers were valid, so long as they did not demonstrably conflict with Scriptural injunction. These were the two obstinately different viewpoints which James had somehow to reconcile if his peacemaker's dream was to be realized.

On all these points Elizabeth not only avoided involving herself in argument, but did her best to prevent any public discussion. To James, on the other hand, they not only offered problems of genuine fascination, but also, since he knew himself to be an expert, a splendid opportunity to show off. The love of theological discussion grew on him with the years, and he was never happier than when exchanging five-thousand word controversial essays with Archbishop Abbot and Dr Grotius, or arguing with Lancelot Andrewes as to whether a man once in a state of grace could ever thereafter be damned *totaliter* or *finaliter*, or both. The Millenary Petition, therefore, gave him a welcome excuse to indulge his favourite hobby; and as soon as the Christmas festivities were over, while the peace negotiations with Spain were still dragging on, and before he had even met his first Parliament, he commanded a representative Puritan delegation from Oxford and Cambridge to meet a selection of Bishops and clergy under his chairmanship at Hampton Court on January 14th, 1604. It seems to have been in his mind that he had only to pronounce his own judgement on the points in dispute and all controversy would be at an end. For it was highly unlikely that men like Dr Reynolds, the President of Corpus, Oxford, or Mr Knewstub of John's College, Cambridge, would be able to demonstrate that he was 'mistaken or wrong informed'.

For the first day of the conference only the Bishops and some of the Council were present; and on that Saturday was sealed what was probably the inevitable, and certainly turned out to be the fateful alliance between King and Bishops, the foundations of which had been laid at Tobie Mathew's dinner table at Durham in the first week of the reign. Monarchy and Episcopacy, the two great institutions which rested their authority on sanctions which were mystical, traditional and irrational, which defied alike the Tridentine certainties of the Papacy and the harsh logic of Calvinism, were forced into alliance by circumstance and were probably bound to stand or fall together.

Whatever difficulties it might raise for him in the political sphere, James's insistence on his Divine Right had a theological value not only for the Bishops, but for a much wider circle in the Anglican Church. Having escaped from the spiritual tyranny of Rome they had now to avoid falling under the alternative tyranny of Geneva. A monarchy directly sanctioned by God was a redoubt which could be successfully defended on both sides. It had been the refuge of the Elizabethan Church against the pretensions of Rome, and James had found in it his only escape from the domination of the Kirk. It is not surprising that the new King and his Bishops greeted each other with gratitude and relief.

But the sympathy and unity of outlook which were so immediately established between James and the men who formulated and embodied Anglican thought were deeper and much more real than a mere matter of necessity or convenience. The churchmen shared with him the whole of that intellectual world in which, outside his hunting, the King chiefly sought relaxation. Pursuing his dream of the *via media* among the warring religions of Europe, James would find in Dr Donne a chaplain who 'never fettered nor imprisoned the word Religion by immuring it in a Rome, a Wittenberg, or a Geneva', but found these 'all virtuall beams of one sun'; and Bishop Williams of Lincoln echoed the same sentiment: 'Is there but one Tree of Knowledge in all the Paradise of the Church of God?' Williams, in many ways the perfect representative of the Jacobean episcopacy, whom James was later to make Lord Keeper, had, besides this large theological charity, much else about him that appealed to the King. 'His well kneaded judgement took delight in clear and solid Divinity', and at the same time he moved in a richly varied circle of antiquarian and learned friends and lived 'in as much pomp and plenty as any Cardinal in Rome for diet, music, and attendance'; and Williams for his part, so his chaplain assures us, 'understood the Soil on which he had set his foot, that it was rich and fertile'. For the first time in his life James entered a world intellectually and spiritually wholly congenial to him, and one which gave him back a welcome as genuine. He could laugh at Dr Tobie Mathew's 'salted wit' and enjoy learned controversy with that 'painful and diligent preacher', Dr Andrewes, 'so noble in his entertainment and so

135

gravely facetious', without being brought face to face with any sense of his own shortcoming. In due course he would find and promote to Canterbury George Abbot, the Master of University College, whose zest for the early fathers and whose mild Calvinism, tempered by much reading of St Augustine, exactly matched his own taste and doctrine. It was thus among his churchmen more than anywhere else that King James found his promised land in England.

It is arguable that some modification of Elizabeth's Church Settlement was by 1603 overdue: that the 1558 concessions to Catholic feeling were now less necessary, and that a timely yielding to the less drastic Puritan demands would have kept the moderate majority contentedly within the Church and have deprived the extremist leaders of their rank and file. 'I did ever holde,' James had written once to Cecil, 'persecution as one of the infallible notes of a false churche'; and again, still more emphatically, 'I will neuer agree that any should die for erroure in faith.' Certainly, if a civil war was ultimately to be avoided, some such policy of Comprehension, rather than a narrow, persecuting exclusiveness, was politically essential. A Tudor sovereign, to whom material unity rather than any particular doctrinal position would have been the paramount consideration, would undoubtedly have seized the opportunity of the Hampton Court Conference to alleviate discontent on the more Protestant wing of the Church. The Puritan demands were more moderate than they had been for the past twenty years, and much more moderate than they would ever be again. Moreover, those who protested were demonstrably the best educated, most zealous, and conscientious of the parish clergy, most of whom had hitherto loyally accepted regulations of which they disapproved for the sake of the unity of the Church. Subsequent history was to show that such men could perfectly well be accommodated as an evangelical body within the Church without impairing her unity on essentials of belief and worship. To have conciliated them before they became embittered with episcopacy and all its works would not only have robbed the nonconformist movement later in the century of most of its strength but would also have deprived the government's political opponents in the House of Commons of the powerful support of Puritanically inclined laymen, who were particularly numerous in those classes directly represented in Parliament.

But all such considerations were wholly remote from the mental processes of King James. He had not that sort of political sense. He could never see another man's point of view; and his vaunted ideal of toleration did not include an admission that a man who differed from him might be right. For him the conference was primarily an opportunity to show off his own skill in divinity to a friendly and subservient bench of Bishops and to settle differences, not by compromise, but by the assertion of authority. He opened the conference, after a 'few pleasant gratulations', with what James Montague, later Bishop of Bath and Wells, described in a letter to his mother as 'a very admirable Speech of an Hour long at least', which left nobody in any doubt as to what it meant to have a theologian as the Lord's Anointed. If he erred in anything, the Bishops were told, 'he would suffer himself to be corrected by God's word; if they erred they must yield to him'. And all hope of serious concessions disappeared in a single sentence in which he congratulated himself that, unlike his predecessors, who 'were fain to alter all things they found established, he saw yet no cause so much to alter and change anything as to confirm what he found well settled already'.

With this basis for discussion fixed in advance, it was clear from the start that Dr Reynolds and his delegation, when they were admitted to the conference on the second day, were unlikely to get a very sympathetic hearing. It is true that James throughout talked a great deal of sound sense. Agreeing that there should be a single revised and authoritative Catechism, he added what William Barlow called 'the excellent, gnomical, and canon-like conclusion' that firstly 'old, deep, curious and intricate questions might be avoided in the fundamental instruction of a people', and that secondly nothing should be excluded from the Prayer Book merely because it was also approved by Papists. He enthusiastically supported the suggestion of a new and authoritative translation of the Bible—a project in which he was to take a direct and expert interest and which was to provide his reign and age with their finest monument. He routed Dr Reynolds with easy good humour on the question of the phrase, 'With my body I thee worship' in the marriage service. 'Many a man,' James said, smiling at the Doctor, 'speaks of Robin Hood who never shot his bow: if you had a good wife yourself you would think all the honour and worship you could do her were well bestowed.' Even the famous aphorism of 'No Bishop, no King' with which he closed up the discussion on the ordination of Bishops and for which he has been much criticized, was really only an emphatic statement of an undeniable fact. But on every controversial issue the King sided with Bancroft, the Bishop of London, who by the end of the conference had been earmarked as the next Archbishop of Canterbury. It was only on the non-controversial points that they reached a genial, though not very practically effective agreement: on the need for raising stipends, recovering lost Church revenues, and providing a better 'teaching ministry'; on the undesirability of pluralities and double benefices, and on the general principle of enforcing a proper observance of the Sabbath. Bancroft's treatment of the Puritans was throughout contemptuous, and James himself was at times insufferably patronizing. 'And surely,' he said at one point, 'if these be the greatest matters you be grieved with, I need not have been troubled with such importunities and complaints as have been made unto me; some other more private course might have been taken for your satisfaction; and withal, looking upon the Lords, he shook his head, smiling.'

Up to this point the conference, though it had achieved very little, had at least done no positive harm. Unfortunately, however, they got on to the question of ecclesiastical discipline and Dr Reynolds, in seeking to sketch out some system less obnoxious than the Archdeacons' courts, suggested as a final court of appeal in each diocese, 'the episcopal synod, where the bishop with his presbytery should determine all such points as before could not be decided'. William Barlow in his book, *The Sum and Substance of the Conference*, noted that at this 'his Majesty was somewhat stirred, yet, which is admirable in him, without passion or show thereof'. But Barlow had his eye on Church preferment and was, in fact, shortly to be rewarded for his sympathetic account with the Bishopric of Lincoln. In reality James was very deeply stirred and his retort, in all the variously reported versions, reeks of the passion and frustration engendered by years of dealing with the Kirk. 'Your Scottish Presbytery,' he said, 'as well agreeth with a monarchy as God and the Devil. Then Jack and Tom and Will and Dick shall meet, and at their pleasure censure me and my Council and all our proceedings. Then Will shall stand up and say, "It must be thus"; then Dick shall reply and say, "Nay, marry, but we will have it thus" . . . Stay, I pray you, for one seven years before you demand that of me, and if then you find me pursy and fat and my wind-pipes stuffed, I will perhaps hearken to you: for let that government be once up, I am sure I shall be kept in breath.' All James's best and worst qualities are to be found in that single, well-known utterance: the coarse, humorous petulance and common sense which made him, for all his lack of dignity and decorum, an endearing figure to his intimates, and which often enabled him, when his personal affections were not involved, to see to the heart of complicated issues; but also the absence of all political sense and of the ability to compromise or to conciliate opposition. The whole of Elizabeth's system of government in Church and State rested on a series of delicate balances which could work in practice only so long as they were not subjected to any harsh dialectic and definition. With a clumsy precision born of too much book learning James was to endanger institution after institution of the Elizabethan State by tactless definitions of claims which, undefined, might well have been enforced by the Crown for another century without serious opposition.

The disastrous effects of James's outburst were in no way immediately apparent. The conference closed on the following day in an atmosphere of outward goodwill, with Archbishop Whitgift asserting that 'undoubtedly his Majesty spake by the special assistance of God's spirit', and Bancroft making haste 'to acknowledge unto Almighty God the singular mercy we have received at His hands in giving us such a King as since Christ his time the like he thought had not been'. The cowed Puritan delegates, when they were called in to hear the complacent conclusions reached by King and Bishops, only dared to put in a humble plea that their brethren 'who were grave men and obedient unto the laws' might be given some time to make up their minds whether they would conform to the new and more rigid enforcement of the Prayer Book ceremonies and the Thirty-nine Articles. James, placidly certain that 'obedience and humility were the marks of honest and good men', and that the mere assertion of a King's authority would suffice to preserve the unity of Church and State, accepted the Bishops' flattery at its face value and treated the Puritans with a scarcely kindly contempt.

But, little though it seemed so at the time, James's threat to Reynolds that, if the aggrieved ministers did not conform, he would 'harry them out of the land' permanently altered the climate of relations between sovereign and subjects. The whole tone of Tudor government had been, however authoritarian, patriarchal and kindly. Lord Burleigh had thought it his duty to stand between the harsh proceedings of Archbishop Whitgift's ecclesiastical courts and those 'poor ministers' who, as it seemed to him, were being made 'subject to condemnation before they be taught their error'. James's intention was kindly and patriarchal, but he lacked altogether Burleigh's large charity and understanding of the difficulties of simple, honest men. When, in due course, three hundred of his beneficed clergy found themselves unable to subscribe to every detail of the Thirty-nine Articles and were forced to resign their livings, neither King nor Bishops seem to have had the slightest inkling that they had condemned to failure Laud's efforts, thirty years later, to restore the Church to 'the beauty of holiness', and had started one of the chains of circumstance which would bring Charles I to the scaffold. 'We have kept such a revel with the Puritans here these two days as we never heard the like,' James wrote triumphantly the day after the Hampton Court Conference closed. 'They fled me so from argument to argument without ever answering me directly, ut est eorum mos, as I was forced at last to say unto them that if any of them had been in a College disputing with their scholars, if any of their disciples had answered them in that sort, they would have fetched him up in place of a reply, and so should the rod have plied upon the poor boy's buttocks.' So, in the happy belief that he had 'peppered them soundly', James brought to an end the first part of his attempt to achieve a 'general Christian union in religion as, laying wilfulness aside on both hands, we might meet in the midst, which is the centre and perfection of all things'.

The simultaneous attempt to deal with the 'wilfulness' of the

Catholics was equally disastrous. By his persistent efforts to define the terms on which he believed a reconciliation with Rome to be perfectly feasible James succeeded only in confusing everybody—the Pope, the English Catholics, and his own House of Commons—as to his real beliefs and intentions. Already he had had one warning, in the Main and Bye Plots, of the effects of injudicious encouragement of Catholic hopes, but his reaction to these was precisely the reverse of what was expected by the majority of his English subjects. In spite of the fact that it had been Catholic disappointment of the hopes of toleration he had raised before his accession which had partly caused these plots, his immediate decision was to allow in practice the very toleration he had refused: to suspend the collection of recusancy fines, allow Catholics to worship in private as they pleased, and close an eye to the immigration of Catholic priests. He may have had some idea that the denunciation of Watson's plot by the Jesuits denoted a change of heart. He certainly hoped to get by toleration the one concession from the Pope which he regarded as vital—the admission that Catholic subjects had a duty of allegiance to their king with which their religion could not interfere. Finally, he was under the delusion that he could make it a condition of toleration that there should be no increase in the number of Catholics in consequence of it.

The immediate results proved that the deep, irrational, anti-Catholic prejudices of the average Englishman were a sounder basis for policy than the theoretically high-minded tolerationist ideas of the King. The revelation of the real numbers of Catholics in the country when they were allowed to disappear without penalty from the back benches of their parish churches of a Sunday, and the large congregations which assembled everywhere to hear Mass, startled even those who had all along cherished the darkest Protestant suspicions, and it thoroughly alarmed the King. The returns which had been collected from every diocese of those who officially stayed away from church had led the government to estimate the total number of Catholics at about eight thousand, five hundred. When toleration allowed them into the open it seemed that the Papal claim to more than a hundred thousand was much nearer the mark; and both James and his most vociferous Protestant opponents be-

lieved, certainly quite wrongly, that most of these were fresh
converts as a result of the government's sudden leniency. This
made nonsense of James's proposed condition that there should
be no increase in Catholic numbers. The other condition, implicit in his mind, if not clear to his subjects or to the Pope, that
the Divine Right even of an Anglican king should be officially
recognized by Rome was equally incapable of fulfilment. The
vast majority of English Catholics were peaceable, loyal folk
who longed only to be allowed to worship after the old fashion
without compromising their patriotic allegiance as Englishmen. To their leaders, men of the Counter-Reformation, such a
compromise was unthinkable. Parsons, Sir Henry Wotton's
'malicious and virulent' Jesuit leader, who largely dictated
Papal policy regarding England, led a school of thought which
made all idea of toleration unthinkable. These men believed all
means justified which might lead to the forcible re-conversion
of England. Their plans were already seriously laid for the
Press censorship which must follow their triumph and the type
of English Inquisition which would be set up, and with them
there could be no question of James's dreamed-of compromise.
They held the betrayal or wherever possible the assassination
of a heretic sovereign not merely permissible but a duty; and,
since it was clearly impossible for the government to distinguish
between loyal and disloyal Catholics when even the most
stringent oath of allegiance could be made worthless by Papal
dispensation, the rank and file had inevitably to suffer for the
views of their leaders. James never saw the logic of the Jesuit
position, constantly begged his Catholic fellow sovereigns to
join with him in denouncing to the Pope doctrines which might
be as dangerous to them as to him, and continued to the end of
his life to believe that lenient treatment would eventually produce a Catholic change of heart. But he was frightened enough
by the immediate results of his policy in the winter of 1603–4
and sufficiently clear-headed to see that he would have no
answer to give an angry Parliament in the spring if he allowed
the Catholic revival to continue. There followed, therefore, the
second reversal of policy within nine months; a proclamation
ordered all Jesuits and priests to quit the country, and several
were hanged by the Assize Judges in February, though without
direct instructions from the government. Soon afterwards, to

the bitter disappointment of the entire Catholic body, whether loyalist or not, the recusancy fines were ruthlessly re-imposed. So began the chain of events which led directly to the Gunpowder Plot.

Thus, as far as religion was concerned, before he had been a year on the throne James had contrived to get the worst of both the available worlds. By refusing to sanction concessions to the Puritans on points which even his Bishops had listed as 'matters indifferent', and by the expulsion from their livings of the 'three hundred silenced brethren', he had identified monarchy and episcopacy with an extremist Arminian standpoint which would tend in the end to make the Church not comprehensive and national, but exclusive and sectional. Whatever view is taken of their protest, it is obvious that the Puritans who protested were all men of zeal, energy, and integrity, while of those who conformed some may have been equally zealous, but many were merely idle and conformed because they did not care. During the next twenty years the expelled three hundred became the first martyrs of a Puritanism far more aggressive and extreme than that of 1603. Their integrity and their disinterestedness were unquestionable, while far too many of those who remained in their livings were a poor advertisement for the opposite point of view, often too unlearned to preach and too badly paid to maintain any dignity or authority in their parishes. Moreover, the very determination of the Puritans to preach, if necessary in the teeth of the law, and their liking for Sunday afternoon disputations and expoundings of the Scriptures gave them an initial propaganda advantage over opponents who as a matter of principle discouraged sermons and threw all the emphasis of religion on to liturgical worship. The Puritan point of view was put far more often and more vociferously to congregations throughout the country than was the Anglican.

The upshot of all this was that moderate Anglicans, especially among the more substantial laymen, who had themselves no fundamental quarrel with the articles or practices of the Church, came to view the Puritan cause with sympathy; to think of the three hundred brethren as righteous and persecuted, and of the Bishops as innovators and tyrants. This point of view was to become increasingly typical of the majority of the members of

the House of Commons as the reign went on and would con-
tribute enormously to the political and financial difficulties
James was to bequeath to his son. The climate of the age in
which he lived made James's determination to have 'one doctrine
and one discipline, one religion in substance and in ceremony'
reasonable and, indeed, inevitable; nor can he and Bancroft be
seriously criticized for insisting that beneficed clergy should
subscribe to the Thirty-nine Articles and conform to the regulations governing forms and ceremonies. What was tragic for
King and Bishops alike was the rigidity of the official outlook at
Hampton Court; the refusal to compromise on what a wiser
statesmanship would have regarded as non-essentials. The
Church as a whole came to be identified with the points of view
of what had hitherto been one of two extremist minorities,
and so lost the allegiance of many whose support forty years
later might have been invaluable. Puritanism became harsher,
more 'railing', and more extreme, while the Bishops were
forced to use their ecclesiastical courts and their powers to silence
preachers and censor books ever more tyrannically in the
attempt to keep control of the situation.

This alienation of moderate opinion was completed by James's
wavering policy towards the Catholics. If his sudden re-en-
forcement of recusancy laws in 1604 exasperated the Catholics
into criminal plotting, the King's tolerationist experiments of
1603—to which he would revert later in the reign in spite of
the Gunpowder Treason—roused all the suspicions of the most
moderate Anglicans. The Puritan thesis, which identified
Bishops and ceremonies with a Catholic reaction, and Catholicism with foreign and tyrannical governments, became almost
a national dogma, held by many who were very far from being
Puritans. The open favour shown to Catholics at Court and the
equivocal statements James was liable to make when he tried
to convince Cardinal Bellarmine and the leaders of Catholic
thought of the reasonableness of his standpoint helped enormously to solidify English opinion against the muddled, benevolent intentions of Stuart government. Thus, with the best of
motives, before he had been a year on his new throne, and before
he had even met his first Parliament, James had already started
one of the processes which in the course of the century were to
destroy English Monarchy, as he understood it, altogether.

CHAPTER VIII

The First Round with Parliament

*

There was something almost magnificent about the confidence with which James launched himself into the successive new experiences of his reign in England: the certainty of his own ability and rightness; the sublime unawareness of difficulties, or of opinions which differed from his own. All this the Conference at Hampton Court had served to strengthen. The mutual esteem and even affection which had sprung up between him and his Bishops had been genuine and heart-warming. It is difficult for the modern mind to grasp how the traditional, semi-mystic feeling for royalty—for the mere fact of kingship—can have risen triumphantly over the lack of dignity and the total absence of any kingly quality which marked James's conduct of any function, public or private: even of a theological conference which he could manage better than anything else. That in the case of the Bishops it did so is, nevertheless, undoubted. This lolling, ungainly figure in the bulky, padded clothes they saw and reverenced as the Lord's Anointed. The sharp, coarsely-worded conclusions of the royal theologian, which matched so well with their own beliefs, they honestly welcomed as divinely inspired wisdom; and neither he nor they were conscious of any inadequacy in their handling of Puritan grievances. Fortified by Bancroft's flatteries, secure in the knowledge of his own wise experience, he faced his first Parliament comfortingly aware, as he blandly informed them, of 'the blessings which God hath in my person bestowed upon you all'. That there would be a factious minority, just as there had been at Hampton Court, was of course to be expected. But he was quite unprepared for a prevailing tone of opinion which was little impressed with his large, generalized wisdom and openly hostile to the theories of kingship which the Bishops had found so readily acceptable.

Some, though by no means all, of James's initial difficulties

145   K

with Parliament were a direct Tudor legacy. Henry VIII and Elizabeth had both used Parliaments to fulfil a dual function: the mobilization of public support for their policies, and the dissemination of government propaganda. The latter years of Henry VIII's reign and almost the whole of Elizabeth's had been periods of national crisis during which it was particularly important for the Crown to be certain of having a united nation behind it. Henry VIII's crises arose out of his breakaway from Rome and were, in a sense, of his own creation. Elizabeth's were forced on her by the internal situation bequeathed by her brother and sister and by the foreign threats which complicated and intensified all her difficulties. But both faced similar problems and solved them by similar methods. When Henry VIII challenged the Papacy he was engaging in a struggle in which some of his ablest and most powerful predecessors had been decisively worsted. In his anxiety to be sure of carrying a majority of effective English opinion with him on this dangerous venture, he made Parliament endorse every step of the break with Rome. With the experience gained from annual sessions and the self-confidence resulting from participation in the business of government the House of Commons had grown rapidly in stature and importance. And since the support of the House was valueless unless it was powerful and influential, this growth had been still further encouraged by Elizabeth.

Inevitably with added experience and self-reliance members became not merely endorsers, but cogent critics of government policy. Elizabeth had had the greatest difficulty in preventing the Commons from interfering in what she regarded as absolutely her own business: projects for her marriage, her foreign policy, and her Church Settlement. In 1597 she had had to give way on one of these points and it was recorded 'that although her Majesty had formerly been exceeding unwilling and opposite to all manner of innovations in ecclesiastical government, yet understanding at this present Parliament of divers gross and great abuses therein, she had . . . given leave and liberty to the House of Commons to treat thereof'. In 1601 there had been the concerted and victorious attack on her wholesale grants of trading monopolies during which Mr Francis Moore had gone so far as to put the question: 'To what purpose is it to do anything by Act of Parliament, when the Queen will undo the same by her prerogative?' There were moments at the end of her reign when even her accumulated prestige and popularity seemed to be waning. As she passed through the Commons on her way out after opening her last Parliament it was noticed that very few voices were raised in the customary cry of 'God save your Majesty'.

The Tudor monarchy had in fact been deliberately made to depend on the close support of the gentry and merchants, and its survival would continue to depend on the sovereign's ability to give those classes the leadership they needed. The House of Commons in 1603 was very far from being competent to direct the day-to-day business of government. Its members had an unrivalled knowledge of the problems of local administration and of England's commercial needs, but in the spheres of foreign and military affairs they had powerful prejudices and little practical experience. The ablest of sovereigns would have found them difficult to handle in the years after 1603, and concessions were inevitable which would gradually give Parliament a preponderant weight in the control of government, unless the King were able, ambitious, and energetic enough to go to the other extreme of benevolent autocracy. But there was no fundamental reason why the co-operation of Crown and Parliament should not continue for another century if the King clearly understood the forces he was dealing with, avoided head-on clashes, and manœuvred so as to preserve the reality of power without bothering overmuch about the theory of it. So far as his relations with Parliament were concerned, the situation which James inherited was, in fact, difficult but by no means impossible. Unfortunately, though, it required just those qualities of tact and flexibility in which James was most deficient.

To start with, he talked far too much. Elizabeth's appearances in Parliament had been rare and impressive: brief statements of policy at the start of a session, an occasional rating, or an engaging appeal to Lords and Commons, as she dismissed them, to collaborate in their counties in giving her subjects good government. Only very rarely was there a studied oration, such as the famous and brilliant speech with which she covered her retreat over monopolies in 1601. James could not resist the temptation to hold forth: to expound not only immediate policy, but large philosophic views on Church and State—'Long orations,' one member rudely said, 'that did inherit but winde.' Royal messages, interrupting debate and seeking to dictate its course, which had been under Elizabeth infrequent and formidable occurrences, became a positive nuisance, seriously interfering with the transactions of business. Complaints of 'many intervenient messages' multiplied as the reign went on, and in 1621 there was a formal attempt to 'moove the King that ther be not so many interpositions'. But when he was opposed James could not resist answering back, and so getting drawn into undignified wrangles. Worst still, he forced the Commons to consider matters which had been much better left undiscussed, pushing them into increasingly extreme statements of their own rights and grievances, and by his own passion for definitions provoking dangerous counter-definitions.

It was an additional misfortune that James's most sensible and constructive ideas broke against the most unreasonable of English prejudices, if only because it made it all the harder for him to do justice to opposition which, on other issues, was more reasonably based. It is true that he had got his peace with Spain in spite of the national prejudices. But the other great project with which he had come south, for a union between England and Scotland which should be something more than a dynastic accident, suffered complete shipwreck. His presentation of the case, though highly characteristic, was not really calculated to appeal to the hard-headed merchants and unimaginative squires who listened to it in the House of Commons. 'I am the husband, and the whole island is my wife,' he told them in his opening speech, after a short historical survey of the growth of the English monarchy. 'I am the head and it is my body; I am the shepherd, and it is my flock: I hope, therefore, no man will be so unreasonable as to think that I, who am a Christian King under the Gospel, should be a polygamist and husband to two wives; that I, being the head, should have a monstrous and divided body; or that being the shepherd to so fair a flock (whose wall hath no wall to hedge it in but the four seas) should have my flock parted in two.' The language and the heavy humour, and above all the highly egocentric approach, were all typical of that aspect of James which least appealed to the men he was addressing, preoccupied as they were with the legal and financial consequences of his project.

They gave way enough in the first session to pass an act setting up an Anglo-Scottish commission to consider how to 'make perfect that mutual love and uniformity of manners and customs' necessary to 'accomplish that real and effective Union already inherent in his Majesty's Royal Blood and Person'. But that was as far as they ever went, and in 1607 James was still complaining in, for him, unusually reasonable terms, of the 'crossings, long disputations, strange questions, and nothing done'. He argued his case on that occasion very ably indeed, but English prejudice was immovable and after 1610 he gave it up. Political union had to be postponed for a century, and the legal union he desired has never been achieved at all. In 1608 the common law Judges, after a masterly summing-up by Coke which quoted every relevant case from that of the Samaritan leper onwards, declared that all those born after 1603 in either country were natural born subjects of both kingdoms, and so avoided the worst effects of the differing legal systems. Further that that nobody in England could be induced to go.

If James had so little success with the Commons in an issue on which he was so clearly right and which he argued on the whole reasonably and well, it is not surprising that on other matters, in themselves less important, which he did not so clearly understand, he quickly ran into serious trouble. The very first episode of the Parliament of 1604 was a squabble which set the tone for relations between Crown and Commons for the rest of the reign. The initial error was the government's. In an attempt, unusual but not unprecedented, to influence the course of the forthcoming elections, a Proclamation had issued from Hampton Court in January admonishing sheriffs and electors 'to avoid the choice of any persons either noted for their superstitious blindness or for their turbulent humours other ways', and also bankrupts, outlaws, and those who evaded taxes. James may well have been personally responsible for the attempt to include Catholics and Puritans as 'disorderly and unquiet spirits'; but he can hardly have understood at the time all the implications of the further proviso, added to the Proclamation, that the election returns should be made, not direct to the House of Commons, but to the Court of Chancery. This was a reversal of the Elizabethan practice by which the House was the sole judge of cases involving disputed elections, and it

149

was the sort of point on which, under the Tudors, the Commons
had learnt to be peculiarly touchy. In fact it was an attempt by
the Crown's legal advisers to recover a piece of Chancery's lost
jurisdiction. It should not have raised any issue with the Crown,
but should have remained, as the Commons respectfully pointed
out, a dispute 'between the Court of Chancery and our Court,
an usual controversy between Courts about their preeminences
and privileges'. But the Commons took the matter up on the
first day of the session the moment the Speaker had finished his
formal, courteous answer to the King's rambling and discur-
sive opening speech. They seized on a disputed election in
Buckinghamshire and after two days of debate nullified the
Chancery return, resolved that a certain Sir Francis Goodwin
had been wrongly excluded as an outlaw, and ordered him to
take his seat. Almost the first political event of the reign was
thus a deliberate challenge to a royal Proclamation.

It was, unfortunately, not in James's nature to avoid an issue.
In this case he went out of his way to provoke another by in-
forming the Commons that their privileges depended on his
good will and advising them to consult the Judges on the
legality of their proceedings. In the subsequent dispute, which
wasted some three weeks of Parliamentary time, both sides
behaved with what was to become uncharacteristic moderation:
James patiently misunderstanding at every point, and the Commons doing their best to avoid a direct clash. They even selected
their precedents with a touch of humour, citing one case of 1581
in which an election, voided on the grounds that the candidate
had died, had to be declared valid by the House when he
appeared to claim his seat, and another in which the Burgess
chosen for Hull had to be rejected as a lunatic. But on the
main issue they stood firm through a long and very wordy
argument, and so drove James to utter with typical petulance
the first of the many phrases in which he was to assert his theory
of kingship. For he ordered the House's committee to meet the
Judges 'as an absolute King'. Though, when the Speaker delivered this message, there was 'amazement and silence', James
won the immediate point since, as the lawyer, Yelverton, remarked, to such a command, 'coming as a thunderbolt', there
was 'no contradiction'. But in the end, when honour had been
saved on both sides by a compromise which annulled all the

previous proceedings and ordered a fresh election in Buckinghamshire, the House at once decided two other similar cases without reference to King, Judges or Chancery; and James, rather than start all over again, let the matter drop, as he ought to have done in the first place. As it was he had roused all the fears and suspicions of the House of Commons and wantonly thrust the nature of royal power itself into the forefront of the controversy, all on an issue which he decided in the end—and rightly—was not worth fighting.

The whole of James's conduct in this otherwise trivial episode, the unnecessarily provoked conflict, the sweepingly generalized claim to power, and the final exhausted withdrawal in the face of determined opposition, were to be only too typical of his handling of Parliament throughout the reign. Typical, too, was the governmental mismanagement which permitted such prolonged waste of Parliamentary time. James had delivered his opening speech on March 19th. The Buckinghamshire election dispute did not finally get settled until April 13th. What is more, it put the House into so unreasonable and touchy a frame of mind that a minor dispute with the Warden of the Fleet Prison was also allowed to drag on for the same three weeks simply because, as Members themselves admitted, their 'privileges were so shaken before and so extremely vilified' that they determined to stand on the extremest point of principle. They showed the same touchiness when they had more or less shelved the projected Union with Scotland and the Bishop of Bristol published a time-serving volume supporting it and criticizing those who delayed it. They promptly took the matter up as a Contempt and complained bitterly to the Lords of the slanderous injury they had suffered. Much of all this must be blamed on the Council rather than on the new and inexperienced King. Better advice in January, when the offending Proclamation was issued, could have avoided the whole irritating issue of privilege altogether. Above all, there had been no proper steps taken to prepare the business of the House of Commons and to guide its debates. Able and experienced though he was, Cecil seems almost wholly to have neglected this important aspect of government by Council. Elizabeth had owed much of her success in dealing with Parliament to the most careful preparation in advance of the Government's programme. Moreover there had always been a *bloc* of Privy Councillors in the House of Commons to initiate that programme and pilot it through. Their experience and authority, their close liaison with the Speaker, and the fact that they knew exactly what they were trying to do gave them an immeasurable advantage over any private member, however factious. They could guide the House through its business with a speed only too welcome to men whose chief desire was to get back to their estates or counting houses; and their expert knowledge made them invaluable to the committees to which Bills were increasingly referred for detailed drafting. It was this continuous close touch with the feeling of the House which largely enabled Elizabeth to dispense with tiresome messages and interpositions. On the rare occasions when, under the stress of religious or financial grievance, the debates got out of hand, the Councillors were admirably placed both to defend government policy and to represent fairly and accurately to the Council the strength and temper of the opposition; and only a major crisis necessitated direct intervention by the Queen.

Either from exhaustion, or because he counted on controlling the course of debate himself from the House of Lords by means of conferences between the two Houses, Cecil entirely abandoned this excellent Elizabethan practice in 1604. It is true that James's lavishness with peerages tended to leave on the Council as Commoners only the less distinguished and unimportant bureaucrats. Whatever the cause, there were in 1604 only two Councillors elected to the House of Commons; and the more important of these was only Sir John Herbert, the Second Secretary of State, who was so permanent a nonentity that he came to be known everywhere as 'Mr Secondary Herbert'. Nor was there any detailed programme of government legislation. After prayers on the first day 'the House settled, in expectation of what should be propounded for the weal of the common subject', and Herbert did not even rise to ask for a subsidy. After an awkward pause private Members began a desultory debate on grievances, and then the House got carried away on the questions of privilege. In due course, lacking a lead from Councillors, they would find leaders among themselves, organize their own business, and draft their own legislative programmes, with results ultimately disastrous for the

Monarchy. In 1604, wholly inexperienced and taken by surprise, they largely wasted time, to the very great irritation of James, who lectured them, but could not provide them with the leadership they needed.

In these circumstances it is surprising that the Commons of 1604 achieved what they did. They wasted, it is true, some more time in rather ineffectual debate on the religious issues raised at Hampton Court. Their Bill to curtail the power of ecclesiastical courts never got beyond the committee stage, and they failed to persuade the House of Lords at a conference held on May 5th to join with them in support of the main points of the Millenary Petitioners. But they got through quite a useful programme of minor legislation, and by June they had clearly found some kind of leadership among themselves. For they drew up and presented to the King an *Apology and Satisfaction* which is one of the most remarkable political manifestoes of English history. There could have been no clearer warning to the King of the danger of starting legalistic disputes with a body the majority of whom had been trained in the law, and of falling back on large general claims to power and privilege to avoid some minor defeat. Everything James had said and every implication of the language he had used was seized upon, and to every one of the claims he had made was opposed a counter-claim at least as large, dangerous, and unhistorical as his own. The issue of ultimate sovereignty, so skilfully kept out of debate in Tudor times, had been thrust by three months of tactlessness into the forefront of political debate.

There was nothing disrespectful in the tone of this remarkable attempt to give a new, foreign King a lesson in English law and history. In cumbersome phrases piled one on top of the other, the Commons emphasized and reiterated their love and loyalty, their gratitude for James's peaceful succession, and their faith in his graciousness and good intentions. But they told him quite firmly that he had been misinformed on several important points, and at great length set out to put him right. For, they said, these 'misinformations' had been 'the chief and almost the sole cause of all the discontentful and troublesome proceedings so much blamed in this Parliament'. The injudicious handling of the business of election returns had gone deep, and it really seemed to the Commons that their privileges, 'and therein the liberties and stability of the whole kingdom', had been 'more seriously and dangerously impugned than ever (as we suppose) since the beginnings of Parliaments'. They retorted, therefore, that those privileges were not a matter of the King's grace, but a 'right and due inheritance' no less than lands or goods, and that the Speaker's formal request for their confirmation at the beginning of each session was 'an act only of manners'. They reiterated in extreme form their claim to complete freedom of speech in the House—an issue on which there had been frequent quarrels in Elizabeth's time; and they mixed in among these assertions of first principles a great deal of long-winded and detailed justification of their proceedings in the various cases which had arisen, along with peevish complaints of the way in which courtiers and time-servers misrepresented to the King what had been said on the floor of the House—another old Elizabethan grievance. Very little of what they claimed was fully justified by historical precedents, even from Elizabeth's time; and their statement that 'the prerogatives of princes may easily and do daily grow; the privileges of the subject are for the most part at an everlasting stand' came strangely from a Parliament which a hundred years before had been little more than a tax-voting machine precariously enjoying the most meagre of privileges and liberties.

But, and here lay the greatest danger of James's habit of making sweeping fundamental statements, the Commons did not stop there. From self-justification they proceeded to attack, with a summary of still unremedied grievances which foreshadowed many of the great disputes looming ahead: matters which, they said rather ominously, they had hitherto refrained from pressing on Elizabeth 'in regard of her sex and age', but on which they now expected concessions. It was out of finance and religion that the whole constitutional struggle between the Stuarts and their Parliaments was to grow. The financial problem created by the Crown's more or less fixed income in a world of rising prices was only glanced at this time. They put on record the exasperation caused by the excesses of the royal purveyors and complained bitterly of the irritating, unprofitable and haphazard burdens laid on landowners by the activities of the Court of Wards, but they shelved the main problem, to be taken up in great detail in the later sessions of this same Parliament. The religious grievances arising out of the Hampton Court failure to meet the Millenary Petition demands seemed to them more pressing, and they stated their view clearly and bluntly: 'For matter of religion, it will appear by examination of truth and right that your Majesty should be misinformed if any man should deliver that the Kings of England have any absolute power in themselves either to alter Religion (which God defend should be in the power of any mortal man whatsoever), or to make any laws concerning the same otherwise than as in temporal causes, by consent of Parliament.'

Here again the Commons were making a larger claim than their predecessors had ever made, and one which Elizabeth would certainly have rejected. She would have preferred to govern her Church exclusively through the two Houses of Convocation without reference to Parliament at all, and only the desire for national unity and the need to repeal Marian legislation had made her embody her Settlement in the Acts of Supremacy and Uniformity. As in other spheres, her instinct was for the avoidance of definition, and even, if possible, of discussion, especially in the House of Commons. But now both sides were moving towards irreconcilable extremes. The Hampton Court decisions had been amplified and embodied in a hundred and forty-one Canons which not only enforced a much stricter discipline and uniformity on the clergy, both in matters of doctrine and in methods of worship, but also decreed the penalty of excommunication for laymen who questioned any detail of the Thirty-nine Articles or in any way challenged the authority of the Bishops. These Canons, passed by Convocation and promulgated by the Archbishop, rested on no other authority but that of a royal Proclamation of July, 1604, which sought to give them the force of law. Thus the Bishops, sure of the King's support, were seeking to revive a legislative power which had not existed since the Reformation, and the Commons reacted at once and violently. Their interest for the moment was purely constitutional and they hastened to deny 'any Puritan or Brownist spirit'. Indeed, their sympathy with the Millenary Petitioners, as shown by the articles on which they sought the support of the Lords, was moderate and restrained. They only sought to have some of the points in dispute—the sign of the Cross in Baptism and the use of the surplice and of the ring in

155

marriage—made optional. On the general principle of enforcing uniformity and obedience they wholeheartedly agreed with King and Bishops, and would have gone much further than they did in persecuting dissenters. But Parliament, not Convocation, must do the persecuting. They could claim with justice that the whole English Reformation had been carried through by Act of Parliament; and they would not admit the King's authority in religious matters to be any different from his authority in other spheres. The Royal Supremacy for them meant the supremacy of the King in Parliament, and they recognized no legislative power in Convocation at all.

So the *Apology and Satisfaction* came to an end, with fresh assertions of loyalty and affection, and a final appeal to James to listen to the House of Commons rather than private persons when he wished to know the truth about England. 'The voice of the people,' they said, 'in the things of their knowledge is said to be as the voice of God.' There was no possibility that James, whose views on the same subject had already been published in *The Trew Law of Free Monarchies* six years before, would accept or act on such a maxim. The protest of the House of Commons had thus no practical significance save as a rallying force: the first attempt to state comprehensively the Parliamentary point of view. It was in fact never formally presented to the King who, exasperated, as he wrote to Mar, by the 'fashious and froward' behaviour of English Parliaments, had gone off to Royston at the end of April to hunt. But he was shown a copy of it and the knowledge of its phrases helped to colour the sharp address he delivered to the Commons when he at length returned to London at the end of July to prorogue them. He would not, he told them sharply, give thanks where he thought no thanks due. 'It were not Christian,' he said, 'it were not kingly.' He made not the slightest attempt to understand the basis of his opponents' case, which for him was but 'humours and respects', and he never perceived that his greatest mistake had been to provoke the Commons to formulate their case at all. For that, of course, he could have pleaded inexperience. In fact he would have pleaded no such thing, being at all times confident in his own judgement and not capable of learning much from his own mistakes. For the Commons it was the last straw to be sent away with a patronizing rebuke which dismissed their serious representations as a sort of schoolboy turbulence. 'You see in how many things you did not well,' James told them, 'and how many things you have done rashly. I say not that you meant disloyalty, only I wish you had kept a better form.'

It was not a good impression that Members carried back to their constituencies; and the discontent, especially in and around London, was increased by the determined following-up of the Proclamation of July, which forced the clergy to conform to Whitgift's new Canons. There is evidence that the Bishops themselves were surprised by the amount of opposition that they encountered, and it was not to be expected that the Puritan ministers would allow themselves to be expelled from their livings without protest. They were indeed anything but 'silenced brethren' and they fought back hard. But there was no Parliament sitting to which they could present their petitions and the Judges ruled that their deprivation was legal. But for the fortunate translation of the over-enthusiastic Bancroft to Canterbury and his replacement in London by the gentler, more careful Vaughan from Chester, there might have been even more trouble and noise in the capital. As it was, even in Puritan circles it was admitted that Vaughan had handled the matter with 'gravitie, wisdome, learning, mildenes, and temperance', though it was still thought wise to postpone the next session of Parliament until October of 1605. The agitation even pursued the King into the country, and on one occasion his hunting was unpleasantly interrupted by the presentation of a petition signed by some eighty gentlemen on behalf of the deprived ministers of Northamptonshire.

To James any interference with his country sports and his card-playing was rapidly becoming intolerable. The habit of idleness formed in those first months when the Plague had kept him out of London was growing on him fast. After one month of bickering with Parliament he had gone off to hunt and left the management of the rest of the session to Cecil; and, apart from a brief interlude when he was entertaining his brother-in-law, the King of Denmark, and the Christmas festivities, he had been at it ever since. In January of 1605 he actually tried to throw a cloak of public-spiritedness over his behaviour by writing to the Council that hunting was the only way to preserve his health and that therefore, for the sake of the health and welfare of the whole nation, they must take the burden of government from his shoulders and see that he was disturbed as little as possible by business. When the plague of petitioners on behalf of the non-conforming ministers and what Chamberlain called 'foolish prophecies of daungers to insue' became intolerable he summoned the Council to Northampton. The ringleaders of the Northamptonshire petitioners were hauled up and rebuked for opposing the King in a manner that was 'little less than treason'. But at the same time, to discourage any Catholic hopes which might have sprung from the persecution of the Puritan elements in the Church, the King gave formal instructions for a fresh drive against recusancy.

Theoretically such a drive had been going on since the previous spring. James, it is true, had intervened when several Jesuits had been hanged in Devonshire and had ordered that there must be no executions merely on grounds of religion. On this point he had long since made his mind clear to Cecil in one of his secret letters from Scotland. 'I will neuer,' he had written, 'allowe in my conscience that the bloode of any man shall be shedde for diuersitie of opinions in religion'. But he had sanctioned the re-imposition of Elizabeth's penal laws and Parliament had passed an Act against Jesuits and Seminary Priests confirming and amplifying them. In practice, however, they had not been at all severely enforced. Now a fresh crop of rumours throughout Europe of his own impending conversion to Rome irritated James into more drastic action. He addressed to the Council a 'longe and vehement apologie', going so far as to say that, if his son should turn Catholic, he would wish him to forfeit his right to the succession. He ordered the rigorous enforcement of fines on all who failed to go to church, and had the decision published in the Star Chamber and in the Court of Aldermen in London.

It was this fresh persecution coming on top of their earlier disappointments that goaded a part of the English Catholic world, always of necessity conspiratorial and humming with designs for rebellion and the seizure of power, to positive action. In fact, of course, the sudden seizure of power by a mere 100,000 Catholics was unthinkable without foreign aid. But it must be remembered that neither Catholic nor Protestant had any exact knowledge of the real numbers of the recusant population, and nobody can tell to this day how many secret sympathizers might have been brought into the open by a successful *coup d'état*. Catholic daydreams and Protestant fears alike exaggerated the figures; and the great Catholic landowner, suddenly faced with ruinous recusancy fines which had hitherto been largely evaded, may be forgiven if he was tempted to take seriously the projects of visionaries who talked with the same certainty as Parsons in Rome of the day that would surely come. Nor did it seem so very unpatriotic to summon even Spaniards to their support if their object was to save their good Anglican neighbours from certain damnation. To make plans and preparations in not very specific detail for a sudden rising was not therefore very difficult. The habit of secrecy was deeply ingrained in households where the priest lay hidden all day with his communion plate and vestments in a room behind the chimney or the panelling and, except in times of settled security, only dared to ride out to his humbler parishioners at night. In such a world the disappointments resulting from James's fluctuating policy made it easy to recruit plotters.

Among these wistful daydreamers there were a few hotheads, like Robert Catesby and Sir Thomas Percy, who saw one thing at least clearly: that there was no hope even for a successful *coup d'état* unless some altogether extraordinary disaster should temporarily paralyse the governing class. Probably nothing short of what they actually projected—the destruction of the nation's leaders, King, Lords, and Commons in a single, devastating explosion—would have created conditions in which their rising could momentarily succeed. The effect of such a blow on a society so closely bound to ties of traditional and territorial loyalty at every level is unimaginable in the twentieth century. But it is at any rate conceivable that the Catholics might have seized power and held it for long enough to bring in foreign aid. At least they could have started a disastrous civil war. The moral considerations which would make even the overwhelming majority of Catholics shudder at such a mass murder do not seem to have bothered this fanatic handful of men. When James asked the newly apprehended Guy Fawkes if he were not sorry for so foul and heinous a treason, Fawkes answered that he was sorry for nothing save their failure. 'A dangerous disease,' he added, 'requires a desperate remedy'; and he spoke for the whole gang who had employed him to guard and fire the thirty-six barrels of gunpowder which they had concealed under faggots and rubbish and iron bars in the cellar so providentially rented immediately under the House of Lords.

So long as the secret was known only to the six men who had planned it all, the gunpowder part of the plot was reasonably sure of success. Salisbury had no complicated network of spies such as had enabled Walsingham to defeat all the conspiracies centred round Mary, Queen of Scots. He had no reason to suspect a plot, and if he had would have had no idea where to start looking for it. In fact all the preparations had been made and the conspirators had quietly dispersed into the country six months before November 5th, the date on which Parliament was eventually summoned to meet; and no hint of them reached the government until Tresham's nerve broke and he sent the famous warning note to Lord Monteagle. Even on the morning of the 5th when Guy Fawkes was already in the Tower the other conspirators, save for Percy, who was known to be Fawkes's employer, were still unidentified. But their own logic which had driven them to the Plot as the only way to give a Catholic rebellion a chance of success forced them to let others into the secret so that there should be a rebellion to take advantage of the Plot. Tresham was one of the wealthy Catholic gentlemen whom they enlisted to gather stores of arms and prepare their friends to rally to their west-country manors when the moment came, and his warning to his brother-in-law had obviously been carefully thought out between them. By having Tresham's letter delivered to him at dinner and read aloud to him then and there Monteagle ensured that the conspirators were informed of the betrayal of their plans before he carried the news to Lord Salisbury.

The warning was a very obscure one. 'I would advise you,' the vital part of the letter ran, 'as you tender your life, to devise some excuse, to shift off your attendance at this Parliament. For God and man have concurred to punish the wickedness of this time. And think not slightly of this advertisement, but retire yourself into the country, where you may expect the event in safety. For, though there be no appearance of any stir, yet I say, they shall receive a terrible blow this Parliament, and yet they shall not see who hurts them. This counsel is not to be condemned, because it may do you good, and can do you no harm, for the danger is past as soon as you have burnt this letter.' If Monteagle gave Salisbury no further hint, it is remarkable that the truth came to be suspected at all. According to James's own account, it was he who first read the riddle; and certainly, of the men who puzzled over the obscure message, the man most likely to guess gunpowder as the solution was Darnley's son. If Salisbury received and passed on a hint, he did it so tactfully that not even James himself seems to have noticed it, so that for the King the shock of the discovery—and it was a very great shock—was mitigated by this singular mark of God's favour, which fitted so well with all that he felt about Kingship and about himself. Moreover for once English public opinion saw the thing in the same light as he did, and for a brief space he found himself something of a national hero, surrounded by men who shared his own slightly awed admiration for the remarkable perspicacity with which God had endowed him.

At three in the afternoon of November 4th Lord Suffolk looked into the cellar, discovered from Fawkes that the faggots in it belonged to Sir Thomas Percy, and went away again. Fawkes knew already of Monteagle's warning letter, and that visit could only mean that the secret was out. But with incredible courage he hung on in the forlorn hope that he might still get his chance; and there at eleven that night Sir Thomas Knyvet, Justice of the Peace for Westminster, found him still waiting, with his touchwood and fuse, tinder box and 'blinde lanterne', and the watch a friend had just brought him so that he might time his explosion accurately the next morning. So on the 5th, instead of a great national disaster, there were only a few wild-eyed gentlemen galloping westward to raise a rebellion which even their Catholic friends could see was now quite hopeless. That evening Chamberlain noted 'as great store of bonfires as ever I thinke was seen', as the first Guys were burnt to celebrate a deliverance which the English were in fact to find it very difficult to forget. The Gunpowder Treason joined the Armada and the Spanish Inquisition, St Bartholomew and Foxe's Martyrs as part of the English Protestant tradition and perpetuated a hatred of Catholicism very puzzling to peaceful and loyal English Catholics who had never dreamed of dabbling in conspiracy.

It also helped to fix in the English mind the particular hatred of the Jesuits, those 'reverend cheaters', 'prowling fathers', and 'caterpillars of Christianity', and mistrust of all they stood for has been one of the hardest to die of the English prejudices. There can be no absolute certainty as to how far the Jesuit leaders were informed, outside the confessional, of the designs of the conspirators. Certainly one of them, Greenway, not only would not reveal the Plot, but failed entirely to discourage it, since at the end he came into the open to 'live or die' with the desperate handful who, after galloping half the length of England, were destroyed or rounded up at Holbeche House in Staffordshire. The bitterest controversy has raged over Garnet, the Jesuit Provincial, who was discovered months later hiding in Worcestershire and tried and executed for complicity in the Plot in the spring of 1606. Catholics then and afterwards revered his memory as a martyr who died because he would not break the seal of the confessional. In Protestant legend he has been the arch-equivocator who would not openly approve the conspiracy, but waited concealed at Hindlip House to take every advantage of it if it succeeded. Even making allowance for biassed reporting of his trial, it seems probable that he himself admitted 'a general knowledge of Mr Catesby's intention', apart from anything he or Greenway learnt in confession, and blamed himself for not having revealed it. It is hard to believe that he and Greenway could not have stopped the plotters altogether if they had really tried; and in any case the whole design sprang from their teaching which held the assassination of a heretic ruler meritorious. Curiously enough the one man in England on whom the Gunpowder Plot had no permanent effect was James himself. Under the immediate impact of it he was to collaborate enthusiastically, though briefly, with Parliament in tightening up anti-Catholic precautions. In the long run, however, he would return to the idea of a friendly understanding with Rome and the Catholic sovereigns. For nothing would convince him that intelligent men would not sooner or later be brought to share his belief in the Divine Right of even a Calvinist king. For the moment, however, he found himself at one with his subjects as never before; and in this brief, halcyon interlude Salisbury was to try, and fail, to solve the other great outstanding problem of the period—that of the inadequacy of the royal revenue.

CHAPTER IX

The End of the Elizabethan Age

*

In 1606 King, Lords and Commons met again in all the consciousness of a shared deliverance. The squabbles of 1604 were forgotten, and the years following the Gunpowder Treason were the halcyon period of James's reign in England, when it seemed as if, after a not too promising start, King and people might after all be able to settle down in comfort to gathering in the rich harvest of the previous century. They were among the most peaceful years of English history, devoid of great events and uncomplicated by foreign crises, since in 1609 even the Dutch and Spaniards stopped fighting and Europe enjoyed a rare, though brief and uneasy interval of almost complete peace.

The fragmentary glimpses which the letters and diaries of this time afford all suggest a secure, unhurried prosperity, with the memories of Elizabethan crises and dangers fading into legend, and no hint of troubles to come. The Puritan Simonds D'Ewes describes a childhood in the agricultural calm of Dorsetshire where his grandfather lived a life typical of the fairly prosperous retired lawyer, with a cellar 'replenished with cider, strong beer, and several wines', since he was 'a great housekeeper', the family coat of arms carefully carved over the dining-room fireplace, and the farm horses brought in to drag the family coach the twenty 'craggy and uneven' miles to Dorchester. For all its calm it was not a static age. But the progress and the steadily growing prosperity were untidy—almost haphazard: the maturing of long-term plans for enclosure and drainage of newly-acquired estates, ceaseless building, and the laying out of walks and orchards and landscape gardens. 'Such a quoile about gardening,' Chamberlain wrote slightly complainingly from Ware Park in October of 1607, 'that a man cannot be ydle

163

though he do but looke on, nor greatly well occupied yt goes so slowly forward, and yet here have ben every day since my comming above forty men at worke, for the new garden is wholly translated, new levelled, and in a manner transplanted.' A more hectic atmosphere pervaded the building and gardening activities at Hatfield, which Lord Salisbury had that same year acquired from James in exchange for his lovely house and snugly-enclosed park at Theobalds. Salisbury was only 44, but cares of State and a frail constitution had pulled him down to what Jonson described, in the *Poetical Exhibition* which he wrote to celebrate James's acquisition of Theobalds, as 'the twilight of sere age'. He built and planned, therefore, against time, and already by 1612 the last of 'the content of 30 great marble stones provided at Carrara' and shipped from Leghorn had been placed, the great fireplaces with their 'fower dorrick columns' were complete, the lions and the naked boys standing on the great carved and gilded staircase, the chapel richly and decorously furnished, the vineyard and fruit gardens, the four hundred sycamores from Flanders, the Dutch bulbs, the melons and roses all planted, so that eight days before he set off on his last fatal journey to Bath he saw it all finished.

While the statesmen and the merchants juggled with endlessly modified trading charters and conditions in the attempt to get the best of both free enterprise and state control in Far-eastern trade and the founding of the first colonies in Virginia, Salisbury's gift of money to be used for teaching 'the art of clothing or weaving or any other suchlike commendable trade' to fifty poor parishioners of Hatfield chosen by himself suggests a similarly casual and haphazard care for industrial progress. The first of the East India Company's voyages, the four ships sent out under Sir James Lancaster in 1601, had returned a few months after James's accession with cargoes which showed 100 per cent profit, and though official economic opinion condemned this trade as impoverishing the country by exporting bullion in exchange for goods, it was clearly too profitable to be suppressed. There had been another expedition in 1604, and after 1607 they became an annual event. The richer peers, courtiers, and politicians joined Sir Thomas Smith and his City friends as regular subscribers to these ventures; and when, in 1609, the charter was renewed and the Company reorganized,

Salisbury and Nottingham and Lord Worcester all joined the new board. Unsupported by a Spanish government too heavily committed elsewhere, the Portuguese gradually lost their hold on the Indian trade; in the Spice Islands of the Malayan archipelago chiefly to the Dutch; on the mainland in India and in the Persian Gulf to the English. Dutch rivalry was to be in the long run a greater obstacle than Portuguese, especially after the peace with Spain in 1609, and half a century of vicious competition lay ahead. But for the moment there seemed to be fortunes in the Indies for the picking up.

In contrast to this, the progress made in establishing settlements in America was much slower and less spectacular, and the Virginia Company, which received its first charter in 1606, never really paid a proper financial dividend at all. In the wholly untried business of establishing colonial settlements at such a distance neither merchants nor politicians were the best men to exercise overall control, and the fact that there was great confusion in men's minds as to the object of such a settlement anyway made the first ventures even more precarious. Raleigh and his half-brother, Humphrey Gilbert, had dreamt of an overseas empire as an end in itself in strikingly modern and purely nationalist terms, and had used the hope of finding gold merely as a lever to secure official support and financial backing. Though this would be the idea which would ultimately triumph, a series of costly failures at Roanoke had discredited it, and by 1603 it was also becoming fairly clear that American settlements were not going to be a means to finding a short cut to India. It was chiefly as a means of disposing of surplus population—the sturdy vagabonds who so haunted the imaginations of Elizabethan statesmen—that the plans were officially taken up again in 1606. The inexperience and jealousies of the pioneers and the hostility of the native Indians all but wrecked this second series of attempts too, and only the adventuring genius of Captain John Smith and the friendship of the Princess Pocahontas, daughter of the most important of the local chiefs, averted total disaster in the first three years. Then, in 1609, there was a wholesale reorganization in which both James and Salisbury took a hand and which brought the ubiquitous Sir Thomas Smith into effective control of the London Company, and the settlement at Jamestown on the Delaware River became permanently secure. Even then the colony succeeded for what was in the eyes of most of its backers pre-eminently the wrong reason, mainly by exporting tobacco. This was a result particularly displeasing to James, whose first publication after coming to England had been a *Counterblast to Tobacco*. But in spite of his recorded opinion that smoking was a filthy habit suited only to heathen Indians, besides being a shocking waste of the nation's money, this deleterious habit first introduced by Raleigh spread so rapidly that 20,000 lb. of tobacco were consumed by Englishmen in 1617, and by the end of the reign the figure had risen to 50,000 lb.

In this setting of a somewhat muddled but steadily expanding and peaceful prosperity the problem of governing England should not have proved so very difficult. Nor, probably, did it seem so to Salisbury and Dorset and their fellow councillors, when they considered the situation as the echoes of the Gunpowder Treason died away. In spite of the occasional difficulties of the lesser landowners, struggling with fixed rent rolls in a world of rising prices, the countryside was prosperous. The volume of trade passing through the Port of London steadily increased. Outlets had been found overseas for surplus capital and energy, and openings for the discontented and the misfits and the ambitious younger sons of an expanding population. There was peace abroad and no threat of any crisis beyond the capacity of experienced and self-confident statesmanship. At home it seemed that the King now sat comfortably in his new saddle. He was extravagant, sometimes tiresome to deal with, and extremely idle. But all the signs suggested that he was settling down and there was every reason to believe that as time went on he would learn more of English law and custom and of the art of managing Englishmen. There were four royal children to secure the succession and a fifth on the way; and James's private life, though often indecorous and always grossly self-indulgent, produced none of the scandals and quarrels such as enlivened and embittered the court of Henry IV and Marie de Medici in France. Puritan discontent was remote still and not vociferous, and there was nothing on the surface of the English scene, political, social, economic, or religious, to suggest the faint premonitory rumblings of what was in fact to be revolution. Secure in his sovereign's gratitude and perfectly content to play the 'little beagle' to his rather heavy-handed banter, his political supremacy buttressed and secured by ramifying family alliances, Salisbury could confront the future with serene confidence.

In fact it was the next six years—the last of Salisbury's life and the culmination of his personal power and prestige—which proved the truth of Bacon's observation that he was fit only to prevent things from getting worse. It could even be said that, in spite of the superficial appearance of success, during those six years the Elizabethan system of government really began to break down. Largely this was James's own fault, unforeseeable in 1606, and outside the control of any minister. At the heart of the trouble was the rapid disintegration of the King's own character in the tempting, easy circumstances in which he found himself in 1603. It had never been safe to leave the government of Scotland, as he put it himself, 'to a Council clerk', and the uncertainties of the English succession and the necessity of earning Elizabeth's good opinion had kept him on his toes and forced him to pay continual attention to the problems of administration. With what seemed by Scottish standards unlimited money to spend, a dependable Privy Council to which it was apparently possible to delegate all the responsibility for day-to-day government, and with Cecil's vast experience of the larger problems to depend on, it was too easy to abandon serious business altogether and live a life of continuous self-indulgence. His physical vitality, never very great, was sapped by too many long days in the hunting field; his intellectual energy by the orgies of over-eating and drinking which followed them. His colds in the head were almost continuous. 'Every day that he hunteth,' Worcester wrote to Salisbury, 'he takes a new cold; for being hot with riding a chase, he sitteth in the open air and drinketh, which cannot but continue, if not increase, a new cold.' There is no extant record of his being incapably drunk, but he can seldom have been wholly sober after dinner time, and the vast quantities of the heavy, sweet wines he loved undermined his constitution with gout. With food and drink he could not be moderate. Every summer he suffered from a 'terrible looseness' as a result of cramming himself all day with every soft fruit in season washed down with Frontignac. Thus he degenerated swiftly into a shambling, flabby, gross and prematurely old man, though intelligent and sensitive enough to be vividly aware of his own unimpressiveness, and therefore all the more inclined to fall back on the sacrosanctity of his kingship which placed him above the petty necessities of cleanliness and seemly behaviour, and equally beyond any obligation to conciliate hostile or critical opinion. This process, too, emphasized in him a tendency, never wholly repressed, though largely in abeyance in these middle years, to an exaggerated preoccupation with young men who possessed the physical perfections and graces which an unkind providence and his own self-indulgence had denied to him.

The disinclination to apply himself to serious business for any length of time had already shown itself clearly before 1606 in the shameless letter to the Council forbidding the interruption of his hunting lest his health, and thereby the well-being of the whole nation, be impaired, and in his leaving London halfway through his first Parliamentary session, when the absence of effective Councillors on the floor of the Lower House made close and continuous supervision of the conduct of government business in Parliament absolutely essential. The very ability of Salisbury made it all the more tempting to abandon the ordinary business of government to him, reserving only the larger decisions of policy, of which there were, as luck would have it, in those uneventful years few to make. A great crisis at home or abroad in the years immediately following the Gunpowder Plot might have saved James's personal situation for him by compelling him to halt the drift into laziness and ineffectuality and employ his undoubted talents. He had a better brain than most of his ministers, and a better understanding of what went on beyond the shores of England. In his youth he had shown occasional flashes of imagination and sympathy which might have enabled him now to penetrate and grasp the difficult and alien processes of the English mind; and on a subject which really roused him he could still, as his speeches on Scottish Union in 1606 and 1607 were to show, marshal a good case with astonishing clarity and cogency. But he was given the fatal opportunity to let his talents lapse into disuse. The routine business of the Council which might have taught him why and how English government worked as it did was neglected. The effort, in the beginnings of a premature middle age, to understand a strange people, adapt himself to their ways and win their affection was abandoned. The assets he had—the cheerful, easy common sense, the tolerance, the occasional flashes of a lovable humour—were overlaid by protective mannerisms as he became aware of failure. The shrewdness and intelligence and energy he directed to trivialities, sending for his printer as often as six times a day to discuss the proofs of his *Apology for the Oath of Obedience*, while wholly neglecting affairs of state. Instead of learning and improving he relapsed in a slothful testiness which refused to make the effort to understand alien minds and dismissed all opposition as factious and disloyal.

All these processes were accelerated by the simultaneous disintegration of his family life. He had never been able to share with the Queen any intellectual activity. Her propensity for intrigue, her hysterical intolerance of opposition, and her dabblings with Rome had made it necessary to exclude her as much as possible from politics, and she had never been able to make any adequate response to the pent-up romanticism, the desire for love and sympathy and a bolstering up of his self-confidence which James had at first so passionately demanded of her. Yet, in spite of their separate households and divergent interests and their squabbles over the upbringing of Prince Henry, they had built up a relationship which was more than just friendly and tolerant, and the later history of James's relations with the Villiers household suggests that, in different circumstances, he would have made a doting and successful husband and father. The death of the infant Princess Sophia within twenty-four hours of her birth in June of 1606, followed the next year by that of the other baby daughter, Mary, seems to have damaged the relationship between James and Anne irreparably. Anne was still only 33, pretty in her fair-haired, vacuous way, perfectly strong and healthy, save that she, too, already suffered from twinges of gout. But having borne James seven children and suffered several miscarriages, she seems deliberately to have decided that she had done her duty. Her life was already given up largely to selfish pleasures. Henceforth it was to be entirely so. Within a fortnight of the funeral of the Princess Mary she was planning with Ben Jonson another of the masques in which she was in the habit of shocking English audiences by acting herself. There were no more births or miscarriages. What intimacy there had been in her relationship with James perished entirely. It remained, as ever, friendly and tolerant—even at times affectionate—but there was no longer in it any emotional solace for James.

An intensely devoted relationship with his eldest son might perhaps have filled the gap in the King's life and prevented much that afterwards went wrong. But, as the character and tastes of Prince Henry began rather precociously to declare themselves, that, too, was denied him. At the age of 12 Henry already showed a cool, clear mind of his own and one very different from that of his father. He was to die before he was 18, and it is not safe to believe the eulogies of his contemporaries on a character scarcely fully formed, and in any case idealized by death and the haunting sense of what might have been. D'Ewes has summed up what became in after years the official opposition view: 'He was a prince rather addicted to martial studies and exercises than to golf, tennis, or other boys' play; a true lover of the English nation, and a sound Protestant, abhorring not only the idolatry, superstitions and bloody persecutions of the Romish synagogue, but being free also from the Lutheran leaven'; and he went on to point out that the Prince had always preferred the company of 'learned and godly men' to that of 'buffoons and parasites, vain swearers and atheists'. But there is enough genuinely contemporary evidence to make it clear that the Puritans were at last basically right in seeing a character sharply different from that of his father and his younger brother. He was much more typically English than either of them, cool and decisive in his judgements, insular and immovable in his prejudices. James had wanted the boy to be all that he himself was not: athletic, self-confident, and attractive. But it was disappointing when he actually grew into just that, incapable of sharing his father's bookish pleasures or of returning his affectionate demonstrativeness. His imagination was caught, not by the blessedness of peacemakers, but by the legends of Elizabethan war. It was disconcerting for James that his son preferred tennis to dialectic; still more so that at the age of 14 he had so profited by his friendship with Phineas Pett, the Master Shipwright at Woolwich, that he knew far more about naval administration and dockyard construction than his father and most of the Council; most bitter of all that, of all living men,

Raleigh, languishing in the Tower, should have become his boyhood's hero.

Ironically enough the Puritan opposition which so grieved for Prince Henry's untimely death probably had every reason to be thankful that he did not live to mount the throne. Behind the sound Protestantism and the hatred of Spain, the naval preoccupations and the athleticism which endeared his memory, there seems to have been a mind deeply imbrued with his father's Divine Right theories of monarchy and also a sharply authoritarian will which would have pushed them in practice to their logical conclusion. There would have been no shifts and evasions and no abandoning the struggle half-way through from laziness, and it seems likely that the fight for Parliamentary liberties would have been much sharper and much more difficult, and that Strafford would have found in Henry IX his ideal master.

Ironically, too, it was the very assiduity and clarity with which Henry absorbed his father's precepts from the *Basilikon Doron* that lay at the root of the estrangement which grew up between them as soon as the boy began to develop a mind of his own. That book had been written in a passionate, almost yearning concern that the Prince should have a fairer start in this business of kingship than his father. But the fact that he agreed with every word that his father wrote made all the more shocking to Henry, as he grew old enough to observe it, the gulf which yawned between James's theory and his practice. Even in 1606 he could see clearly that James had failed to make his 'Court and company to be a pattern of godliness and all honest virtues to all the rest of the people', and less and less in the years that followed, as the tone of the Court steadily deteriorated, could the King claim to 'cherish modesty, banish debauched insolence, foster humility and repress pride'. He was very far from being what he advised his son to be—'an ordinary sitter in his secret Counsel'. In defiance of his own strict precept he had already acquiesced in the Queen's apostasy to Roman Catholicism. Before long the advent of the first great favourite of the reign, Robert Carr, was to make nonsense of another, which had warned the Prince to 'employ every man as ye think him qualified, but use not one in all things, lest he was proud and be envied'.

171

So the fussy, voluble, fond affection which James would have loved to lavish on his eldest son met no response. Henry showed himself loyal and dutiful, but perfectly capable of managing his own life. By the time that he was 14 his separate establishment at St James's was already sharply differentiated in tone from the Court, and before he died it would become almost an official centre of opposition to James's government. Moreover, with the tacit withdrawal of Henry into a disapproving aloofness, James lost too the only other of his children who might have responded to his petting and spoiling, his daughter Elizabeth, who adored 'her most worthy and dearest brother', Henry, to the exclusion of all other affections. His only other surviving child, the six-year-old Charles, was too young and still too sickly and backward to fill the gap thus created in his father's life; and this was the gap into which, in the summer of 1607, Robert Carr was to step with such fatal consequences.

The rapid decline of the tone and behaviour of the Court from Elizabethan standards which was largely the result of the deterioration in James's own character from 1606 onwards cannot be dismissed as unimportant gossip and scandal, for it had far-reaching and serious results. The growth of personal extravagance alone in which the King gave the lead, wildly exaggerated as it was bound to be by rumour, went far to explain the hostility and suspicion with which the House of Commons received any financial proposition from the Government; and the decline of the moral tone of the Court as a whole did much to crystallize into a solid and permanent opposition those Puritan elements already half alienated by the Hampton Court religious policy. The Queen's debts were a perpetual source of trouble: in ten years she ran up a bill of £40,000 with the jeweller George Heriot alone, and the *Masque of Blackness* which Ben Jonson and Inigo Jones put on for her in January, 1605, to celebrate the creation of Prince Charles as Duke of York cost something over £3,000.

James, too, spent absurd sums on jewels—some £92,000 in the first four years of his reign. The masques and banquets which celebrated every Christmas season became one of the largest charges on the Exchequer, and the King's erratic generosity made life even more difficult for the harassed Lord Treasurer. 'I heare,' Chamberlain wrote to Carleton in February, 1607, at a moment when all the City knew that money was low in the Exchequer, 'the Kinge hath undertaken the debts of the Lord Haye, the Vicount Haddington and the earle of Montgomerie to the value of fowre and forty thowsand pounds, sayeng that he will this once set them free, and then let them shift for themselves. In the meane time his owne debts are stalled to be payed the one half in May come two yeares, the residue in May following.' Haddington was that John Ramsay to whom James believed he owed his life on the day of Gowrie's conspiracy and so, of course, had a special claim. But merchants and tradesmen who were to wait over two years for money already long owing might well feel aggrieved when, less than a year later, the King marked the occasion of that same Haddington's marriage not only by giving the bride the gold cup in which he had drunk her health, 'a bason and ewer, two livery pots and three standing cuppes all very fayre and massie, of silver and guilt,' but also by granting the young couple a joint annuity of £600 out of the Exchequer. Five years later, in the midst of an even worse financial crisis, he would give the Countess of Somerset £10,000 worth of jewels as a wedding present. Cumulatively the totals of these grants and presents became formidable. By 1610 a little over £220,000 had been given away in hard cash, mostly to Scotsmen, and the pensions granted amounted to £30,000 a year. That is to say that the presents represented more than a quarter of his total indebtedness and the annuities about six per cent of his yearly expenditure.

Gradually a more and more vulgar ostentation pervaded Court life, when great ladies would appear at functions wearing jewels worth over £100,000, and the wife of an ambitious civil servant would think it worth while to spend £50 a yard on the trimming of a dress. Even the value of presents became a matter of calculation and haggling: when de Beaumont, the French Ambassador, was recalled in 1605 he complained bitterly because his parting present of plate weighed only 2,000 ounces, quoted precedents, and made such a fuss that he got 500 ounces more. Old-fashioned folks might deplore such 'mecanicall tricks', but they were increasingly the rule. Corrupt practices inevitably grew out of a system which depended on perquisites and commissions of all kinds in place of salaries and pensions and in which the reversions of even minor offices were for sale. James's own conscienceless attitude in money matters encouraged laxness and open peculation throughout his household and in every department of state. Every government contract was the subject of endless underhand transactions, and more and more public money found its way into the pockets of tax farmers and government officials.

Along with this alarming decline in the general standard of financial probity there went a sad falling-off in manners and taste for which, too, James must personally be held largely responsible. Himself lacking dignity and any sense of decorum, he allowed the most ceremonial occasions to become drunken and disorderly orgies. It did not matter so much that he liked in private to be surrounded by riotous young men who would enliven an evening's card-playing by riding races on each other's backs. That the public occasions were allowed to become overcrowded and riotous did matter. A Court banquet, so decorously conducted in Elizabeth's time, became an indecent scramble for free food and drink which quickly degenerated into a debauch. It was an excellent thing that great occasions should be marked by the engagement of the King's or the Prince's servants to act a play by Shakespeare, or by Inigo Jones's elaborate staging of Jonson's and Campion's masques. But only too often the performances were drowned in the din and disorder and overcrowding, and once at least the lawyers of Gray's Inn, arriving by water at Whitehall to give the *Masque of Flowers* which it had cost Sir Francis Bacon £2,000 to prepare, could get no space cleared to dance and had to be sent away. Sir John Harington wrote for his friend, Barlow, a description which has become famous of what must have been the worst even of the debauches over which James presided without apparent embarrassment: the performance of the Masque of Solomon and Sheba in honour of the visit of Christian IV of Denmark in 1607. By the time the masque came on at the end of the banquet both kings and all the performers had had far too much to drink. The Queen of Sheba fell over the steps as she sought to offer Christian a present and deluged him in wine, cream, jelly, cakes and spices; and when the King, having been roughly cleaned up 'with cloths and napkins', then tried to dance with her both fell down and had to be carried out and put to bed. Incredible though it may seem, James sat on through the rest of this lamentable performance, so expensively prepared as an offering to the royal visitor by Lord Salisbury.

'The entertainment and show went forward,' Harington wrote, 'and most of the Presenters went backward or fell down, wine did so occupy their upper chambers. Now did appear in rich dress Hope, Faith and Charity; Hope did essay to speak, but wine rendered her endeavours so feeble that she withdrew, and hoped the King would excuse her brevity. Faith was then all alone, for I am sure that she was not joined with Good Works, and left the court in a staggering condition. Charity came to the King's feet, and seemed to cover the multitude of sins her sisters had committed; in some sort she made obeisance and brought gifts, but said she would return home again, as there was no gift which Heaven had not already given His Majesty. She then returned to Hope and Faith who were both sick and spewing in the lower hall. Next came Victory in bright armour and presented a rich sword to the King, who did not accept it, but put it by with his hand; and by a strange medley of versification did endeavour to make suit to the King. But Victory did not triumph long; for after much lamentable utterance she was led away like a silly captive and laid to sleep in the outer steps of the ante-chamber. Now did Peace make entry and strive to get foremost to the King; but I grieve to tell how great wrath she did discover unto those of her Attendants; and much contrary to her semblance rudely made war with her olive branch and laid on the pates of those who did oppose her coming.'

Even allowing for Harington's desire to make a good story and show off, and the fact that he owed James a grudge for having patronized him insufferably, it was clearly the sort of evening to cause the greatest possible scandal among sober City merchants and taxpayers and in such remote manor houses as might boast a London correspondent to keep them in touch with the gossip of St Paul's. The House of Commons had only just voted £400,000 to relieve the King's necessities, and Harington was not the only man to point the obvious moral that 'in good soothe, the Parliament did kindly to provide his Majesty so seasonably with money'. The spreading tales of Court scandals and Court debauches had a direct political consequence, in that they largely helped to wreck the delicate financial negotiations which Salisbury was about to open with the Commons. They also marked the beginning of that rift between Court and Country which was to be James's worst legacy to his descendants and was to make the pattern of politics for the next century.

But visits from foreign royalty were very rare and the Danes were such notoriously heavy drinkers that it would anyway have been difficult to keep the celebrations reasonably sober. Normally such festivities were confined to the Christmas season —the only period when the King was ordinarily in residence at Whitehall. Salisbury might hope that this was an isolated episode which would not be repeated and would in due course be forgotten. The appearance of Robert Carr at Court and his almost immediate rise to the position of sole favourite with the King added a permanent and much more dangerous element to the situation. Only a year before it had seemed that James had quite outgrown the need to lavish an exaggerated affection on some good-looking young man. James Hay had come south in 1603 with the reputation of a favourite, and in the first months of his reign in England James had made a great fuss of Philip Herbert, Pembroke's handsome younger brother, who was created Earl of Montgomery. But there is no evidence at all that Hay's relations with the King were ever indecorous, and Montgomery was far too tough, smelt too much of the stables, and was too single-mindedly preoccupied with hounds and hunting to fill the part. If James ever made any emotional advances to him they were soon abandoned, and Montgomery became a hunting companion only, always in favour, but never of any political, or any great social importance.

Nevertheless, though there is no positive evidence of it at all, enough of James's original tendency must have survived for an old friend like Hay, who knew him well, to think it worth while to introduce Carr to the King's notice with the deliberate intention of gaining an indirect ascendancy for himself and the Scottish interest to counter-balance the all-powerful Cecil–Howard influence. This he did by an excellent piece of stage management helped by a stroke of luck. Carr was a tall, brainless athlete with the slightly effeminate fair-haired good looks most calculated to catch James's eye. He was well-connected

ROBERT CARR
EARL OF SOMERSET
by Cornelius Johnson

and had served for a time as a royal page in Scotland, a post from which, so Queen Anne said, he had been dismissed for clumsiness. Since then he had been abroad and had acquired better manners and a fluent knowledge of French, though he does not seem to have grasped very much of the political situation and background; and now he was back seeking another opening at Court.

Hay chose a tilting match to launch him, giving him his shield to carry into the ring; and he seems to have attracted instant attention even before his horse began to give trouble. He was a fine horseman, but in the end the animal came down with him and broke his leg. From that moment his career was made. James gave personal instructions for proper medical attention and could hardly wait until the jousting was over to rush to see that the invalid was comfortably settled in Master Rider's house at Charing Cross. From then on he visited the young man every day, interfering fussily in the details of his treatment and convalescence, and giving jealous orders for the exclusion of all other visitors, as the Court sensed what had happened and flocked to inquire after this hitherto unknown young Scot. It is surprising how little James had learnt, for all his shrewdness and wit, of human beings and their follies and limitations. That, lonely and starved of affection as he was, he should have fallen for youth and good looks is at least understandable. Rebuffed by wife and children, he was able now to lavish on Carr a possessive affection which sought to exclude every other influence on the young man's life. 'Remember,' he was to write much later, when their relationship was on the verge of shipwreck, 'that all your being except your breathing and soule is frome me.' Robin Carr was to be, as he liked to phrase it, his 'creature': a thing created by himself. But the infatuation which led him to believe that he could turn Carr into a statesman, the pathetic delusion that by teaching the young man Latin he could make him an adequate intellectual companion, and the blindness to the political and social consequences of his behaviour were all unforgivable. Nevertheless, at the age of past 40, as he stood by the bedside with a rod playfully clutched in his hand hearing his pupil conjugate Latin verbs, he cherished every silly romantic daydream possible in such a situation. There were those who, in mockery of Carr's

Scottish accent, suggested that James had been better employed teaching him English, since he had 'much need of a better language'. But there was no mockery or intrigue that could halt this favourite's rise, and when he emerged again into public life it was as the King's inseparable companion.

Thus, by James's folly, in one afternoon the whole pattern of English politics and of English history was changed, immeasurably for the worse. Carr's rise to official pre-eminence was slow and carefully graduated. Some nine months after the fatal tilting match he was knighted, and Chamberlain, writing on December 30th, 1607, to tell Carleton of his appointment as Gentleman of the Bedchamber, refers to him only as 'Sir Robert Carre, a yonge Scot and a new favorite'. For any advancement to larger honours some endowment was necessary. Carr could not be expected to support a peerage on an Exchequer grant of £600 a year and a stream of casual presents of jewels and clothes and golden tables set with diamonds. In January of 1609 this problem was solved in the worst possible way by the grant of Raleigh's estate at Sherborne, the only property saved from the wreck of his fortunes for the support of his wife and family. A criminally careless flaw in the deed conveying the land to trustees laid it open to forfeiture. There was no Crown property available to meet the case, when so much was already having to be sold to meet the King's most pressing debts, and James's long-nursed hatred and fear of Raleigh made this for him the obvious solution. So he persisted in the teeth of a public opinion outraged by this final act of meanness against the last survivor of a legendary past, deaf to the appeals of Raleigh and his wife, of Prince Henry, and even of the Queen. The habit of merely disregarding opposition to his immediate wishes and ignoring unpalatable facts was growing on him; and all he would say to those who protested was: 'I mun hae it for Carr.' So Sherborne was handed over, and a little over a year later Sir Robert was created Lord Rochester, a Privy Councillor, and a Knight of the Garter, and in May, 1611, Keeper of the Signet and virtually the King's private secretary. Two years later he was to complete the climb by becoming Earl of Somerset and Lord Chamberlain.

But Carr's real power and influence increased very much more quickly. He was very soon in a position in which he could make or block almost any public appointment, and the pace at which his influence increased was only limited by his own uncertainty and inexperience. He had, however, provided himself with an adviser who had an older and better brain than his own: a chance-met acquaintance of his early days in Scotland named Overbury. This man, a minor poet and littérateur whose ambition far outran even his undoubted abilities, eagerly seized the chance of a short cut to power and wealth offered by Carr's friendship and, though the King never really liked it, the two became inseparable. Overbury had all the disreputable skill in suits and intrigues and Court racketeering to make the alliance a profitable one, and enough diplomatic knowledge and experience to pilot his patron through the deeper waters of statecraft in which James so ingenuously involved his new favourite. 'Carr and his governor' rapidly became a real force, not strong enough, it is true, to weaken the massively-based position built up by Lord Salisbury, but one which he could not eliminate and which he had always to take into account not only in the internal politics of Whitehall, but on larger issues of policy as well.

In small things as in great this new development accelerated the deterioration of James's character and Court, and of his reputation in the country at large. The cheerful, unaffected and unselfconscious ordinariness of James's behaviour in public, though it lacked dignity, had hitherto been in many ways an asset in his dealings with his subjects. But now it led him to treat Carr in public with the same exaggerated, gross affection as in private, and what had already been a little odd in a sixteen-year-old boy when he was worshipping at the shrine of Esmé Stuart, became grotesque in the middle-aged man. He appeared everywhere with his arm round Carr's neck, constantly kissed and fondled him, lovingly feeling the texture of the expensive suits he chose and bought for him, pinching his cheeks and smoothing his hair. It does not seem that there were many in that hardened Court who were morally shocked by these displays, but there can have been few who did not find them ludicrous and unseemly. The Queen resented it from the start and took a particular dislike to Overbury, to whom she always referred in letters as 'that fellow', and whom she twice had arrested for gossiping indiscreetly about her debts. It completed, too, the estrangement between Prince Henry and his father. The Prince disliked Carr personally and several times quarrelled with him in public; and as he grew older his rather harsh, clear-cut mind saw only too clearly all that was reprehensible and deplorable in the situation. Inevitably, too, in circumstances which he knew to be indefensible, the consciousness of disapproval made James even more obstinate and inaccessible to criticism than ever, and more inclined than ever to ignore opposition.

The Court adapted itself quickly enough to the new state of affairs. It consisted, after all, almost entirely of professionals: men who hoped to make a fortune, or at least a living, out of the public service. Sir Francis Bacon, still seeking desperately to secure the advancement to which he knew his great talents entitled him, set the tone for the careerists and place-hunters, not only by flattering Carr, but by 'habitually stooping and crouching' to Overbury. Parliament men were less complaisant, since Carr for them was another object on which the King wasted public money. In the country at large, where knowledge of Court doings penetrated only slowly and uncertainly, there was little reaction until later on, when Carr's career was to involve the monarchy in really serious scandals. His advent did nevertheless throw the whole ramshackle machine of Elizabethan government out of balance. A certain arbitrariness and chanciness were bound to influence the composition of the government in any political system in which the King still retained executive power and a free choice of ministers. But the groupings and calculations and intrigues of Elizabethan statesmen had at least always been based on the solid realities of territorial or commercial interest. The rules, as they understood and played them, did not ensure that the ablest men got into office, but did make more or less certain that only those exercised power who were accustomed to it and whose standing in the country compelled them to use it with some sense of responsibility. To this system favourites, so long as they remained the companions of the King's leisure only, could do little or no harm. But when James, as his infatuation increased, insisted more and more on referring political decisions and important appointments to a young man of no intelligence, experience, or consequence, chosen only for his 'smooth outside', the results were serious. By 1612 even the entrenched and irremovable Salisbury was beginning to find his policies cramped and vitiated by this new influence which he could neither control nor eliminate, and which after his death would be disastrous.

So the golden age which had seemed to be opening after the Powder Plot became instead the beginning of a fatal decay in the whole tone of Court and government. Processes had been set in motion which in a very short space of time would completely estrange Court from Country and leave Stuart Kings normally opposed, for one reason or another, by an overwhelming majority of their politically minded subjects. It was particularly unfortunate that this should have happened at a moment when the King had already committed himself to a religious policy unpopular with a large number of Englishmen and was about to embark on vital and tricky financial negotiations with Parliament. For, while James hunted and junketed and indulged his infatuation for Carr, he was simultaneously engaged in a series of disputes with the House of Commons in which there emerged clearly for the first time some of the issues which were to lead thirty years later to civil war. For over these, too, King and subjects became rapidly and alarmingly estranged.

CHAPTER X

The Financial Breakdown

*

The pattern of James's relations with his Parliaments in the years between the Gunpowder Plot and the death of Salisbury followed the same general trend as the developments in Court and government. A situation which seemed at first full of promise for the future degenerated fast into one of continual bickering and misunderstanding, with the King less and less prepared to learn from his mistakes or to compromise with an opposition which he would not make the effort to understand. Not unnaturally the session postponed from the 5th of November to January of 1606 opened in an atmosphere of warm self-congratulation. The King, not yet recovered from the worst fright of his life, was for once prepared to forget his dreams of universal tolerance and collaborate wholeheartedly with Parliament in harrying the Catholics; and Parliament men, feeling that they all owed their miraculous preservation to the King's detective ability, were genuinely ready to forget the disagreements of 1604 and hope that in future James would show a better knowledge of the legal limitations of his prerogative and of the liberties and privileges of the House of Commons.

In this mood, without disputing the Treasurer's argument that the expenses of the succession and the coronation had been exceptionally heavy and had to be met by exceptional means, they voted unprecedentedly large subsidies amounting to nearly £400,000, to be spread over the next four years. This was not, in fact, nearly enough to pay off the debt already accumulated. It would not even meet the normal annual deficit for the next four years. But it relieved immediate necessities and allowed the King to believe that the Commons had now come to their senses, so that they could proceed in joyful co-operation against the Catholic menace. The *Act for the better discovering and re-*

pressing of Popish Recusants and the further *Act to prevent and avoid dangers which may grow by Popish Recusants* were the high-water mark of anti-Catholic persecution. The first tightened up all the existing penal legislation, making it obligatory on all not merely to go to church every Sunday, but to take Communion as prescribed in the Prayer Book. The King was given the right, at his discretion, to refuse the ordinary recusancy fines and take instead two-thirds of the offender's landed property. A more stringent Oath of Allegiance was imposed which, in clear terms, repudiated the Pope's claim to 'any power or authority to depose the King, or to dispose any of his Majesty's kingdoms or dominions, or to authorize any foreign prince to invade or annoy him or his countries, or to discharge any of his subjects of their allegiance and obedience to his Majesty, or to give licence or leave to any of them to bear arms, raise tumult, or to offer any violence to his Majesty's Royal Person, State, or Government'. Anybody who twice refused to take this oath was to suffer outlawry and forfeiture, and finally the Act made it High Treason not only to convert others to Rome, but to be converted. The second Act anticipated the Test Act by trying to exclude known recusants from public life altogether, barring them from the learned professions, the army and navy, and all the lower reaches of the administration. They were forbidden to come to Court, or within ten miles of the City of London, without a warrant from King or Council.

This was the policy which James set himself to defend in his next published work, the *Apology for the Oath of Obedience*, convinced in theory that this was the right way to deal with an impossible class of persons, and that the leaders of Catholic Europe would agree that on this issue he was right and the Pope wrong. A special edition was offered to every crowned head, and James was genuinely hurt and surprised when Catholic rulers ignored it, or even refused to accept it. Sir Charles Cornwallis, writing from Madrid, ruefully reported that the Duke of Lerma would not even let him present the volume to the King of Spain as a leaving present, wishing 'with a great sighe that those rare and singular parts of his Majesty, (whereof all the world took so great a notice) had been employed upon a better, a more sound and pleasing subjecte'. Furthermore James himself quickly reacted away from a policy into which he had only been stampeded in the hysteria following the Gunpowder Treason. He hated persecution anyway, and the policy as laid down in the Acts was largely unworkable. Had the penalties been fully exacted, and had the magistrates used the inquisitorial powers conferred on them, social life in many counties of the north and west would have been quite disrupted. There were many Catholics whom the King liked personally and the conversion of the Queen to Rome, unostentatious though it was, had made Catholicism fashionable in some Court circles. Thus, after the preliminary panic, the lot of Catholics became in practice very much what it had been before. The exaction of the fines from recusants, especially when they were allowed to compound to save forfeiting two-thirds of their property, became one more complicating factor in the Jacobean financial system. It was cheaper to grant a courtier the right to mulct one of his Catholic neighbours than pay him a salary or pension, so that there grew up a vested property right in recusants. Sir William Anstruther would regard the death of 'my recusant, Master Talbot', as a valid ground for claiming a pension from the Secretary of State, and it would be a proper exercise of political influence for Lord Southampton to invoke Salisbury's protection 'in the behalf of my poor aunt, Kathryn Cornwallis, who by your Lordship's favour hath hitherto lived free from trouble for her recusancy', especially since, as Southampton candidly admitted, he was 'in the expectation of some good from her'.

In consequence this penal legislation of 1606, which had appeared to be the foundation of a new harmony between King and Commons, became in a very few years one of their most bitter and recurrent causes of dispute. The Commons never changed their view that 'Jesuits, seminary priests and Popish recusants' were at the root of all English troubles, and that the Acts of 1606 were 'good and provident laws'. When they presented a list of religious grievances in 1610, the first and most important was that 'although your Majesty by your Godly, learned, and judicious writings have declared your Christian and princely zeal in the defence of the religion established . . . yet the laws are not executed against the priests, who are corrupters of the people in religion and loyalty'. They laid a finger accurately on the core of the abuse, which was letting recusants 'compound with those that beg their penalties', and begged the King to take back into his own hands 'the penalties due for recusancy, and that the same be not converted to the private gain of some, to your infinite loss, the emboldening of the Papists, and the decay of true religion'. The gap between James's theory and practice in this matter became one of the most nagging of Parliamentary grievances, and in 1621 was to lead to a major quarrel.

Thus the apparent harmony of 1606 was only superficial and temporary. There was even a determined body of opposition to the unprecedentedly large subsidy, which denounced its opponents as men 'who studied to please'. The same error had been made as in 1604: 'I think,' one member wrote, 'the State scorneth to have any Privy Counsellors of any understanding' in the Lower House. From his place in the House of Lords Salisbury was increasingly unable to control the course of Commons debates. Indeed it was sometimes difficult for Councillors themselves to know what was in the King's mind; at one point in 1606, on a matter admittedly not very important, the Commons were reduced to taking Sir Francis Hastings's word that 'my Lord Chief Justice told him that my Lord of Kinlosse delivered unto his Lordship that the King is well pleased that the Bill shall passe'. There had never in Elizabeth's time been the slightest doubt of her views on any piece of business before the House. But now there were signs that the Commons were finding their own leaders: men of decisive character who might have spent their lives merely as critics of government in the old days, but who now stepped into the vacuum created by Salisbury's carelessness. In default of a government programme of legislation, members had to take the initiative themselves, lest they return to their constituencies 'with nothing for the good of the commonwealth', to become, as one of them put it, 'a mock and scorn to the country'. Inevitably they began by marshalling their grievances and then appointed committees to draw up bills to remedy them, which would again be considered by the whole House in Committee. Thus the negligence of James and his ministers led directly to many of the modern techniques and procedures of Parliamentary government; and since they were complicated techniques, there inevitably emerged the experts who could work them: the clear-headed men with legal or

business experience who could marshal a case and draft the
required bills.

Their progress was slow and obscure. But it is clear that by
1610 Sir Edwin Sandys, the magnate who was taking Sir
Thomas Smith's place on many of the boards of the great City
companies, had established a recognized leadership over the
House which the ablest of Privy Councillors would find it hard
to shake. The beginnings of this process and its significance
can be seen in an episode as early as 1606 when, against the
King's expressed wish, the Commons revived their old grievance against Purveyance and appointed a committee to draft a
bill abolishing it. James asked them, quite mildly for him, to
drop the matter, and it was Sandys who in a long speech swung
the House to a direct and clear defiance of the will of the sovereign
such as it would never have dared to make under Elizabeth.
'Touching our Bill against Purveyors, I thinck we ought not to
let it sleepe,' he said. Elizabeth had already once quashed a Bill
on the same subject in 1598. But, through idleness, or because
he simply failed to grasp the importance of what was happening,
James let it go at that. Sandys had argued that it would be a
dangerous precedent to let the King stop their debating what
they liked. But in fact the precedents were all the other way, and
never before had the Crown allowed freedom of speech to mean
more than freedom to say, in reason, what they liked about
government measures. Though they would probably stoutly
have denied it, Sandys and his friends were here the innovators;
and when James, seeing the danger, tried with Bacon's help in
1610 to re-establish the Elizabethan practice he found that it
was already almost impossible to cut off debate on subjects
which embarrassed him.

Everything that happened on the Parliamentary front during
these years served to strengthen James's belief that Parliament
was being deliberately and obstinately unco-operative. In his
highly simplified view he was personally responsible to God for
the good governance of England and Parliament was there only
to help him to do so. It was no part of its duty to oppose his
measures or to propose its own remedies for the grievances he
was graciously pleased to allow them to state. He felt the same
about finance. 'The only disease and consumption which I can
ever apprehend as likeliest to endanger me,' he wrote to his

Council in 1607, 'is this eating canker of want, which being removed, I could think myself as happy in all other respects as any other king or monarch that ever was since the birth of Christ.' In these circumstances it was Parliament's plain duty to relieve his necessities and enable him to govern properly; and, given his basic, simple proposition of his direct responsibility to God rather than to his people's representatives, his case was unanswerable. All criticism and interference became a sin as well as a crime—a clear infringement of the divine will. But instead of settling down to the hard work of finding his own remedies for abuses and injustices, and patiently working out a technique which would enable him either to master Parliament or to collaborate with it, he fumed and lectured, and dismissed as maddening English prejudice the obsession with a system of laws which seemed only designed to prevent him from governing as he wished, wisely and well. 'We are sorry of our ill fortune in this country,' he burst out in one letter to the Privy Council, 'that having lived so long as we did in the Kingdom where we were born, we came out with an unstained reputation, without any grudge in the people's hearts but for wanting of us. Wherein we have misbehaved here we know not, nor we can ever yet learn: but sure we are that in all the Lower House these seven years past . . . our fame and actions have been tossed like tennis balls among them and all that spite and malice durst do to disgrace and infame us hath been used. To be short, this Lower House by their behaviour have periled and annoyed our health, wounded our reputation, emboldened all ill-natured people, encroached upon many of our privileges and plagued our purse with their delays'.

Nothing did more to strengthen this conviction in James than the long, abortive debates on Union with Scotland which occupied so much Parliamentary time in 1606 and 1607. James was so clearly right in his desire for 'a perfect union of laws and persons, and such a naturalizing as may make one body of both kingdoms', that all opposition seemed to him stupid or wilful prejudice, as most of it was. Much time was wasted in the Commons on 'scandal and obloquy not pertinent to the matter in hand'; on fears that the rich English pasture would be eaten up by the herd of famished Scottish cattle, and pure invective such as the speech which ended with the remark that the Scots had 'not suffered above two kings to die in their beds these two hundred years'. But there were some real objections, too. The legal systems of the two countries were not easy to reconcile and, indeed, never have been entirely reconciled. The single Church of which James dreamed was equally quite unattainable. Even on the vexed question of naturalization there was a real difficulty, since Members were obsessed with the thought that, had Philip of Spain and Mary Tudor left an heir, every Spaniard might have claimed the rights of a natural-born Englishman and used them to subvert both Church and State. So, in spite of the brilliance with which Bacon supported the King's case, it was rejected, and only a very small part of James's original ambitions was salvaged by Coke and the Common Lawyers for him. Parliament never gave way.

But it was over money that all the main difficulties arose in 1607 and again in 1610. For the big subsidy of 1606, so cheerfully voted in the aftermath of the Gunpowder Plot, did nothing but postpone for a couple of years a financial crisis which was inevitable. Neither James nor his opponents and critics in the House of Commons ever really grasped the basic factors underlying the Crown's poverty in the early seventeenth century. The ramifying and confused system of taxation, the bribes and the perquisites, and the overlapping functions of so many officials and departments made any proper system of accounting impossible. Combined with the operation of economic laws which were understood imperfectly or not at all, they baffled every successive Lord Treasurer who tried to discover exactly where he stood and why. Some scribblings of Lord Burleigh's, in which he jotted down the cost, item by item, of a Star Chamber dinner in 1588 which came to £18 5s. 2d., and noted gloomily that such a dinner in 1559 had only cost £5 9s., and in 1509 only £1 10s. 7d., show that he had at least grasped that the rise of prices was at the root of his problem. Lord Dorset, mildly and benignly corrupt and secure in the possession of his own vast fortune, never in his occasional memoranda on the subject really mastered what he called 'the anatomy of many miseries for lack of money'.

Dorset died in 1608, in the middle of telling a funny story at the Council table, leaving a situation so serious that it could no longer be ignored. His last 'accompt' showed debts totalling more than £700,000 and revealed, according to Salisbury, that James's expenditure exceeded his ordinary revenue by about £80,000 a year. Partly because there was nobody except himself obviously qualified to succeed Dorset, partly, probably, because he wished to gather all the threads of policy into his own hands for an attempt at wholesale reform, Salisbury added the Treasurership to his already exacting Secretaryship of State —a burden which was very quickly to break down his frail constitution. But before his health collapsed he had time and energy to make his attempt at the complete financial reorganization which would alone enable the Elizabethan system of government to survive into the seventeenth century. For, unless the Crown could be provided with an adequate permanent income, Parliaments would have to meet almost every year to vote the subsidies needed to cover the deficit, and this would inevitably mean the end of government by the King in Council. Increasing experience coupled with the knowledge that the need for subsidies gave them the whip hand was bound to lead the Commons to interfere in royal policy and try to gain some control over the expenditure of the money they voted. The process was indeed already observable. Parliament had sat for about eleven months only during the forty-four years of Elizabeth's reign. There were five sessions of James's first Parliament between 1603 and 1611, and that fact alone accounted for much of the new initiative shown by the Commons and the new procedures which they were elaborating. Grievances remained fresh as they were carried forward from session to session, and projected Bills which had been left uncompleted were sometimes picked up and carried through the following year. Unless the Crown could secure a revenue large enough to govern in times of peace without Parliamentary grants, sovereignty—that is to say control of national policy—must surely pass fairly quickly to the tax-voting House of Commons.

By the time he had disentangled the situation Salisbury found that he had nearly a million of debts, and his first task was if possible to liquidate these, with their crippling burden of annual interest. In this he was surprisingly successful. He sold Crown property to the value of £400,000, and he dug out old debts due to the Crown to a total of £200,000 and got them paid. The revival of various lapsed dues and fees, and uncollected fines, gave him another £100,000. With the help of the subsidy of 1606 he was thus able in two years and in the teeth of the annual deficit to pay off £700,000 of the debt. But that left the problem of the annual deficit itself still unsolved. Dorset had done something to increase the yield of taxation in his last years by centralizing the collection of the Customs duties and improving the administration of Crown lands. Salisbury had done even better by increasing the Customs duties themselves. His opportunity to do so arose out of the collapse, early in the reign, of the Levant Company, which had been paying the government a handsome yearly sum for its monopoly of trade with the Eastern Mediterranean. To compensate itself the Treasury had imposed an extra duty of 5s. 6d. a cwt. on imported currants, and this in 1606 a merchant named Bate had refused to pay. In the subsequent lawsuit in the Exchequer Court the whole question of the Crown's right to 'impose' such extra duties was thoroughly argued, and with sound Elizabethan precedents behind them the Judges decided unanimously for the King. Salisbury seized the opportunity thus offered and, after careful discussion with leading City merchants as to what the trade would stand, issued in 1608 a new *Book of Rates* which levied Impositions of duty calculated to bring in to the Treasury another £70,000 a year. But, although these various improvements, together with the steady rise of the Customs duties as the total volume of the nation's trade increased, brought the Crown's revenue up from £264,000 in 1603 to £366,000 in 1608, expenditure was going up even faster—from £290,700 in 1603 to £509,524 in 1610.

Thus, calculate and economize as he would, Salisbury could not foresee any possibility of reducing the annual deficit below £56,000, and there was every reason to suppose that expenditure would continue to rise faster than revenue for causes outside the control of any English government. Since there was also the £300,000 of outstanding debt to be liquidated, Parliament had to be called again in 1610, though if all went well Salisbury might hope that it would be the last session for some time. For he proposed that they should not only vote subsidies to pay off the remaining debt, but should strike a bargain with him known as the 'Great Contract' which should make the Crown normally solvent without reference to Parliament, at any rate for some years to come. Broadly speaking, the plan was to surrender for ever the vexatious and inequitable feudal revenue from wardships, knights' fees, and the rest, which brought in on the average about £65,000 a year, and against which Parliament had already vigorously protested, and also to give up the right to Purveyance, which was reckoned to be worth another £50,000. In return Parliament was asked to grant the King an additional permanent revenue of £200,000 a year for life.

The Great Contract was thus not a very far-reaching or revolutionary measure. It was the work of a tired and ageing statesman whose mind was in any case embedded in the habits and systems of the previous reign. It would have tided over the current crisis and perhaps have secured the immediate future. Something much more drastic was needed if the situation of 1610 was not simply to recur; and Sir Julius Caesar, the Chancellor of the Exchequer, for one, thought the King was offering to strike a very bad bargain. But it was very much a step in the right direction. What James had to avoid at all costs if he could was the temptation to use the surviving prerogative rights of the Crown to screw every possible penny out of his subjects so as to meet his rising costs without ceaseless application to Parliament. This was just what Sir Julius Caesar was proposing to do as an alternative to Salisbury's Contract: to tighten up and extend the feudal demands which were already a crying grievance, and to screw another £20,000 out of Purveyance by using it to support the households of his children as well as his own. Already the use of such methods was arousing bitter complaint, and they led to a vicious circle in which each successive Parliament met in a less reasonable frame of mind, with new grievances piled on old ones, and with the chances of any real and permanent relief of the government's difficulties steadily diminishing. From the King's point of view the Great Contract was at least a statesmanlike beginning to a solution of the problem and its failure to get through a disaster.

A number of different causes combined in the sessions of 1610 and 1611 to defeat Salisbury's plans and so to make James's final and petulant dissolution of this tiresome Parliament in February, 1611, a turning point in English history. For by then he had committed himself and his successors to policies both in religion and finance which would lead directly to the Civil War and make the struggle for sovereignty with the nation's representatives in Parliament the dominating theme of Stuart history in England. In the first place there were two converging streams of religious dissatisfaction: there was the growing Puritan opposition to the encroaching power of the Bishops, and especially to the Court of High Commission through which that power was ultimately exercised; and there was a far more widespread resentment of the mildness which was in practice being shown to Catholics in spite of the severe legislation and high-sounding royal pronouncements of 1606. There was also a growing mistrust of James's good intentions on purely financial grounds: the known extravagance and corruption of Court and government, and a conscious realization that only the necessity for periodical subsidies made James listen to Parliament at all, on finance or anything else. Finally there had been some alarming arguments used by the Judges about the royal prerogative, especially during Bate's case, which re-aroused all the critical-defensive mood of 1604.

Salisbury opened the ball in 1610 with a very able survey of the financial position to a conference of both Houses on February 15th, tracing the origins of their difficulties back to the Irish wars of Elizabeth's last years, and detailing his own recent attempts at reform. 'The Grounds and Strength of his Arguments were so energeticall,' one observer wrote, 'and his Speech so persuasive, as it seemeth to have given very good Satisfaction both to the Minds and Judgements of all the House'. But the reaction of the Commons shows how far-reaching already were the effects of the government's seven years' negligence to control debates and procedure. They gave a tepid assurance 'that the House had an inclination and willingness to give his Majesty satisfaction', but hesitated, 'to engage themselves in any offers or promise of Contribution to the King, afore they were sure of some certain and sound Retribution from him; least that after they had given over the one, they should also be in danger to lose the other'. The subsidy needed to pay off the debt they relegated at once, as was indeed normal, to the end of the session. As for means to cover the annual deficit, they referred the whole business of the return concessions to be granted by the King to what had clearly already become a

Standing Committee of General Grievances. Under the leadership of men like Sandys, members had already clearly rooted in their minds the principle that redress of grievances should precede supply, even if it had not yet been formally enunciated. They proposed now, not only that the Crown should give up the feudal revenues and the right to Purveyance, which Salisbury was prepared in advance to concede, but that the laws against recusants should be properly enforced and that all grants and pensions to courtiers should be cancelled. Already the dangerous effects of Carr's rise to supreme favouritism were making themselves felt. When the King forced Sir Henry Neville to answer the straight question whether it was not his subjects' duty to relieve his wants, he got the characteristically cautious reply: 'Where your Majesty's expence groweth by the Commonwealth we are bound to maintain it; otherwise not.' Before the Committee of General Grievances the member for Oxford City demanded to know 'to what purpose is it for us to draw a silver stream out of the country into the royal cistern, if it shall daily run out from thence by private cocks?' He added that he would never 'consent to take money from a poor frieze jerkin to trappe a courtier's horse withal'. Finally they confused the whole issue which Salisbury was trying to keep so clear and simple by raising the further question of the legality of Impositions.

It is this series of debates on Impositions which show most clearly how far opinion in the Commons had advanced in the last seven years, and also how much more clearly they understood the implications of the King's actions than he did himself. For James was not deliberately and coherently attempting to subvert the liberties of England, but merely taking the most convenient way Salisbury could find to deal with 'the eating canker of want', so that he could govern as he ought and enjoy himself as he wished. But the Commons saw two implied dangers very quickly. The first and more obvious was that the King might very soon raise far more by Impositions than the mere £70,000 a year so far brought in by the Book of Rates. In that case the Crown might cease to be dependent on the Commons for money even in a crisis, and the financial lever by which they could obtain redress of grievances in Parliament would have gone. 'If this power of imposing were quietly settled in our Kings,' Whitelocke said, later in the session, 'considering what is the greatest use they make of assembling of Parliaments, which is, the supply of money, I do not see any likelihood to hope for often meetings in that kind because they would provide themselves by that other means.'

The other danger raised by the lawyers in the House sounded much more academic and remote, but was real and practical enough when they were dealing with a logician like James. The Judges in Bate's case had endowed the Crown with a legal right to take any action to control foreign trade in the general interests of the nation. They had further laid down that only the King could be judge of what those interests required, and that this emergency prerogative, even though it might sometimes mean an interference with the liberty and property of the subject, could not be more closely defined or limited without so weakening the Crown that in a crisis the whole safety of the nation might be endangered. They were inclined to scoff at the argument that this gave the King by implication an unlimited right to tax his subjects without reference to Parliament. 'The King may pardon any felon,' Chief Baron Fleming pointed out; 'but it may be objected that if he pardon one felon he may pardon all, to the damage of the commonwealth, and yet none will doubt but that it is left in his wisdom'. But it was just this sort of reasoning that Members like Mr Hakewill feared. He admitted that the Judges' logic was perfectly sound, but said that in that case the law was 'most unreasonable, improvident and contrary to itself'. In making this stand he was perfectly right. For James's grandson, the second James, was to do just what the Chief Baron had scoffed at as unthinkable: to interpret a legal right to dispense individuals from the anti-Catholic laws as a right to suspend those laws altogether, exactly as though, by pardoning every murderer, he had in effect legalized murder. But in fact James himself indirectly justified Mr Hakewill's alarms even sooner, by coming down to the House on March 21st and making the largest claims he ever made for his royal prerogative: claims which would make all common law safeguards for the liberty of the subject entirely valueless.

'The state of Monarchy,' he said in the most famous passage of that speech, 'is the supremest thing upon earth; for kings are not only God's lieutenants upon earth and sit upon God's throne, but even by God himself they are called gods. There be three principal similitudes that illustrate the state of Monarchy: one taken out of the Word of God and the two other out of the grounds of policy and philosophy. In the Scriptures kings are called gods, and so their power after a certain relation compared to the Divine Power. Kings are also compared to the fathers of families, for a king is truly *parens patriae*, the politic father of his people. . . . Now a father may dispose of his inheritance to his children at his pleasure, yea, even disinherit the eldest upon just occasions and prefer the youngest, according to his liking; make them beggars or rich at his pleasure; restrain or banish out of his presence, as he finds them give cause of offence, or restore them in favour again with the penitent sinner. So may the King deal with his subjects.'

It was all very well for James to go on to assure them that God would punish all kings who nevertheless failed to govern according to the laws; the Commons wanted more immediate and obvious safeguards for liberty and property. The only effect of the King's ill-timed and ill-judged intervention was to broaden the whole front of the dispute and to produce a ramifying series of debates and petitions on every accumulated grievance, in the course of which Salisbury's modest and sensible Great Contract proposals got thrust into the background. Four years too late, James tried to revive the Elizabethan method of forbidding all further discussion of the powers and rights 'inherent in the persons of princes', and merely provoked a solemn Petition of Right which raised the whole question of freedom of speech. Partly from the growing natural indolence which made it impossible for him to fight a dogged battle through to a finish, partly because his need for ready money was all the time increasing, the King gave way and the debates dragged on through June. On July 7th the Commons presented their religious grievances, asking for the rigid enforcement of anti-Catholic penalties, the re-instatement of the three hundred ejected clergy, the abolition of all pluralities, and some restriction on the activities of the ecclesiastical courts. At the same time they presented a much larger petition demanding that all Impositions without consent of Parliament should be 'quite abolished', that the powers of the Archbishop's Court of High Commission should be drastically curtailed, that the King should be more sparing in the use of Proclamations which interfered with the normal process of law, and that the powers of the Council of Wales should be curtailed.

Thus, in the course of those six months' debate, all the issues on which the Civil War was ultimately to be fought had been brought out into the open. On almost all of them James was technically in the right, and the doctrines put forward by the House of Commons were, by Elizabethan standards, dangerous innovations. Nevertheless James had so mismanaged his case and had used such unfortunate language in developing it that the Commons undoubtedly believed sincerely that they were only defending their ancient liberties against new and dangerous encroachments. Moreover they were supported by a growing public opinion outside the House. Chamberlain, as always faithfully reflecting the gossip of St Paul's, recorded a general discomfort 'to see our monarchicall powre and regall prerogative strained so high and made so transcendent every way, that yf the practise shold follow the positions, we are not like to leave to our successors that freedome we received from our forefathers, nor make account of anything we have longer than they list that govern'.

The financial discussions which were the cause of it all degenerated meanwhile into a prolonged haggle. The Commons offered only half the £200,000 a year Salisbury had demanded as compensation for the surrender of the feudal dues and Purveyance, and further stipulated that the King should also surrender his claim to Impositions. Salisbury in the end was prepared to offer that, too, if the King was given an adequate subsidy and a total additional income of £300,000 a year in compensation for all. But by then the Commons were so mistrustful of the King's whole theory of government that they feared any bargain which might weaken their hold over royal policy. A fresh series of debates on the scandals of Scottish favourites and Court extravagance finally exhausted James's patience; he prorogued and finally, in February of 1611, dissolved his first Parliament with nothing achieved. Financially he was thrust back on the sort of expedient proposed by Sir Julius Caesar: the exploitation of his prerogative powers to screw the uttermost farthing out of the existing sources of revenue, which could only intensify every grievance. How little he had learnt in general by this year of ill-tempered debate was shown by his immediate elevation of Carr to the House of Lords as Viscount Rochester and a scattering of another £34,000 in indiscriminate gifts, mostly to Scotsmen.

Salisbury had still a little over a year to live, and outwardly his hold over the government remained as sure as ever. In fact the whole Elizabethan system for which he stood was breaking down, and he was already losing control of events. The Parliamentary failure left him with no financial policy but a number of dangerous and not very remunerative expedients, only one of which turned out successfully: the creation of a new order of Baronets. These were 'gentlemen of good family and estate' who were prepared, in return for a hereditary knighthood, to subscribe a total of £3,240 each towards the maintenance of the army in Ireland, which normally cost the English exchequer about £11,000 a year. The idea caught on well and in the first three years raised over £90,000. But, even so, Salisbury found that his financial situation was deteriorating again very fast and, worse and more decisive still, he was at last losing his control over the King. As the years went on James stood less and less in awe of Cecil, and his gratitude for a miraculously peaceful succession gradually evaporated. Ironically enough, at this moment, when the monarchy's control over the course of English politics was being seriously shaken for the first time for a century, James's confidence in himself as 'an old and wise King', perfectly capable of governing England successfully, was steadily growing. At the same time, under the influence of his passion for Carr, he was becoming noticeably more irresponsible. A capricious and unpredictable influence was upsetting the delicate Cecilian political balances as the new Lord Rochester began to feel his feet and to realize that James's infatuation could mean for him complete control over English policy at home and abroad.

Under the impact of this fresh factor Salisbury's widely entrenched position began to crumble. His Howard allies saw a shorter and less difficult channel of access to the King opening up, and began to use it to further policies of which Salisbury heartily disapproved. It was almost certainly from the tortuous mind of the Earl of Northampton—the old '3' of James's Scottish correspondence, and all his life a secret Catholic—that there sprang the idea of a Spanish alliance secured by the marriage of Prince Henry to a Spanish princess. Unrestricted toleration for the English Catholics would be an inevitable condition of such an alliance, and it was an idea thoroughly to James's taste. He was about to open negotiations for the marriage of his daughter, Elizabeth, to the Calvinist Elector Palatine. To marry his son simultaneously into the heart of the Counter-Reformation would precisely illustrate his conception of himself as the peacemaker of Europe and of the Church of England as the mediator, reaching out to reconcile the two extremes. But it would utterly destroy Salisbury's carefully maintained position of a neutrality equally friendly to Dutch and Spanish, and it would be wildly unpopular with an overwhelming majority of Englishmen.

For the time being this project was wrecked on the uncompromising hostility of Prince Henry himself, who roundly declared that two religions should never lie together in his bed. That the idea was seriously mooted at all shows how Salisbury's hold on policy was weakening, even before his health broke down altogether in the spring of 1612. That April, as a last, desperate remedy for the dropsy which was gaining on him, he went down to try the waters at Bath. The cure was a failure, and on May 24th, in the parsonage house at Marlborough on his way back to Hatfield, he died. The event created the greatest political vacuum men could remember. He left behind him no carefully trained son, as his father, Burleigh, had, to pick up the major threads of his policy. Lord Cranbourne, on whom he had once set such hopes, had grown up a dull, second-rate young man, and in his offices there were plenty of well-trained, conscientious diplomats and administrators, but no statesmen. There was now only Raleigh in the Tower and the almost senile Lord High Admiral to represent the legendary glories of the old reign. A year before Shakespeare had retired to Stratford, where he would write no more plays, and the Elizabethan sun was really setting at last. For the handful of lesser survivors from the great days and for the younger men who looked forward to a new era which should revive the glories of the old there was now only the Prince of Wales; and in November, 1612, only six months after Salisbury, Prince Henry too, sickened and died, and the last hopes of that kind of revival died with him. The publication of the new great Bible, commissioned eight years before at Hampton Court, with its elaborate, contorted sentences of dedication 'to the most High and Mighty Prince, James', marked the transition. Henceforward the age was unquestionably, almost aggressively, Jacobean.

To James the changes which were thus symbolized came predominantly as a relief. He had begun to feel Salisbury's great position as hampering and confining the statecraft which he felt himself so perfectly capable of exercising. The obligation of gratitude and deference had become tedious, and the restraints imposed on his conduct and policy galling. Morover, complacent though he was in so many ways, James can never have been entirely unaware of the unflattering contrast he presented personally to all that Salisbury and his generation had stood for; and his sense of escape from an irksome tutelage was even officially reflected in the inevitable reshuffle of offices which followed. No new Lord Treasurer was appointed to restrain and criticize the lavishness of his impulses, but the office went to a Commission, of which Northampton was the most influential member. He did not even choose a new Secretary of State. For a brief space he was captivated by the idea that he would administer his kingdom himself and demonstrate how infinitely better qualified he was to do so than any of his subjects. All correspondence was to be conducted through Carr, as Keeper of the Signet, and 'Bedchamber men', who were mostly Carr's nominees. So the transfer of effective power to the new favourite, which Salisbury had unobtrusively, but on the whole effectively resisted, was now complete.

The dissolution of his first Parliament and the end of the Salisbury régime were something more than an episode in English political history. They marked an epoch. During the next ten years Parliament only met for two entirely futile months of debate in 1614, and James was making an experiment just as deliberate, and in its way just as decisive in its results, as that of his son in the so-called eleven years' tyranny twenty years later. He sought to show that he could very well govern England without the help of the House of Commons, either as a forum for the ventilation and remedy of grievances, or as a tax-voting machine; and so he destroyed the only effective link between Court and country, government and people. The activities of Court and Council which made up the surface of

English activity became more and more remote and scandalous to the ordinary countryman, and even to the City merchant intent on profiting by the long era of peace. The annual Summer Progress, which Elizabeth had exploited as an opportunity to show herself to the mass of her subjects and to keep her in touch with a wider public, degenerated under James into a hunting tour of the southern counties during which he shut himself away as much as possible from crowds and publicity. Stringent proclamations forbade the common people to intrude on his Majesty's desire to be 'very private and retired', as he moved each summer on an almost settled beat, first to the Marquis of Winchester at Basing, and then on a leisurely tour of Hampshire, Wiltshire, and the borders of Gloucestershire and Somerset, ending up generally with Lord Southampton at Beaulieu in the New Forest. In the north and west men never had a chance of a glimpse of their King. Scotland would only see him once again before he died; and even in the south and on the road to Royston and Newmarket it was the royal purveyors, the Clerk of the Market who fixed local prices and the carttakers who requisitioned transport, who provided the only direct link between the ordinary Englishman and the Court.

Thus the grievances left unremedied in 1610 simmered, very slowly but none the less cumulatively, for ten years, while the old Elizabethan governmental machine, less and less efficient and increasingly corrupt, managed the day-to-day business of the country. More than ever before the nation's history became bound up with the personal doings of the King and of the men, wildly unsuitable in the eyes of most Englishmen, whom he gathered round him as advisers and intimates. Court gossip took the place of serious news, and of this only the major scandals would penetrate to the remoter countryside. An occasional inflammatory sermon or pamphlet might give the King a clue as to what was passing through the minds of his subjects. Round the board tables of the big companies and in the incessant negotiation of loans the worlds of Court and City made contact. Otherwise Whitehall was cut off from the life of the rest of the country: remote, alien, and at times almost incomprehensible.

CHAPTER XI

Experiment in Personal Rule

*

For a very short time after Salisbury's death the excitement of finding himself his own master and of trying himself to manage the routine of government rekindled James's interest in politics and his old ambition to startle his subjects by the excellence of his king-craft. But he had lost the energy and skill which had once so surprisingly enabled him to master the feuds and disorders of his native Scotland, and there was now no industrious, long-headed Maitland to see to all the details for him. Eight years of self-indulgence, during which his attention to business had been testy and intermittent, had left him without the capacity for hard work, and the experiment of governing through the Bedchamber was a disastrous failure. Throughout the year 1613 the exasperated Council was petitioning for the appointment of a Secretary to deal with accumulating arrears of business, while the new Treasury Commissioners helplessly watched the financial situation, so promisingly restored by Salisbury, collapse again to the verge of insolvency.

The truth was that James was ageing prematurely and fast. He was still well under 50, but he was degenerating physically, becoming more clumsy and unwieldy, and more and more careless in his personal habits. He looked out on the world from tired, disillusioned eyes, and he wrote no more poetry. More and more he was tending to withdraw himself from a world which obstinately refused to dance to the tunes he piped: from Popes who would still not recognize the sacrosanctity of heretic princes, and European rulers who would not even read his book; from the demagogues of the House of Commons whose sheer perversity denied him the revenue he needed to be a proper King, and from the railing complaints of Puritans who rejected the well-intentioned efforts of his Bishops. But disillusionment was to pursue him even in the comparatively closed circle of the Court into which he sought to withdraw. For he was never to learn the lesson that disappointments and difficulties cannot successfully be met by ignoring them; and once he had caught the habit of running away he could never recover the courage to turn and outface them. His intelligence, when he exerted it, remained as clear as ever, and he saw far more clearly than most of his contemporaries the deeper implications of the growing struggle between Crown and Commons. But he could only muster energy for an obstinate defensive; a slow and in the long run fatal retreat. His infatuation for Carr, and the still greater infatuation for Villiers which followed, were his last daydream refuge from a world which had proved itself cold and unkind. Surrounded by young men who were, as he loved to call them, his 'creatures', he could make a last attempt to escape into a fantasy which would behave as he wished.

But even within the narrowing circle of these interests and commitments harsh facts persistently obtruded and thwarted his benevolent intentions, bringing out in him that streak of callousness which had shown itself over Cobham's plot and in the persistent persecution of Raleigh, and which appeared again in his handling of the very minor crisis of Arabella Stuart's marriage in 1610. For the first few years after his accession he had treated his cousin Arabella much better than Elizabeth had done, despite the fact that she had more than once been put forward by factions at Court and by Catholic intriguers as a better claimant to the throne than himself. For once his touchiness about his own legitimacy had been in abeyance, and Arabella's honourable refusal to mix herself up in plots of any kind had been rewarded. She had been allowed to take her proper place at Court and accorded her proper precedence as a member of the royal family, and had been promised an adequate settlement and establishment as soon as she should decide whom she wished to marry. This she did not do until she was 35, when she fell headlong in love with William Seymour, a bookish young man of 23, whose descent from Henry VIII's sister, Mary, made him another of the people whose claim to the throne had been canvassed in 1603. Neither of them seems to have possessed a spark of ambition and they were both, it was said, 'ungraceful both in their Persons and Houses'. Dynastic intrigues were in any case unreal and out of date in the England of 1610, and the pair might perfectly safely have been allowed to marry and live out together the obscure, retired life which was all they both wanted.

Unfortunately, however, this threatened union of two rival lines of royal blood threw James back into a world which had nothing to do with the England of 1610. In the Scotland of his youth, which had been kept for centuries on the verge of civil war by bands of discontented feudatories, such a union would have been a real threat. The dark fears of usurpation and assassination which had haunted the life of every Stuart King leapt out of the past to cloud James's judgement and harden his heart. Memories came flooding back of the dark hints of Gowrie's possible claims to sit on his throne, and of the bonny Earl of Moray, 'who might ha' been a king'. He remembered the futile Catholic intrigues and Cobham's criminal folly, both centred round Arabella, and forgot the ignominious failure of both, which was the best guarantee of the harmlessness of that gentle, not very intelligent young woman. James's rage when he discovered that, in the face of his express order that they were never to meet again, the lovers had been secretly married was pardonable. Seymour was clapped into the Tower and Arabella ordered north in the custody of the Bishop of Durham. Normally there would have been forgiveness and relaxation when anger cooled. But Arabella had 'eaten of the forbidden tree', and it was not the defiance of his orders, but the much more serious, if obscure, threat to his kingship which hardened James's heart. The pair almost pulled their happiness out of the fire in spite of him. By pretending to be much iller than she was Arabella escaped on her way north and contrived the simultaneous escape of Seymour from the Tower. But he missed the ship in which they were to have crossed the Channel together and took another to Ostend, and she, lingering at sea in the hope of picking him up, was caught and brought back to four years of imprisonment in the Tower, where she first went mad and then died. She had committed the one sin which to James was unforgivable, and it does not seem that it crossed his mind to take pity on her. It was easier just not to think about her, just as it had been easier to think as little as possible about his mother.

But no streak of callousness and no habit of ignoring unpleasant facts could protect him from the blow that fell in 1612
with the death of Henry, Prince of Wales. The doting affection
which had inspired the *Basilikon Doron* was, it is true, a thing
of the past, and father and son were fast growing apart. It was
on his friend, David Murray, and on his beloved sister, Elizabeth, that the Prince called continuously in the lingering deli-
rium of his typhoid fever; and the Princess Elizabeth constantly
visited his apartments in disguise in the hope of being admitted
to his bedside. After one visit James and Anne retired, the one
to Theobalds and the other to Somerset House, to escape as far
as possible from the sort of spectacle neither could bear; the
King showing his grief 'with more impatience then was expected', while the Queen sent round to the Tower to beg off
Raleigh a 'quintessence' of his own invention which, very re-
luctantly, the physicians tried as a last resort. In fact Raleigh
had more real cause for mourning than any of them, for with
Prince Henry there died his best chance of getting out of
prison. Neither James nor Anne grieved for long. Both were
resilient by nature, and once they had recovered from attacks of
gout which laid them up simultaneously, very soon resumed
their divergent rounds of pleasure. Indeed, they were forced to
do so rather more quickly than was decent by the fact that the
young Elector Palatine—the Palsgrave Frederick—was already
in England when Henry died, waiting to be betrothed and
married to the Princess Elizabeth, and he could not be asked
to wait too long.

This wedding, which took place on St Valentine's Day, 1613,
was an event of more than merely family and social significance
in the history of England. Not only did it found the Hanoverian
dynasty a hundred years later; within a few years it was to involve complications in foreign affairs which were almost disastrous. For the moment, however, it was an excuse, merely, for a
new climax of extravagance and ostentation, and an opportunity for much genuinely popular rejoicing. Frederick was not a
very impressive young man: 'a slight edifice on an ill foundation'. Chamberlain, who paid a special visit to Court to see the
young pair together, found him attractive, but 'too young and
small timbred to undertake such a taske'. But Elizabeth, who
was by far the most attractive, and now the only really popular

member of her family, had fallen deeply in love with the young man. He was, moreover, a Calvinist, and therefore acceptable even to the severest Puritan critics of the Court. There were thus no misgivings to mar the exceptionally expensive celebrations which went with the marriage: the £9,000 worth of spectacular fireworks and shows on the river; the Lords' Masque, outstanding for its extravagance, but 'long and tedious'; and the elaborate entertainments prepared by the Inns of Court. This was the occasion on which Lady Wotton flaunted her trimming at £50 the yard, when Lord Montague spent £1,500 on frocks for his two daughters, and the more important noblemen so vied with each other in their dress that Chamberlain was driven to the sad conclusion that 'this extream cost and riches makes us all poore'. It is not surprising that James's debts were again mounting fast towards the million mark and that ambassadors and public officials applying to the Treasury for their 'Extra-ordinarys' were met increasingly often with the statement that 'the King is now disfurnished of money'.

The events of these few months of 1612–13 thus served to emphasize most undesirably the King's absolute dependence on Carr. He was deprived suddenly of the only statesman whose wisdom and prestige might have acted as a check on his self-indulgent impulses and of the only two members of his family who might have offered some alternative intimacy. Prince Henry's death in particular destroyed the only centre round which some effective opposition to Carr's exclusive influence might have gathered. Throughout 1613 James kept the Treasury in Commission and refused to appoint a Principal Secretary. The effective government of England was carried out literally from the Bedchamber, where despatches were considered and letters drafted while the King changed after hunting; and the exasperated Privy Council in London had to wait on the favourite's whim for every decision of policy and every important public appointment.

In the Court and government world it was the massive Howard grouping which was most immediately affected. Deprived of the Salisbury alliance on which their power had rested, Suffolk and Northampton were bound gradually to lose their hold on the administration unless they could in some way get control of Carr; and it was out of their intrigues and manœuvres to achieve this that there arose the most damaging scandal of James's whole reign and one which completed the isolation of Court from country. At the beginning of 1613 they found their way blocked by Sir Thomas Overbury, who maintained a jealously exclusive control over the favourite which gave him, in effect, control over royal policy, while the Howards were quite unable to force into the vacant Secretaryship their nominee and protégé, Sir Thomas Lake. They had, on the other hand, one great asset in the fact that Carr was conducting a love affair with the Countess of Essex, who had been born Lady Frances Howard, and who was longing to be rid of her husband and married to the favourite. This situation Northampton set himself to exploit with brilliant cunning. The Essex marriage had been a disaster from the start. A foolish, fatherly whim of James's, sprung from gratitude to the memory of the late Lord Essex and more immediate gratitude to the Howards for supporting and easing his succession, had united them in 1606, when Essex was only a dull, backward boy of 14 and his bride a precocious, spoilt beauty a year younger. Essex had then been sent abroad with tutors to finish his education, while his wife was allowed to run wild at Court under the criminally careless guardianship of her mother, the Countess of Suffolk. He returned to find her entirely unmanageable, head over heels in love with Carr, and obstinately unwilling to have anything to do with him. After two years of misery he had become as sick of the marriage as she was and willing to fall in with almost any plan which would set him free. What Northampton wanted was the dissolution of the marriage by a decree of nullity based on Essex's inability to consummate it, so that the lady, untouched by scandal, should be free to marry Carr and bring him safely into the family grouping.

The plan did not work out quite as smoothly as Northampton had hoped. James, besotted with Carr, and more than ordinarily fond of Frances Essex, cheerfully agreed to the appointment of a Divorce Commission. It was one more peculiarity of his relationships with his young men that he was delighted that they should marry and took a close interest in the whole proceeding, and even in their subsequent domesticities. But when it came to consideration of the very shaky case for a nullity put together by the Countess's lawyers, Northampton and Suffolk found that there were limitations even to their family influence. George Abbot, whom James had appointed Archbishop of Canterbury in succession to Bancroft in 1611, was long-winded and muddle-headed, but scrupulously honest. As President of the Divorce Commission he became extremely suspicious of the Countess's evidence and more than doubtful if the sort of divorce which she was claiming existed in canon law at all. He could not carry all the eight Commissioners with him in this view. Lancelot Andrewes, for one, had convinced himself that there was nothing but misery for the young people in prolonging such a marriage and was prepared to ignore any canon law arguments in favour of a commonsense solution. Three others, the time-serving Bishop of Coventry, Richard Neile, Sir Julius Caesar, the Master of the Rolls, and Sir Daniel Dunne, Chancellor of the Exchequer, knew that the King had helped Lady Essex to gather her evidence and supported Andrewes for purely selfish reasons. But Abbot was able by the middle of the summer to split the Commission exactly equally and reduce the matter to a deadlock.

The conscientious scruples of the Archbishop were not Northampton's only worry. As soon as he heard of the divorce project, Overbury perceived the threat to his own hold over Carr and determined to break it. Since he had been writing Carr's love letters and poems for him and had supervised the whole intrigue with Lady Essex, he almost certainly had evidence which would destroy the whole basis of the Countess's claim for a nullity, and he made it clear that he intended to use it. Northampton dealt with this threat in April, before the Divorce Commission met, using Lady Essex's hold on Carr and Carr's on the King to get Overbury offered a mission abroad, and at the same time encouraging Overbury to expect Carr's powerful protection if he refused. Overbury fell into the trap. Rather than cut himself off from the source of all his influence, he refused the offered embassy, insolently certain that he was invulnerable. Carr, acting under Northampton's instructions, made the most of the insolence when reporting it to the King, and James, who had never liked Overbury anyway and was glad enough to have him out of the way, punished his contempt by committing him a close prisoner to the Tower. Since Northampton had dependants and nominees of his own in the key jobs at the

Tower, the plan worked very well. Overbury was prevented from communicating his dangerous knowledge and spent the whole summer in the Tower, where he became very ill; and there in September he died.

Meanwhile, at the end of June, Northampton and Suffolk applied directly to the King to get the Archbishop's objections overruled. James seems to have handled the whole matter throughout with extraordinary *naïveté*. Where the happiness of those he loved was concerned his habitually tortuous, suspicious, and critical mind was in suspended animation. He knew nothing of Carr's damaging intrigue with the Countess and never suspected that there was anything fishy about her case. He only wanted the young people to be happy, and rather easily he satisfied himself that canon law was on their side. Characteristically he assumed that he had only to let this be known for all concerned to bow to his judgement—what he called 'some skill I have in divinity'—and his wishes. To his surprise, and somewhat to his perturbation, Abbot made a fight of it. But Abbot made it a theological fight; and in the pleasure of bombarding the Archbishop with five-thousand word dissertations on the law and practice of the early Church, James missed the real point, which Abbot himself had much obscured, that the Countess had not really made out a case on the facts. Equally characteristically, in a case where he thought that anyway common sense should override legalistic objections, James made sure of getting the right decision by appointing two reliable Bishops as additional Commissioners, with instructions that they were not to waste time by re-hearing the evidence, but only to review it and then to take part in another vote. So in September, just after the news of Overbury's death in the Tower, the divorce was pronounced, Abbot and his three still faithful supporters abstaining from a verdict.

So the Howards achieved their object, but at what was destined to be a fearful price. The Archbishop's courageous, if muddled, stand had made the world outside the Court aware that there were doubts about the honesty of the Essex nullity proceedings. The fact that Carr and the Countess were almost openly living in sin had leaked out in the spring and become common knowledge by the autumn, except, apparently, to the King; and there were some nasty rumours flying about Overbury's illness and opportune death which Howard power could stifle for the time, but not kill. Outwardly, however, the triumph was complete. The vacant Treasury was given to Suffolk. Northampton became Lord Privy Seal; and Carr, promoted Earl of Somerset to make him the equal of the lady he proposed to marry, was made Lord Chamberlain so that the King, as he said, might be sure of having him constantly about his person. The wedding which was the climax of the whole affair on December 26th, 1613, was extravagant and ostentatious, even by the standard James had set, in spite of the emptiness of the Treasury. James bestowed £10,000 worth of jewels on the bride and put on a lovely masque by Campion for them. Every man who had any hope of office or preferment gave a present much more costly than he could afford, and the junketings, prolonged over several days, in the end exhausted even James himself. In the circumstances the Somersets and their Howard relations could afford to ignore the great success Laurence Lyle, the printer, was having with a posthumous poem by Overbury called *The Wife* which, it was widely said, had been written to discourage his patron from marrying the Countess, whom he had once described as 'a filthy, base woman'. All their influence could not prevent the book from selling out five editions in less than a year, and the continuous dark rumours that Overbury had been murdered while he lay helpless in the Tower were sapping the Howard supremacy even before it was fairly established.

In theory and on paper James had at last achieved his heart's desire. He had freed himself from all the restraints which had hitherto trammelled his personal power, and could now demonstrate the benefits of a paternal government controlled by an 'old and wise king'. The oppressive memory of the old Queen and the tiresome comparisons which it provoked were almost forgotten. The last of the statesmen of the great age, with prestige and power enough to limit his extravagances and influence his policies, was dead. Supreme power under himself was vested in a subservient Council and a favourite entirely of his own choosing. It was even possible to think that he was emancipated from the irritating arguments and pretensions of a House of Commons which had challenged his ecclesiastical policy and restricted his expenditure. The Addled Parliament in the spring of 1614—a last brief and half-hearted attempt to come to terms with the exasperated gentry and merchants—had come to grief on all the old issues. Lacking all guidance from King or Council, the Commons had spent two months wrangling among themselves or with the Lords, and had failed to produce a single statute, a coherent statement of grievances, or a subsidy. 'There never was knowne a more disorderly house,' Chamberlain wrote, 'many times more like a cockpit than a grave counsaile, and many that sat there were more fit to have ben among roaring boyes then in that assemblie'. Parliament as an institution was, temporarily at any rate, discredited, and the field seemed open for a demonstration of benevolent despotism. The only concrete difficulty was, as always, 'the eating canker of want'. Since Salisbury's death the King's debts had again risen to over a million, and he would spend the rest of his reign on the verge of bankruptcy. But even there it was possible to hope that competent administration could avert major disaster without making the religious and financial concessions on which the Commons had taken their stand.

But the sad truth was that now he had achieved power James had no real desire to do anything with it. The only prerogative in which, by now, he was vitally interested was that of doing as he pleased and spending what he needed without interference from anybody, and the divine right he would defend most tenaciously was a right to do nothing. Unwilling himself to shoulder the daily burden of hard work on which alone a benevolent despotism could be built, he had delegated power to men who were also, in effect, without a policy. The Howards and their friends were in office merely to keep others out and to ensure for themselves a monopoly of governmental profits and perquisites. They would oppose the calling of a Parliament on exactly the same grounds as the King: to avoid interference and criticism. Beyond that they had no home policy. In foreign affairs they did indeed continue to champion a Spanish alliance, though the Prince whose marriage to an Infanta could alone give some substance and meaning to such a policy was dead. This had some potential advantage for the Spaniards, who were using an uneasy interlude of European peace to build up their strength for a final assault on Dutch independence. For England it had no practical meaning; and the tedious negotiations for the betrothal of the young Prince Charles in his turn to an Infanta, when they became known, served only to make Court and government still more unpopular wherever in England rumours of politics penetrated at all.

There were, it is true, the rudiments of an opposition policy. One of the more unexpected consequences of the triumph of the Somersets had been the appointment of the Puritan Sir Ralph Winwood to the vacant Secretaryship of State, thanks largely to his timely gift of four superbly matched black horses for the Countess's ceremonial wedding visit to the City of London. He wanted not merely to frustrate the closer alliance with Spain, but to revive the memories of Elizabethan maritime and colonial war. He cherished, too, Salisbury's dream of re-uniting King and Commons on the basis of a financial settlement, along with concessions to moderate Puritanism within the Church and whole-hearted persecution of Catholics. But with his failure to manage the debates of the Addled Parliament the more serious parts of his policy had in fact already broken down; and he himself had neither the ability nor the personal standing nor the wealth to re-establish a Salisbury régime. Moreover there was little influential backing for his ideas. Raleigh, still frustrated and hopeless in the Tower, might dream of Orinoco and Cadiz. The rich Protestant peers showed their disapproval of Spanish politics only by standing aloof from the political world altogether. At Court there was in effect only a rival gang, intriguing to get the Howards out merely to get themselves in, which to some extent found a focus round the Queen, who detested Somerset and was jealous of his hold on her husband, and the Archbishop, who could not forgive the fraudulence of the divorce over which he had presided.

But even within the closed circle of the Court, more remote and isolated from the country than ever after ten years of Stuart government, James could not achieve the comfort which had become the major object of his life. For Robert Carr was not only a ridiculous choice as a statesman; he turned out in the end to be useless even as a favourite. The daydream world which the King had conjured up years before round the young man's sick bed at Charing Cross crashed into disillusionment within a few months of its apparent achievement. Immediately after the Somerset marriage, during the spring and early summer of 1614, all seemed to be going well. James was allowed to indulge his peculiar delight in the domestic intimacies of his favourites and fussed over the Countess almost as much as he did over her husband. When she fell ill after a wedding banquet in May, Chamberlain wrote that there had been 'much care and tender respect had of her, both by her Lord and the King'. The picture was idyllic. Even the plan, formulated when he first began to teach Carr Latin grammar, to share with him the secrets of statecraft, seemed to be working well enough. The Spanish Ambassador, Gondomar, who was one of the shrewdest observers of the English Court, informed his government that Somerset 'at the Council Table showeth much temper and modesty, without seeming to press or sway anything, but afterwards the king resolveth all business with him alone'. With no great crisis to be faced at home or abroad and Northampton's long experience to steer him through the details, Carr did indeed for a time fulfil his boast to Overbury during one of their quarrels a year before that his own legs were 'straight and strong enough' to bear him up without assistance.

But neither James nor the Howards had reckoned with the fatal vanity to which royal favourites have always in the end succumbed. Somerset was a stupid young man and he became insolent and overbearing more quickly than most. Above all he lacked the intuitive skill to handle his necessarily very complicated personal relationship with the King. James's love was essentially possessive. He loved to lavish it, and with it all its outward manifestations of rich presents and honours and intimacies. But they must always remain centred upon himself, and their glories must emanate from him. In no circumstances could he allow himself to be possessed: to be bullied, or humbled, or enslaved. That personal independence of his royal self was what he had fought all his life to establish and maintain. He would be the slave of his own infatuation, but not lie at the mercy of another's whim. Somerset, once sure of the infatuation, failed to realize that a continuous return of gratitude and deference was the price which had to be paid. He took for granted what still always had to be earned, became rude and exacting when he could not instantly have his own way, sulked and threatened when he should have cajoled. Overbury, whose whole career had depended on Somerset's playing his cards right, might have restrained him. His Howard connections, intent on lining their own pockets and in any case securely based on wealth and influence which were independent of the favourite, did not bother. Northampton, the only one of them who might have seen the danger and countered it, was caught out in the spring of 1614 in treasonable correspondence with Rome and forced to withdraw into the country. So, though the King's idyll continued, it was by the summer sufficiently disturbed to make it worth the while of Somerset's enemies to launch the only sort of counter-attack possible against the complete and apparently immovable monopoly of power by the Howard grouping.

The intrusion of George Villiers into James's life was a much more gradual and less spectacular affair than Carr's abrupt appearance in the tilting yard. He seems first to have been noticed hanging about the racecourse at Newmarket, the threadbare but ambitious younger son of an impoverished family, for whom a scheming, silly mother had planned a career at Court, but who had so far only been able to afford the essential finish to a polite education in Paris. It was Sir John Graham, one of the Gentlemen of the King's Bedchamber, who first persuaded him to try to get his foot in at Court, and organized for him a walking-on part in the comedy of *Ignoramus* which the Cambridge undergraduates were to produce before the King that summer. There James saw him for the first time, and to those who knew him well it was clear at once that he was interested. Graham was able to enlist more powerful backers for his protégé: notably the Herberts, who resented the Howard monopoly more actively than any other of the great noble families, and Sir Thomas Lake, the junior Secretary of State, who had risen under Howard patronage but sensed a changing tide and was anxious to secure his future. Lord Pembroke, the senior of the Herberts, and Lake between them managed the next phase—the actual presentation of the young man to the King at Apthorpe on August 3rd. Again all the signs were propitious. Philip Herbert, Earl of Montgomery, Pembroke's younger brother, himself a prime favourite for a time in 1603 and secure in a sort of semi-favouritism ever since thanks to his passionate interest in horses and hounds, was called in to pronounce a final verdict, and it was favourable. So at Baynard's Castle, the London headquarters of the Herberts, the final syndicate was formed. Apart from those already involved there were Winwood and Archbishop Abbot, and both Russells and Seymours were represented. They decided to buy Villiers a wardrobe and an office close about the King's person. Once there his good looks and his charm must do the rest.

So James was provided with the last and greatest love of his life, a creature infinitely superior to Carr both mentally and physically. It has been the fashion to talk of Villiers's effeminate charm, but he was in fact well-built and athletic and his good looks, though startling, were in no way womanish. It was, actually, a boyish charm which he never quite lost: a frolic-some, adolescent gaiety which degenerated in its worser moments into petulant immaturity. To his mother, to his inti-mate friends, and above all to the King he would always be, in what he himself called his 'old free and frolicke stile', 'that same naughtie boy, George Villiers'. The King would be his 'dear Dad', and to both King and Queen he was their 'Dogge' or, because he reminded James of a picture he had once seen of St Stephen, their 'Baby Steenie'. Nothing could have suited the prematurely ageing King better. He surrendered gladly and easily to a paternalistic dotage, and seems to have been genu-inely hurt and surprised that Somerset did not immediately share his feelings and enter gladly into the exciting business of making the young man happy. For James went out of his way from the start to make it clear that Somerset's position was in no way threatened and that he hoped to see the new favourite rise under the mantle and protection of the old, so that they could all three be happy and gay together.

Somerset would certainly have done well to accept a situa-tion which was in any case out of his control, and so have pre-served, for a time at least, the reality of his power. But he was too stupid and too vain to admit any rivalry in the King's affections, and he was without a competent adviser. Overbury was dead and Northampton died that summer before the crisis arose. Left to himself he tried to block every step of Villiers's advancement, and at first with some success. In November the young man's backers had planned to get him a vacancy in the Bedchamber, which would have suited their purpose very well. Somerset fought the appointment with every weapon that he had, sulked and stormed and threatened, and succeeded in the end in putting in a bastard kinsman of his own. But it was a Pyrrhic victory. The syndicate was able to purchase instead the office of royal cup-bearer; and already the gossips of St Paul's were referring as a matter of course to 'Villers, the new favorit' and talking widely of the serious squabbles which were undermining Somerset's position with the King. By the end of that month it was known that, in spite of the state of the Exchequer, the King was giving £1,500 towards the expenses of a Christmas masque, 'the principall motive whereof is thought to be the gracing of yonge Villers and to bring him on the stage'.

So disturbance and ill-temper and opposition pursued the poor King even into the privacy for which he had sacrificed so much. There were ugly little scenes in public, as when a servant of Somerset's, probably deliberately, spilt a bowl of soup over Villiers's new suit: Villiers struck the man in a rage, and Somerset made a fearful scene because the proper penalty for brawling in the King's presence was not exacted there and then. He seems seriously to have expected that James would allow the young man's right hand to be struck off while he himself stood by to exercise the Lord Chamberlain's duty of searing the stump with hot pitch. But it was the private sulks and rages which James found hardest to bear, and the measure of them and of his own goaded unhappiness can best be taken from the enormous letter of complaint and warning which he wrote to Somerset in January. It was over two thousand words long—a complete, unselfconscious revelation of himself, without shame or reticence. Much of it was taken up with tedious recapitulation of past scenes and accusations, pouring scorn on Somerset's tales of a 'court faction' working against him, which were in fact well enough founded, and pointing out how many great concessions had been made to him as compensation and reassurance for the very trivial favours so far shown to Villiers. There was much insistence, too, that Somerset was still the 'inwardly trusty friend and servant' whose merits were still unsurpassed. But the complaints when they came were clear and unequivocal, delivered in that homely, hard-hitting language which James could still always command.

'These before rehearsed rich and rare parts and merits of yours,' he wrote, 'have been of long time, but especially of late, since the strange phrenzy took you, so powdered and mixed with strange streams of unquietness, passion, fury, and insolent pride, and (which is worst of all) with a settled kind of induced obstinacy, as it chokes and obscures all these excellent and good parts that God hath bestowed on you.' All this was an abuse of the 'infinitely great liberty and freedom of speech' always allowed to him, and it was, James insisted, of comparatively recent origin: 'And do not deceive yourself with that conceit, that I allowed you that sort of licentious freedom till of late. For, as upon the one part, it is true you never passed all limits therein till of late; so, upon the other, I bore, God Almighty knows, with those passions of yours, of old dissembling my grief thereat, only in hope that time and experience would re-claim and abate that heat, which I thought to wear you out of by a long-suffering patience and many gentle admonitions; but the circumstances joined to them made them relish ten times worse to my taste than otherwise they would have done, if they had only remained *in puris naturalibus* of passions.' After that James relapsed into a revealing pathos, complaining of scenes 'uttered at unseasonable hours, and so bereaving me of my rest', so that it seemed that they were staged 'of purpose to grieve and vex me'. He accused Somerset of 'a continual dogged and sullen behaviour' and of 'a kind of distrust of the honesty of my friendship for you'. And finally he put his finger on the really vital point in his relations with those whom he loved: 'Fourthly (which is worst of all), and worse than any other thing that can be imagined, you have, in many of your mad fits, done what you can to persuade me that you mean not so much to hold me by love as by awe, and that you have me so far in your reverence that I dare not offend you, or resist your appetites'.

As he wrote on James became more and more egotistical and the self-pity mounted within him: 'I leave out of this reckoning your long creeping back and withdrawing yourself from lying in my chamber, notwithstanding my many hundred times earnestly soliciting you to the contrary, accounting that but as a point of unkindness.' But he did not, in fact, leave them out of account, for they were, he said, the greatest grief that he had ever yet experienced, and one which he could no longer bear 'without admitting an unpardonable sin against God in consuming myself wilfully, and not only myself, but in perilling thereby not only the good estate of mine own people, but even the state of religion through all Christendom, which almost wholly, under God, rests now upon my shoulders. Be not the occasion of the hastening of his death through grief, who was not only your creator under God, but hath many a time prayed for you, which I never did for any subject alive but for you. But the lightening my heart of this burden is not now the only cause that makes me press you undelayedly to ease my grief; for your own furious assaults upon me at unseasonable hours hath now made it known to so many that you have been in some cross discourse with me, as there must be some exterior signs of the amendment of your behaviour towards me.' These themes of complaint, and the threat which lay behind them, were reiterated and elaborated until they must have been clear even to Somerset's limited intelligence. 'It lies in your hands,' the letter ended up, 'to make of me what you please—either the best master and truest friend, or, if you force me once to call you ingrate, which the God of heaven forbid, no so great earthly plague can light upon you. In a word, you may procure me to delight to give daily more and more demonstrations of my favour towards you, if the fault be not in yourself.'

This—the most extraordinary letter, probably, that any king ever wrote to a subject—had not the slightest effect. For six months James continued, undeterred by his failure with Carr, to seek, in Wotton's phrase, to mould Villiers 'as it were Platonically to his own Idea', and 'make him a Masterpiece', and he continued to hope that his old favourite would co-operate in the advancement of the new, while Court and country were treated to the degrading spectacle of an open and ostentatious rivalry between two good-looking young men for the favours of their ageing and unattractive King. There was a severe tussle on St George's Day when the Queen, reluctant, but urged on by the Archbishop, appeared in James's bedroom to wish him the compliments of the day and to ask him to mark it by knighting this 'noble gentleman', Villiers, whose name was George, and making him a Gentleman of the Bedchamber. James, who was probably in the plot anyway and only wanted his wife to give some sign of her official approval of his new favourite, pretended to hesitate and to turn the matter over in his mind, and he made his usual fuss over the production of a naked sword for the ceremony. Out in the anteroom Somerset heard what was afoot and, since he could not intrude into the royal bedroom, sent in a message that Gentleman was far too much, and that Groom of the Bedchamber would be quite enough. Overhearing this, the Archbishop, too, sent in a message, insisting that nothing less than Gentleman would do. In the upshot, of course, Villiers got his knighthood and his appointment, since this was what the King had intended all along. The whole scene did not probably strike the Jacobeans as particularly grotesque or indecent; but even the Jacobean world was aware of a further cheapening of public honours.

A month later, on May 22nd, there was another silly piece of public rivalry, when Lord Knollys and Lord Fenton were to ride in state down to Windsor to be installed as Knights of the Garter. The normal friendly competition as to which of them could produce the larger and more distinguished train of followers wearing his colours became, because Knollys was another Howard son-in-law, a trial of political strength: an episode which, as Chamberlain said, was 'not worth the repeating, but that the matter is come to that passe that every little thing is observed now that they are growne as yt were to siding and to open opposition'. In the teeth of it all James persevered in his project of getting the two young men to work in collaboration until it finally shipwrecked at Lulworth in August, during the summer Progress. After getting Sir Humphrey May, who had a great reputation as a peacemaker, to prepare the ground, he sent Villiers to make a direct request for Somerset's favour and protection. Somerset's answer was short and sharp: 'I will none of your service and you shall none of my favour. I will, if I can, break your neck, and of that be confident.' So James was brought face to face with irreconcilables which not even divinely appointed kingship could bring together. What was more, since he himself still remained obstinately non-committal, Villiers's backers had to face the fact that to achieve anything of real value they had to remove Somerset altogether.

Two circumstances combined to end that deadlock in the late summer of 1615. The first was the feeling, which soon spread beyond the Court, that Somerset's hold on power was weakening. James, in a last attempt to bring the spoilt young man to

his senses, and to put an end to the continuing scenes of recrimination and reproach, tried the effect of a small series of
rebuffs. Somerset's friend and protégé, Henry Gibbe, got into
trouble and he could not save him from being expelled from his
Bedchamber appointment. He brought Bishop Bilson, who had
been so useful over the divorce proceedings, up to London and
pushed hard for his appointment as Lord Privy Seal; and after
long delay the Bishop was kindly but firmly ordered back to his
diocese by the King. Finally, in July, the Wardenship of the
Cinque Ports, which Somerset had held provisionally since
Northampton's death, was taken from him and given to Lord
Zouche, who was of the Archbishop's party. But this sense of a
weakening of the favourite's hold, which soon spread from Court
to City, did no more than create a climate favourable for a
direct attack on the Somersets. It produced a sudden revival of
the ugly rumours about Overbury's death and a fresh and ex-
panded edition of his *Poems* and *Characters*. It was a stroke of
pure luck which provided the opposition with material which
might be deadly. Trumbull, the English envoy at Brussels,
asked to be recalled to impart some information too dangerous
to be committed to paper, and he told Winwood that he had
heard the confession of an apothecary's boy named William
Reeve, who had believed himself to be dying at Flushing, and
who alleged that he had poisoned Overbury in the Tower in
circumstances which seemed inevitably to implicate the Countess of Somerset, if not also the Earl. The unsupported evidence
of an apothecary's boy who was, in any case, not available for
cross-examination was poor material for an attack on an all-
powerful favourite, and Winwood moved cautiously. But now
that he knew what he was looking for it was fairly easy to
collect corroborative evidence, and by the end of the first week
in September he felt justified in laying what he had found before
the King. It was reasonably certain that Overbury had been
poisoned and reasonably probable that one or both of the
Somersets had been accessory to the murder. Winwood had
every interest in taking advantage of the situation. He had been
one of the earliest backers of Villiers. He had seen Somerset
do all in his power to wreck his attempted accommodation with
Parliament in 1614, and he loathed the Spanish politics and
toleration for Catholics which the Somerset régime involved.

EXPERIMENT IN PERSONAL RULE

Once he had the King's permission for a cautious and discreet investigation there was a real chance of bringing the favourite down, and with him, perhaps, the whole fabric of Howard supremacy.

CHAPTER XII

The End of the Howard Supremacy

*

Winwood had to proceed with the greatest caution in exploiting his potentially valuable information. In that age any mysterious or sudden death was liable to be attributed to poison. Little was known of the strength and action of poisons and nothing at all of their detection. Wildly exaggerated accounts of the poisoners of Renaissance Italy, of Catherine de Medici's dark activities in France, and the genuine poisoning scandals which had convulsed Paris only a few years before made almost any story credible. Dorset's sudden death had been said to be due to poison; and so had the more lingering sickness of the Prince of Wales. Wise men—and in this context James was generally wiser than most—discounted all such popular rumours and were reluctant to have them seriously investigated. But Overbury's case was different because the rumours happened to be true. Northampton, working through Sir Thomas Monson, the Master of the Armoury, and playing on the desire of Sir Gervase Elwes, the newly appointed Lieutenant of the Tower, to ingratiate himself with authority, had arranged to put a man of his own in as gaoler to ensure that Overbury was effectively isolated. But he had not attended sufficiently to details. His great-niece, the Countess of Essex, had been able to slip in as Overbury's keeper a disreputable man of her own named Richard Weston; and since nobody else had access to the prisoner except the Lieutenant, she had the wretched man at her mercy. Enraged by his last-minute threat to prevent her divorce, and afraid that even if he were silenced until the divorce went through he might still contrive to prevent her marriage to Carr, she had decided that he was best out of the way altogether.

A great deal of sympathy and sentiment has at different times

221

been wasted on Frances Howard, Countess of Essex and Somerset. She was bewitching to look at, with all the social graces and charming, kittenish manners, the old Lord Treasurer's favourite daughter, Prince Henry's first love, and the acknowledged beauty and pet of King James's Court since she was fifteen. But even her neglected upbringing by a dishonest and unprincipled mother and the years running wild at Court cannot be held wholly to blame for her complete and irresponsible selfishness and her total lack of any moral sense. She was, almost literally, venomous. Her first impulse when her somewhat loutish young husband came back from his travels to claim her and interrupt her love-affair with Carr had been to have him poisoned. She dealt largely with the riff-raff of the medical world for charms and love-philtres to inflame Carr's passion and dangerous sedative doses to frustrate her husband: notably with the celebrated and wholly wicked Simon Forman, and a good-looking, dissolute, ignorant, bombastic fellow called Franklin who passed for an apothecary; and her link with that world was a certain Mrs Anne Turner, widow of a not very reputable doctor and mistress to Sir Arthur Mainwaring, who lived on the fringes of the Court as a dressmaker, a purveyor of a secret recipe for yellow starch, and a go-between in every kind of scandalous intrigue.

It was Mrs Turner and Franklin who between them organized the death of Overbury for her, with great incompetence, and a remarkable disregard of the need for secrecy. In spite of a number of experiments on cats, they so under-estimated the doses of arsenic all through the summer that they only succeeded in making the man desperately ill. What was more Weston, on the night that he was appointed, was caught by Sir Gervase Elwes carrying up a bowl of soup in one hand and a glass phial of poison in the other, and, thinking the Lieutenant to be in the plot, brazenly asked: 'Shall I give it to him now, sir?' Elwes, new to the job and lacking experience of Court life generally, and in any case too weak a character for what was always a dangerous and responsible post, feared to be ruined whatever he did. He knew that Northampton, Suffolk and the favourite were all involved in some sort of plot against Overbury. Were he to denounce the poisoning, these would be the very men who would sit in the Star Chamber to investigate the matter, and his story would depend on the unreliable evidence of a known rogue. To attack powerful men in that world was to court disaster unless the attack was pushed home to complete victory, and Elwes could see little chance of that. So he set himself the impossible task of serving both masters: of keeping Overbury close, but frustrating any attempt to poison him. Weston he terrorized into promising to bring everything sent for Overbury first to him, and he had to turn his cooks to duplicating the stream of tarts and jellies which came round as presents from Lady Essex to the unsuspecting prisoner. But Weston, too, was serving two masters, and he slipped enough under the Lieutenant's guard to make Overbury very ill, though not enough to kill him. In the end, when the divorce proceedings reached a crisis, the conspirators suborned the apothecary's boy, William Reeve, who was employed by one of the physicians regularly attending Overbury to administer a periodical enema. They filled one of these with a large dose of mercury sublimate and killed him almost outright.

There would have been rumours about that sort of death in any event. In this one so many people had been in the plot, Franklin was by nature so boastful, and Mrs Turner and Weston were so carelessly certain of protection from great personages, that the rumours spread persistently, and instead of dying down during the following eighteen months multiplied and magnified. It was they which were chiefly responsible for Overbury's *Poems* and *Characters* running through two editions in the first year; and they were not confined to humble folk. The Archbishop admitted that he had heard strange stories and murmurings on the very day that Overbury died, and King James must have been one of the few people in his own Court who was wholly ignorant of what was being said. But when they came to exploit the situation Somerset's enemies found themselves still held by the reasoning which had kept Elwes silent two years before. Any great man, and still more a royal favourite, was a constant target for malicious attacks, and James was known to be particularly suspicious of such attacks and prone to discount them. An unproved accusation would still recoil in total ruin on the accusers. So, wisely, Winwood consulted the King at every stage; and his first step was to get in touch with Elwes to discover if he had had any suspicion of foul play.

Elwes was quite unaware that he himself might be regarded as criminally involved. At a dinner party with Winwood and the Earls of Pembroke and Shrewsbury he let himself be drawn out, under the impression that he was securing the favour and backing of these powerful men and clearing his own good name of some ugly rumours; and his account of his interview with Weston alone justified Winwood in returning to the attack with the King. Fatuous and partial though he could be when his favourites were involved, there were certain fundamentals on which James never wavered. He might be unreasonable and intolerant about the Common Law, but that was a very different thing in his mind from the King's Justice, which was an integral part of his kingship itself, for which he was responsible directly to God, and with which he could tamper only at peril of his immortal soul. Overbury had been his prisoner and therefore under his protection. His honour as well as his justice were involved in an investigation into his death, and once he was sure that there was something more here than malicious rumour and jealousy of those whom he had so highly favoured, he did not hesitate. He demanded a full written report from Elwes, which was submitted on September 10th, and then set on Lord Chief Justice Coke to investigate the statements it contained. He was still determined not to be stampeded and suspicious that the whole accusation was a political manœuvre. 'There be,' he told Coke, when he gave him his charge, 'two things in this cause to be tried and the verity can be in but one of them. First: whether My Lord of Somerset and My Lady were the procurers of Overbury's death; or, that this imputation hath been by some practised to cast an aspersion on them. I would have you diligently inquire of the first; and if you find them clear, then I would have you as carefully look after the other, to the intent such practices may be discovered and not pass with impunity.'

Weeks before Coke started his inquiries the rising tide of all too accurate rumour had already thrown all those involved in the murder into a panic. There were hurried tavern conferences between Mrs Turner and Weston in July, and Weston was sent round to the Tower to find out how much Elwes knew and how much he had told, or was going to tell. But the man who behaved most foolishly and most suspiciously was the one least certainly implicated of all of them—Somerset himself. No evidence has ever been produced implicating him directly in the murder, or even proving that he even knew of it until afterwards. It is fairly certain that by the spring of 1615 he had discovered his wife's part in it, and this knowledge may well have helped to make him react so hysterically to the rise of Villiers and James's attempts to make him behave sensibly. He must have been vividly aware, too, that his conduct during the summer of Overbury's imprisonment would look extremely incriminating. His part in Northampton's plot had been to keep Overbury quiet by writing ceaselessly of his attempts to mediate for him with the King, while at the same time inflaming James's anger with tales of Overbury's unrepentant insolence and disloyalty. He had certainly hoped that Overbury would die when he fell ill, and had said so in several letters to Northampton, and many of Lady Essex's presents of food and wine had been sent round in his name. The political situation made it certain that his enemies would try to involve him in any inquiries which might develop, and his wife's guilt made it almost impossible for him to defend himself.

But, granted that his situation was dangerous and the nervous strain appalling, Somerset could scarcely have behaved more foolishly than he did. He started collecting up and destroying or falsifying all the surviving letters between himself, Northampton, and Overbury which might be given an incriminating twist, and at the same time approached the King for a general pardon for any irregularities which he might have committed during his tenure of the Privy Seal. There was nothing unusual in such pardons, which were designed to protect public servants against accidental or technical legal lapses in the conduct of King James's rather haphazard business. But the moment when inquiries were pending into Overbury's murder was a bad one to choose, and it was particularly unfortunate that this pardon had very large special clauses written into it covering felonies and misdemeanours, so that the law officers refused to certify it as fit to pass under the Great Seal. On this issue Somerset had managed to get the King on to his side. He wanted to be protected, he said, from the malice of his enemies, especially in case the King should die. James was vividly enough aware of the malice and found the request entirely reasonable. He was also always infuriated when the law was set up against his expressed wishes as a challenge to his sovereignty. In consequence there was a furious scene at the Council Table on July 20th, when Somerset explained his reasons for wanting the pardon and the King peremptorily ordered Lord Chancellor Ellesmere to affix the Seal. Ellesmere's opposition brought out all the worst in James. He refused to listen, even when the old man fell on his knees and, on the grounds that such a pardon would put Lord Somerset out of the reach of the law altogether, said that he must first have a pardon himself from His Majesty for sealing such a document. But Somerset's victory was worse than barren. Ellesmere delayed and argued for weeks while the Queen got to work to shake James's resolution, and the matter was still being argued when the first official moves against Overbury's murderers made it impossible to pursue it any further. Somerset was thus left not only unprotected, but had allowed his enemies to see that he was frightened. The story made a stir even outside Court circles and provoked the inevitable suspicion. 'Yt is a signe,' Chamberlain wrote, 'they feare themselves when they procure such kinds of pardons.'

More foolish even than this was Somerset's insistence in harrying the poor old King, in spite of the decisive warning he had received in January. The rebuffs of the summer he treated only as further grounds for reproaches and recriminations. Every minor attack, every small favour shown to Villiers, and every malicious rumour circulated by his enemies to damage him he made the excuse for rushing to James and making a scene, demanding immediate and spectacular revenge. At the end of July he provoked the King into writing again to protest that he had been 'needlessly troubled' with his 'desperate letters' and assure him that he might still stand on the old footing, but only 'by expressing that love to my person and respect to your master that God and man crave of you, with a hearty and feeling penitence of your by-past errors'. But Somerset was driven by furies and beyond the reach of warnings. While Coke in London pursued his relentless way through three hundred separate examinations, slowly forcing the truth out of first Weston, and then Mrs Turner, interviewing the apothecaries who had attended Overbury and everybody who had ever carried presents and messages to him in the Tower, James was being constantly plagued to arrest the course of justice and break off inquiries which, Somerset said, were only part of a plot by his enemies to implicate him and bring him down. He tried to convince the King that his own credit was equally involved in avoiding public trial, and even threatened him with the enmity of all his Howard connections if he did not intervene to protect his old favourite. When the Lord Chancellor, the Duke of Lennox, and Lord Zouche were joined with Coke in a strengthened Commission of inquiry he complained bitterly that the King had deliberately selected his personal enemies; and when this Commission summoned him from Royston to London for questioning he railed that he would not go, until James stopped him with a characteristic phrase.

'Nay, man,' he said, 'if Coke sends for me, I must go.'

It is very hard to fathom what was in James's mind during these difficult months, in spite of the self-revelation of his letters to Somerset. Certainly he was delighted with his new young favourite and quite determined that nothing should stand in the way of his advancement. But his fondness for Somerset remained genuine enough, too; and he sincerely hoped to be able to keep him about his person, still, as Sir Humphrey May put it at Lulworth that summer, 'a great man, though not the sole favourite'. About the murder he kept an open mind. In the world he had lived in all his life it was perfectly possible that the attempt to implicate Somerset was indeed an elaborate plot to ruin him. But in his heart he seems to have felt that the man, if not guilty, was certainly doomed. Their parting at Royston was as cloyingly affectionate as even James could make it. He accompanied Somerset all the way down the stairs to his coach, embracing him, demanding over and over again when he might hope to see him back, and then giving him more kisses to be passed on to his wife. But all this seems to have been an elaborate make-believe, for as the coach drove off he was heard to mutter:

'Now, the de'il go with thee, for I shall never see thy face more.'

But he was very far from the end of the discomforts brought on him by his rash elevation of Robert Carr. He had to write yet another long letter of rebuke and self-justification, pointing out sharply that 'both ye and your father-in-law have ever and at all times behaved yourselves quite contrary to the form that men that wish the trial of verity ever did in such a case', saying stoutly that he never meant wittingly to bear any man's sins but his own, and ending with the instruction: 'Fail not to show this letter to your father-in-law, and that both of you read it twice over at least.' Lord Treasurer Suffolk, at any rate, took the hint, left his daughter and son-in-law to their fates, and concentrated all his energies on salvaging what remained of the family supremacy. Somerset was beyond taking hints or advice and continued up to the very day of his trial to make things as difficult as possible for King and government.

Eight months were to elapse before the scandal reached its public climax in the trials of the Earl and Countess. The small fry, Weston, Mrs Turner, Franklin, and the luckless Elwes caught in the meshes of his own revelations, were all hanged by Christmas. But then there was a long delay, due partly to the fact that the Countess was pregnant and could not be moved into the Tower until after Christmas, partly to the great difficulty the Attorney-General, Sir Francis Bacon, found in building up a convincing case against Somerset at all. In the absence of all effective medical evidence a poisoning charge was almost impossible to prove in the seventeenth century anyway. Inevitably in all the earlier Overbury trials the evidence offered by the Crown had been largely circumstantial and hearsay, and Coke had had to resort to a good deal of bullying and rhetoric to get the verdicts he wanted. Guilty though they undoubtedly were, no modern court would have accepted the case presented against them. This absence of any direct proof, and the fact that, in spite of great pressure, none of the small fry had made confessions implicating Somerset, made it extraordinarily difficult to bring home a charge of complicity against him. There would be no Coke to bully and browbeat prisoner or jury: as Bacon wrote ruefully to James, 'it is one thing to deal with a jury of Middlesex and Londoners, and another to deal with the peers'. Lady Somerset made things easy and tidy for them by confessing her guilt and making no defence. This was the ideal of Stuart justice, satisfactory to all parties, since confession was held greatly to mitigate guilt, and so made it possible for the King, if he wished, to exercise his prerogative of mercy with less risk of outraging public opinion. But Somerset, despite all kinds of pressure and temptation, truculently refused to admit his guilt, and so forced them to a trial which, even if the verdict was not seriously in doubt, would expose the weakness of the Crown case to a very wide public.

It is doubtful if James ever realized the extent to which the Overbury exposures damaged the prestige of the Crown, the reputation of the Court, and his own personal standing among folk outside the official circle who were yet very far from being Puritans. Bacon, a much better and clearer-headed monarchist than the King and the only man at James's Court with the ability to have turned divine right kingship into a practical possibility, saw it clearly enough: 'Since the first nullity to this instant, when justice hath her hands bound, the devil could not have invented a more mischievous practice to our state and church than this hath been, is, and is like to be. God avert the evil.' It was James's habit to treat all opposition and criticism as factious or unreasonable, and he learnt no useful lessons from the disaster of his relationship with Somerset, caught up as he was in the toils of his own personal sufferings.

These, in all conscience, were acute enough. When he had committed himself emotionally as he had to Somerset, he could not shake himself callously free merely by a process of falling out of love. That had been apparent enough during his long struggle to elevate Villiers and make a companion of him without irretrievably hurting or losing the love of Somerset. And Somerset in the Tower proved almost as big a reproachful nuisance as he had been at Court. An enormous correspondence passed between Bacon and Villiers for the King's consideration during the four months after Christmas, as they gloomily considered what they would do if Somerset remained truculent and defiant and tried to build up a convincing proof out of what Bacon contemptuously called Coke's 'leavings of a case'. The King in the end intervened personally, sending Somerset's secretary, Mr James, round to the Tower with a very secret letter for Sir George More, the new Lieutenant, and a private verbal message to the prisoner promising to spare his life and show some grace and favour to his wife and child if he would but plead guilty. When this was indignantly rejected, James even resorted, again through More, to telling Somerset the downright lie that his wife's confession had directly implicated him and that it was useless to defend himself. The end of the letter to More was very characteristic and very revealing of the King's unhappiness: 'You must not let him know that I have written unto you, but only that I sent you private word to deliver him this message. Let none living know of this, and if it take good effect, move him to send in haste for the Commissioners to give them satisfaction, but if he remain obstinate, I desire not that you shall trouble me with an answer, for it is to no end, and no news is better than evil news.'

But there was worse to follow for James. Sir George's attempt only provoked Somerset into a wild outburst of threats of what he would reveal if they were so foolish or inhuman as to bring him to trial and a demand to convey some secret message to the King. There was, of course, some substance in the threat. There were no secrets of state that could be damagingly revealed, but a public suggestion that the King himself was privy to Overbury's murder would be infinitely damaging, however convincingly it were refuted. Even if Somerset stopped short of that, he still inevitably had it in his power, after years of the sort of intimacy James had allowed him, to make extremely injurious and wounding revelations. James saw the most private part of his private life in danger of exposure to an unsympathetic, sniggering world. This was, however, the inevitable penalty of favouritism and there was nothing he could do to prevent it, save to arrange with More to have two men standing by Somerset throughout his trial with cloaks in readiness to muffle him if he started any really dangerous outburst. To the last minute Somerset could not believe that the master who had loved and indulged him would compel him to go through the danger and humiliation of a public trial. He whose word had once seemed law could not grap the fact that there were some laws which were beyond the reach even of a king's divinity. When finally he was warned on the evening of May 24th that his wife had that day pleaded guilty and been sentenced to death and that he was to face the Lords on the following day he gave way to an outburst of fury and announced that he would not go to Westminster at all unless he were dragged there by brute force. The agitated Lieutenant foresaw a degrading, impossible scene and, remembering how 'immovably fixed' in the King's love Somerset had been, was not at all sure that James's sensibilities would be able to stand it; and he wrote off in haste to Whitehall for further instructions. But James, roused from his bed to face this last crisis, behaved with dignity and sense. Events must take their course. Unless Somerset were clearly 'sick or distracted of his wits', More must get him to Westminster Hall somehow. If there were a last-minute confession, he wished to hear of it immediately. Any other news could wait until the trial was over.

In the end Somerset behaved with perfect dignity and made no attempt to confuse the trial with awkward revelations. He persisted in his innocence, but he defended himself, as Bacon put it, 'modestly and wittily', and there were no recriminations. But James spent one of the most miserable days of his life. He tried to distract himself with business, and had a long discussion with Gondomar on possible terms for a marriage treaty. But he could not keep his mind away from Westminster Hall where the man whose company, he had once told his Council, he more valued than any man's living, was fighting for his life. No courtier had ever seen him 'so extreme sad and discontented'. He watched the landing stage at Whitehall eagerly for any boat which might bring news and would neither dine nor sup until he heard what line Somerset had taken in his defence. Bacon spent nearly the whole day presenting his case and it was not until late that night that James heard at last that all had gone well. The Lords had vindicated the King's justice by a unanimous vote of 'Guilty', and nothing had been said by anyone to make the situation worse than it was already.

Inevitably the Somerset trials were two of the greatest shows ever put on in Jacobean England. A public fed on wild rumours for two years and with its appetite whetted by the vast publicity with which Coke had invested the earlier trials, was at last to have a real glimpse of the legendary wickedness of a remote, scarcely comprehensible Court. Westminster Hall was crammed for both days, even with seats costing 10s. and family boxes £10. There was all the elaborate medieval ritual designed not so much for justice, as to let it be seen that justice was being done; and indeed the only purpose served by these two trials was to present a good enough case for the Crown to convince the world that the Somersets were not the victims of false charges trumped-up by political enemies. In this they were not wholly successful. The Countess, having confessed, had no alternative but to plead guilty and ask the Lords to intercede for her with the King. Some of the audience found her grief and penitence unconvincing, but mostly it was agreed that her behaviour had been 'noble, graceful, and modest'. The King's main purpose was thus served. Her guilt was demonstrated, but her confession and penitence gave him grounds to pardon her, as he had always intended to do anyway, without too seriously outraging public opinion.

The Earl's trial was less satisfactory from both points of view. Bacon's case was not wholly convincing to all those present and has never since been found convincing by historians or lawyers. Many of the gossip writers of the day recorded a 'general wish' that his life should be spared, and though his defence of himself was not skilful—'poor and idle' one observer called it—his persistence in asserting his innocence carried a good deal of conviction. On the other hand it made it a good deal more difficult for the King to exercise his prerogative of mercy, and Somerset truculently refused to the end to make it any easier for him. His request to the Lords for intercession was little more than a perfunctory formality. He would do no more than write to the King asking to be beheaded rather than hanged, and that his daughter might be provided for out of his forfeited lands. When, therefore, his life was spared and his close imprisonment gradually relaxed, when he was left with the Garter and some £4,000 a year, reunited with his wife, and finally released from the Tower to live out the rest of his life in exile at Lord Knollys's house at Grays, James got the worst of both worlds. Those who thought poorly of the Crown's case concluded that there must have been some undisclosed facts implicating the King to account for the hesitations of the prosecution and the leniency with which the prisoners were treated afterwards. Moralists who thought the Earl guilty were shocked that the King condoned such wickedness in high places. Though there can be no foundation for it, the suspicion that James had some sort of hand in Overbury's death has lingered on to this day. But it was not necessary to believe that to be shocked by the disclosures of the trials. Untold harm was done to the reputation of Stuart Court and government among sober taxpayers normally unaware of the doings of Whitehall, and even the London mob several times riotously demonstrated their expectation that the Somersets should be executed. But of this James was probably very little aware. His principal feeling seems to have been relief that the emotional wear and tear of Somerset's downfall was over without a major disaster. Though it is said that he once did see him again secretly in the garden at Royston and that they wept on each other's necks, there was never any question in the King's mind of a return of the Somersets to Court.

So the syndicate which had planned the advancement of George Villiers at Baynard's Castle two years before had achieved their immediate object. The old favourite was irretrievably ruined and their man was securely established in his place. Modest, unassuming, and charming, Villiers still remained in the background of politics, acting, indeed, as a sort of private secretary to the King through whom a great deal of public business had to be handled, but not yet noticeably influencing decisions and only making the first, tentative plans for the advancement of his devoted family. But his personal triumph with the King was complete. He had provided for James the perfect antidote for the misery and humiliation of Somerset's long-drawn-out ruin: a private haven of sympathy and gaiety in which he could forget the public degradation and an outside world which he knew must be either censorious or mocking. In those few months Villiers built up a hold on James which no previous favourite had ever achieved and which was never afterwards even threatened. He had become indispensable to the King's happiness. 'Christ,' James was to say, sublimely unaware of blasphemy, 'had his John, and I have my George.'

But Villiers's backers got very little reward for their efforts, either immediately or later. Pembroke, it is true, got the reversion of Somerset's office as Lord Chamberlain. Raleigh was released from the Tower early in 1616 and allowed to start seriously implementing the plans for an expedition to the Orinoco which he had been nursing for twelve years, and which he dreamt would make his fortune and the King's and perhaps re-open the chapter of Elizabethan glories. Sir Ralph Winwood might begin to furbish up his old dream of King and Commons happily united on the basis of a popular war with Spain. But there was in fact to be no great change of policy, and not even a reshuffle of important offices. The Howards proceeded blandly on their way, undisturbed by a disaster to one son-in-law, and the Spanish Ambassador was easily able to draw in advance any sting there might have been in the plans of Raleigh and Winwood. And even later, when Villiers moved into the foreground of politics, there would be no spectacular triumph for those who had started him in his career. The Queen, when Archbishop Abbot first approached her to intercede for his protégé with the King, had warned him that, this young man once brought in, 'the first persons he will plague will be you that labour for him'. Anne herself in fact became another victim to the Villiers charm, and he would be in due course her 'kind Dog' too. But Abbot lived to recall 'how like a prophetess' the Queen had spoken. As George Villiers rose to Viscount in 1616, to become Earl of Buckingham a year later and Marquis a year after that, it became clear that he was self-sufficient. He would advance his family and help his dependants, but he would need no backers.

Probably the root cause of Raleigh's pathetic last expedition is to be found in James's financial embarrassments. Since Salisbury's death things had gone from bad to worse. The expedients resorted to in default of Parliamentary assistance were the worst imaginable. Monopolies, originally intended to function as a rudimentary system of patents to benefit inventors and those who were opening up new markets for English goods, had in fact become a tax on all initiative. Profits which should have been ploughed back into expanding trade and industry were drawn off, partly to meet the expenses of a very incompetent administration, partly to support the King's personal extravagance, but very largely to enrich courtiers who had contributed nothing at all to the national well-being. Forced loans which, though common under Elizabeth, had always been repaid now became a sort of capital levy which undermined government credit and drove merchants not only to put up their rates of interest, but to charge exorbitant prices for every commodity sold to Court or government, so that the remedy nearly always intensified the evil.

It is true that the nation was getting steadily richer while the government got into increasing difficulties. But more intelligent planning could have balanced James's budget at vastly less cost to industry and commerce. In 1614, for example, a typical piece of mismanagement did serious damage to one of the most important sources of English wealth, the export of cloth. For years the Merchant Adventurers had enjoyed a virtual monopoly of the export, mostly of coarse and unfinished cloth, which was dyed and worked up on the Continent, chiefly in Holland. A syndicate of courtiers and merchants, of whom Alderman William Cockayne was the guiding light, now extracted from the government a patent to dye and finish all cloth before export. James and the Council were induced to agree, partly by straight bribery, partly by the dazzling prospect of additional revenue of £300,000 a year, which was to be the government's cut of the extra £700,000 the new company expected to make in profits. But the English dyeing industry could not cope with the sudden new demand. What cloth Cockayne and his friends did get dyed was mostly so badly done that it was unsaleable. The Dutch and others had a monopoly of the market for finished cloth and were furious at the threat to their own dyeing industry and, unable to import English undressed cloth, began to manufacture it for themselves. Fortunately the scheme shipwrecked before the English cloth industry was totally ruined and the Merchant Adventurers were reinstalled. But they had lost much of their market, and some of it they were never able to recover.

The result of such ill-judged policies was that, in spite of a rising revenue from the Customs, the ordinary expenses of peace-time government entailed a permanent deficit, and when he had exhausted every expedient James found himself still, and apparently permanently, in debt to the tune of something over £750,000. A wholesale administrative reform, coupled with economies at Court and an overhaul of royal grants and pensions, would probably have sufficed to meet the ordinary deficit. A purge of monopolies and a revision of the list of Impositions might have done even more by releasing much-needed capital for the expansion of trade and industry which would alone in the long run produce a substantial increase in the royal revenue. But James had always been too idle and self-indulgent to apply himself to such problems, and he was now too old to start. He preferred expensive and entertaining companions to efficient administrators who would certainly have resisted his extravagances and curtailed his personal pleasures. Instead, therefore, he dreamt always of some lucky windfall which would solve all his problems without any undue effort on his own part. This was the dream which was to ruin Raleigh, and which was at the bottom, really, of the Spanish marriage negotiations. At the back of James's mind all the time there was the thought of the dowry an Infanta might bring, drawn from the fabulous output of the gold and silver mines of South America. Sarmiento, now Count Gondomar, one of the most brilliant diplomats of his age, had learnt after an intensive study of James's character to play on his every weakness, and whenever there was any question of the actual amount of the dowry shrugged it off as a sordid detail beneath a gentleman's consideration and, of course, a matter almost of indifference to a sovereign as rich as the King of Spain. James fixed the figure in his mind at a million pounds, which would nicely get him out of all his difficulties; and for ten years Gondomar was able to keep him nibbling off and on at this bait.

In 1616 the Spanish negotiations were more or less at a stand. Somerset, their most eager advocate on the Council, had gone; and the Spaniards had made such demands for toleration for English Catholics, for the Infanta's Catholic household, and on the subject of the education of any children who might be born of the marriage, that James felt that he could go no further. When, therefore, Raleigh, in his passionate desire to get free of the Tower, dangled before him Indian legends of the golden city of Manoa and of the gold mines already discovered up the Orinoco, James saw at once a possibility of solving all his financial difficulties for ever, and at the same time bringing the Spaniards to more acceptable terms for the marriage. He wanted a closer alliance with Spain anyway, and it was only his need of the dowry that forced him to negotiate for it on terms so very favourable to the Spaniards and so unlikely to find any enthusiastic support among the English tax-paying classes.

To establish an English colony on the mainland of South America, between the Portuguese in Brazil and the Spanish Main, was, as has since been proved, a perfectly feasible proposition. Raleigh had sailed a hundred and twenty miles up the Orinoco in 1595 and certainly believed that there was gold there. He might claim that he had then established English sovereignty, and it was common knowledge that the whole area of Guiana between the Amazon and the Orinoco was not effectively occupied by anybody. What was kept always in the background of discussion was the fact, known certainly to Raleigh and almost certainly to James, that by 1596 the Spaniards had established a village settlement at San Thomé, exactly where the English hoped to start prospecting for gold. As soon as Gondomar heard of the projected expedition he protested vigorously, to be assured by James that if Raleigh harmed a single Spaniard he should be sent to Spain for King Philip to hang. Thus Raleigh sailed under a condition which both he and James knew was almost impossible to fulfil. But it was his only hope of escaping from prison and re-making his fortunes, and he accepted it as the desperate gamble that it was. James was less deeply involved. There was an outside chance that he might become suddenly rich beyond his wildest dreams. If not, he had always hated Raleigh. He believed him to have plotted against him both before and after his accession, and he found the aggressive, masculine vitality of the man repulsive. Moreover there had been criticisms of kings and of the institution of monarchy in Raleigh's *History of the World* which James found dangerous and subversive. So Raleigh sailed, after many difficulties, in the summer of 1617, with the sentence of death of 1604 still hanging over him unrepealed, and knowing that he would pay for any failure with his head.

James, meanwhile, had suddenly been seized with the desire, after fourteen years' absence, to revisit Scotland. He could scarcely have chosen a worse moment. There was not the money in the Treasury to pay for the journey and no likelihood of any more coming in; and the whole Council, including Buckingham, rallied behind Suffolk and begged the King on their knees not to go. But James would not have his whims interfered with. The more the difficulties with supplies and transport mounted, the more bad-tempered and obstinate he became. But the moment he was on the road north with his great cavalcade of several thousand courtiers and attendants he recovered not only his temper, but something of his lost youth. All the way up the Great North Road he hunted and feasted with the zest and lavishness that had marked his journey south fourteen years before. He went out of his way to hunt round Lincoln, was received once again in state by the mayor and citizens of York, and on May 16th was greeted by the burghers of Edinburgh with an enthusiastic loyalty and generosity far greater than anything they had shown when he had been their King and had lived among them. Soothed and flattered by loyal addresses and by the wild enthusiasm of the people wherever he went, he recovered some of his lost energy and his old pungency. 'His Majesty, God be thanked,' Buckingham wrote to Bacon, 'is in very good health, and so well pleased with his journey that I never saw him better nor merrier.' He spent a honeymoon summer, which included a hunting tour of the north by way of Falkland, Dundee and Perth, and two visits to the scene of his strange, unhappy childhood at Stirling. The whole affair nearly ruined both his kingdoms. The official welcomes and pageants in every city, the cost of putting seven royal palaces into a state of repair, and the mere expense of housing the English Court and its horses for four months taxed Scottish resources to the uttermost; and the English Treasury faced that year a deficit of £137,000, most of which was due to the journey.

The honeymoon atmosphere did not actually last even to the end of the tour. Right from the start a note of alarm had been sounded in the Kirk when an organ decorated with gilded statuettes of apostles and patriarchs had arrived, in advance of the royal party, for the redecoration of the Chapel at Holyrood. The Anglican service which James had insisted on holding the day after his arrival in Edinburgh with its choir and its surplices, and the injunction that all should kneel at Communion, had roused all the old Presbyterian hostility and suspicion. James had last left the country at the moment of his most spectacular triumph over the Kirk, and he had fallen into the habit of under-rating the strength and obstinacy of its leaders. He had successfully insinuated Bishops into their organization, though he had not yet dared to invest them with much power; and he tried now to use the popularity of his sudden visit for slipping in the complete Anglican ritual. In consequence he faced a very stormy session of the Scottish Parliament before he left, had an even stormier dispute with an assembly of divines at St Andrews, and ended up with a royal row with David Calderwood, the man on whom Melville's mantle had descended, and who now found himself hounded into exile by a Scottish Court of High Commission. By the time James made his way south again by Glasgow, Carlisle, and the west most of the old bitterness had crept back into Scottish politics and he himself was crippled by gout and arthritis. He found the Queen, too, ill, and spent a miserable, dull winter, wrestling in Council with his debts and outside it with the growing feud between Buckingham and the Howards. It was into this atmosphere that Raleigh sailed back in June of 1618 with a report of utter disaster.

The Orinoco expedition had probably been doomed from the start anyway but it had been made much more disastrous by the fact that Raleigh, who had never been an easy man to work with, even in his heyday, was unable to control his subordinate captains. They forced him to remain with the ships covering the mouth of the river while his second-in-command, Keymis, took the landing party up in boats. The intention had been to surround San Thomé while search was made for the mines, thus leaving the responsibility for opening hostilities to the Spaniards. But Keymis let himself be provoked into attacking and capturing the village—an attack in which Raleigh's beloved son, Walter, was killed—and then spent a month there, half besieged, making no serious attempt to find gold, and, having returned to report his miserable failure, killed himself. Raleigh's promise was broken now and his only chance of snatching something from the ruin would have been a successful attack elsewhere and perhaps the capture of a treasure galley or two in the old Elizabethan manner. Winwood, anxious to provoke war with Spain anyway, had actually suggested this, and conceivably it might have saved him. But by now crews as well as captains were mutinous. Two ships had already sailed home to spread alarm and despondency, and there was no fight left in the rest. Heartbroken and hopeless, Raleigh sailed home to his death. Gondomar had already so worked on James that he was even prepared to fulfil his rhetorical promise to send the culprit in chains to Madrid, and it was only King Philip's refusal which prevented him.

It would have been difficult to find grounds for executing Raleigh merely on the strength of what had happened at San Thomé. The immediate responsibility had lain on the disobedient and incompetent Keymis; for the overall plan which made such a disaster almost inevitable King and Council shared responsibility with Raleigh. Indeed, though Winwood was dead, the Council was openly opposed to the King's decision, and James knew full well that all informed opinion in the country was against him. He did not even dare to stage any sort of public trial, which would merely have inflamed the nation still further on Raleigh's behalf. A small Commission held a perfunctory private investigation and James, dismissing public opinion and the arguments of his Council alike as 'the advice of fools and badly disposed persons', insisted on executing the sentence of death which had hung suspended since the monstrously unfair treason trial of 1603, thereby making his enemy a national hero. Raleigh, composedly writing his last poem on the flyleaf of his Bible the night before his execution, and smoking his pipe to 'settle his spirits' before going out to make a superb end on the scaffold, stood in small things as in great for all that James most detested. But England preferred them to the shabby spectacle of a debauched and rapidly ailing King truckling to Spain and showering honours and rewards on those whose only merit was a 'smooth outside'.

So ended James's dream of American gold, and with it the brief flutter of anti-Spanish politics on the Council. For the next seven years the Spanish marriage negotiations were to be the permanent background to English diplomacy, while Gondomar's insolent charm established a hold over James which gave him more real power than anybody except Buckingham, and enabled him entirely to dispense with the Howard support on which the project had at first depended. From his point of view it was just as well, for the Howard supremacy in Court and government was on the verge of collapse. They had easily survived the loss of Somerset and could probably have retained for some years longer a major share of power, but the rise of Buckingham gradually deprived them of their patronage, and the attempt to recover that ruined them. Too late, when Buckingham had already established an unshakeable hold on the doting King, they tried to substitute a protégé of their own by the same sort of method as had first been used to lift George Villiers from obscurity, though more crudely. The Suffolks brought to Court a very beautiful, effeminate young man named William Monson, who seems to have had none of the charm, brains and character which lifted Villiers out of the ruck of good-looking

GEORGE VILLIERS, DUKE OF BUCKINGHAM
Artist unknown

young men. They bathed him in posset curd, dressed him splendidly, and thrust him vulgarly and ostentatiously into James's notice, until the King was goaded into sending a sharp reprimand by the Lord Chamberlain forbidding him his presence and suggesting that he leave the Court altogether. This open attempt to supplant Buckingham proved fatal to its authors; for it roused the favourite to his first major intervention in politics and resulted in Suffolk's ruin.

The corrupt practices of the Treasury had been a byword for years, and there had been constant rumours since the summer of 1614 of a pending inquiry. Everyone, except possibly King James, knew that, in order to get a bill settled or to draw overdue expenses from the Treasurer, a hard bargain must first be driven with the Sub-Treasurer, Mr Bingley, and with Lady Suffolk. Only when one of these two expressed themselves as satisfied would there be any hope of Suffolk setting the machinery for payment in motion. But Suffolk's conduct continued to pass unchallenged for the same basic reason that his daughter's murder of Overbury so long went uninvestigated: the great danger of attacking those who were secure in the possession of powerful friends round the King and among the Lords of the Privy Council. In spite of ceaseless complaints and rumours Suffolk held on his course, and in January of 1618 Bingley even got a knighthood. But in the summer of 1618 Suffolk's failure to find adequate funds for the Scottish journey provoked some uncomfortable inquiries. At the same time he lost the valuable shield of Sir Thomas Lake who, in the Secretary's office, had been able to fend off the more dangerous attacks, and who now found himself doomed to resignation by a vicious and indefensible slander launched by his wife against Lady Exeter. Simultaneously Buckingham's attitude changed from a careless tolerance to hostility, and it suddenly became safe to attack the Treasurer. In June the stories of Lady Suffolk's transactions reached the King. He ordered her out of London, and when she returned threatened to have her whipped out again at the cart's tail like a common whore. A month later he demanded Suffolk's resignation.

It took another eighteen months to complete the Star Chamber inquiry which culminated in sentences of imprisonment in the Tower for both the Suffolks and a crippling fine. Their two sons lost their Court appointments and Lord Knollys, as a son-in-law, his office as Master of the Wards. Lake duly fell, after a *cause célèbre* over which James himself delightedly presided, as he said, like Solomon, and demonstrated his wisdom by personally proving that the vital evidence of one of Lady Exeter's maids was perjured. He took her to the room at Wimbledon where she said she had overheard a compromising conversation and demonstrated that the arras behind which she claimed to have hidden fell far short of the floor and left her entirely exposed. By November of 1619 it was a current jest in London that the Howard faction might set up a Privy Council of their own in the Tower, since they had there a Lord Treasurer, in Somerset a Lord Chamberlain, Lord Howard de Walden for a Captain of Pensioners, Lake for Secretary, and Lord Knollys. A threat of an inquiry into Admiralty and Dockyard accounts sufficed to procure the resignation of the senile Nottingham, and the work was complete.

In the place of this complicated family grouping which, with various adjustments, had dominated politics since 1603 there was now only Buckingham. He himself, already Master of the Horse, took over the Admiralty, where he launched a well-advertised campaign of reform, though it was not thorough enough to produce an efficient fleet when it was needed a few years later. But there was no new grouping of family alliance to replace the old, for Buckingham wanted no rivals near the throne. For the key jobs he preferred industrious, efficient civil servants who would not aspire to make policy or control patronage; as Secretaries Sir Robert Naunton and George Calvert; and to restore the shaken finances Lionel Cranfield, later Earl of Middlesex, a self-made, hard-headed and loyal City merchant whose only ambition now was to balance the King's budget. Such arrangements suited the King well. He had always preferred 'conformable men with but ordinary parts', and Cranfield in particular perfectly matched the recommendation James had written for Prince Henry twenty years before: 'And specially choose honest, diligent men, but mean men, to be your receivers in money matters.' He preferred, too, to be free of the great nobles whose wealth and territorial influence gave them a certain independence of the Crown. Henceforward all effective power would be vested in Buckingham who was his own creation; and it was unfortunately at this moment, when the King's own faculties were failing fast and there was no experienced statesman at the centre of power, that England was faced with the first serious political crisis of the reign.

CHAPTER XIII

Crisis Abroad and at Home

*

At the moment when Buckingham took over the virtual direction of English affairs the Spanish negotiations, so long the centre of all English political activity, had just acquired a new context and a new importance. Hitherto the Spanish desire had been merely to neutralize England in the event of an outbreak of war with the Protestant powers of Northern Europe. Spain never intended the twelve-year truce signed with the Dutch to be more than a breathing-space. She still commanded vast resources. The silver of Peru could still pay for the finest army in Europe; the southern Netherlands gave her an admirable base; and her general, Spinola, was reckoned the best alive. If the Dutch could be isolated they were virtually doomed. At the same time it was extremely improbable that they could be isolated: an outbreak of war in the Netherlands would almost certainly touch off other great issues in which the whole of Europe was likely to become involved. The Counter Reformation had recovered for Rome almost all the south of Europe, but was now halted before the political organization of the north, which defied peaceful penetration and could only be overcome by force. The general war of religion, abandoned in exhaustion by Charles V in 1555, was therefore liable to break out again at any moment on a still larger scale. The accession of Ferdinand of Styria, who in 1619 was to become the Emperor Ferdinand II, to the headship of the Austrian branch of the House of Habsburg meant that there was now a ruler in Vienna who not only meant to be master in his own hereditary dominions, but would certainly provoke a showdown with the German Princes in an attempt to make the Imperial authority a reality. The long struggle between France and Spain, laid aside during the French Wars of Religion, would break out again as soon as the government of Louis XIII of France felt itself strong enough at home to challenge the encircling Habsburg power. In the far north there was Gustavus Adolphus of Sweden, young, ambitious, and extremely efficient, nursing dreams of Baltic empire and ready to take advantage of any general conflagration.

In this situation, which had been simmering uneasily since 1609, it was difficult to formulate a coherent and effective English policy. The tradition of support for the Dutch inherited from Elizabeth was being weakened year by year as Dutch merchants and fishermen crowded the English out of market after market, gradually monopolized the carrying trade, and threatened to seize all the most valuable East Indian possessions of the decaying Portuguese Empire. On the other hand it was doubtful if England could safely stand aside and allow first the Dutch and then the Protestant North German Princes to fall victims jointly to the Habsburgs and the Counter Reformation. More than once James dallied with the idea of placing himself at the head of a northern Protestant league, into which it might have been possible to weave France, whose fear of the Habsburg would outweigh the Catholicism of her government; and such a policy might have had value as a deterrent to Spanish intrigues and ambitions. But it was not compatible with James's other dream of establishing himself firmly in both camps and becoming the arbiter and so the peacemaker of Europe. In fact the very limited time and energy which James was prepared in these years to devote to serious politics was dissipated in the simultaneous pursuit of both these policies. Relations with the Dutch were vitiated by periodic outbursts of peevishness at their fishing in the North Sea without English licences and by James's testy Protestant heresy-hunting which resulted in impertinent interference in the affairs of the Dutch Church. In the one or two minor crises when his Protestant allies required solid help and leadership James invariably left them in the lurch, while he ceaselessly pursued the mirage of a Spanish marriage for Charles which was to counterbalance that of his daughter, Elizabeth, to the Calvinist Elector Palatine and so establish him firmly astride the powers of Europe.

It would seem that Gondomar so seriously misread the minds of Englishmen that he really thought the reconversion of England to Catholicism by means of a royal marriage a possibility.

Like all Catholics at that time, he greatly over-estimated the numbers of English recusants and was entirely unaware of the depth to which hatred of the Roman Church, and of Spanish Catholicism in particular, had taken root among the mass of Englishmen. In his vision the abolition of the penal laws would bring into the open vast numbers of secret Catholic sympathizers, and so make it possible to legalize Catholic worship in public. Englishmen of all classes, he thought, encouraged by the example of the great church which the Infanta was to be allowed to establish for herself, and by the conversion of Prince Charles, which he regarded as a certainty, would come flocking thankfully back to the faith of their forefathers, and the recalcitrant minority could then be coerced. Needless to say, James knew all this for the dangerous nonsense that it was and had no intention of abandoning his own religious beliefs or of allowing his son to do so. But James in his turn was equally deluded; for he still thought that the marriage could be used as a lever to screw out of the Pope a denunciation of the Jesuit doctrine that it was a pious duty to assassinate Protestant sovereigns, and that the Spaniards so valued English friendship that they would accept very limited concessions to English Catholics in exchange for what they regarded as the sacrifice of the Infanta.

All these cards had been on the table since 1615, when Philip of Spain, much less dazzled than his ambassador by impossible day-dreams, defined the terms on which he was prepared to ask the Pope for a dispensation authorizing the marriage. James's answers, point by point, showed that he knew them really to be unacceptable. On the non-enforcement of the penal laws he postponed decision, knowing well in his heart that this could never be accepted by Parliament. On the education of the children of the marriage, which the Spaniards demanded exclusively for the Infanta, James wrote: 'It is clear that I, too, shall be careful to instruct my children in my religion since I am as confident of its goodness as the King of Spain is of the goodness of his; yet there shall be no compulsion on the one side or the other.' This was James's great delusion: that a gentleman's agreement to differ was as possible to the Counter-Reformation mind as it was to his. But even his characteristically commonsensical note that wet nurses should be selected for their health rather than their religion made no sense in the Spanish world of blacks and whites. From 1615 onwards even Gondomar must have seen that there was no real hope of a successful treaty. But from the diplomatic point of view the mere fact that James did not see this was enough. Even if England could not be an ally in the coming struggle, she could be neutralized by the skilful prolongation of the negotiations. It was even possible for Spain to make unthinkable concessions if James seemed to be wavering, since in that case the Pope could always be counted on to refuse a dispensation; and that, too, James never realized, thinking that the Spaniards so valued his alliance that at a pinch they would do without a dispensation.

Thus in 1618, when the expected European crisis burst unexpectedly soon, it found England isolated and powerless, without an effective policy of any sort. What was worse, it materialized in a form which made a policy of isolationism for England impossible. When the Bohemians revolted against Ferdinand of Habsburg as their King elect, they did so partly on nationalist, but also partly on religious grounds, and it was on these last that they appealed to all the Protestant powers, including England. Had all the Protestants behaved as prudently as the great Lutheran Princes of North Germany and refused to meddle, or even, like James, through laziness and indecision postponed an answer, the Bohemian revolt might have been isolated as a domestic problem. But Frederick of the Palatinate and his Calvinist friends threw themselves into it at once, encouraging the Bohemians with wild promises in the hope of organizing the downfall of the whole Habsburg power in Germany. Since the Spanish Habsburgs were bound to come to the rescue of their cousins in Vienna, this automatically brought about an international crisis. And when, in October of 1619, Frederick accepted the crown of Bohemia from the rebels he inevitably plunged his father-in-law into the thick of issues which in England were very imperfectly understood.

In characteristically muddled fashion James was already personally involved. He had leapt at a suggestion, thrown off carelessly by Gondomar in the hope of keeping England inactive for a few more vital months, that he should mediate between the Bohemians and Ferdinand: it precisely suited his conception of himself as the peacemaker of Europe. So James Hay, now Lord Doncaster, was sent off with a train of a hundred and fifty followers on a grandiose mission to Prague which cost £30,000 and achieved nothing save ridicule. There was in fact no basis for mediation. James was, however, given a chance for effective action in August, 1619, when Frederick sent the Baron von Dohna to London to ask his advice on the Bohemian offer of the crown. From James's point of view—and from the Elector's—it was vital to prevent him from accepting if possible. Frederick, with 'a mind rather fitted for the little besoignes of Accounts and Reckonings than any vigorous or masculine heat to shoulder up the crackt title of a Crown', was bound to run into major trouble and would probably drag England after him. Not only would his personal honour oblige James to intervene to help his daughter. The whole of English public opinion would demand that he should. Elizabeth had the sort of charm which could not only win individuals to a lifetime's devotion without reward, but could catch the imagination of the masses. She was, furthermore, married to a sound Protestant whose Calvinism would command the support of a majority of an English House of Commons; and Puritan England, more conscious than ever before of identity with European Protestantism, nursing the memories of Foxe's Martyrs and Elizabethan legends of the flouting of the Inquisition dogs of Spain, would clamour to support so good a cause without pausing to think how this might be effectively done. But James let things drift, and by the time he made up his mind to advise Frederick to refuse the crown it was too late. In October Frederick and Elizabeth arrived in Prague. In November of 1620, after a year of playing cheerfully and incompetently at being a King and Queen, they left in headlong flight amidst the remnants of their army, destroyed at the White Mountain by the troops of the Catholic League. At the same time Spinola began the systematic conquest of Frederick's own dominions in the Palatinate, and the young couple quickly became, and remained for the rest of their lives, homeless pretenders to both crown and electoral hat.

When he dismissed the Addled Parliament in 1614, James probably intended never to call another. As long as he could, by Forced Loans and Benevolences, by the sale of honours and Monopolies, and by the judicious levying of Impositions, cobble together an income just sufficient for his ordinary needs—and with Cranfield as Treasurer he just could—there was no object in inviting a fresh outburst of unwelcome criticism and intolerable pretensions. He had no wish to know what the grievances of the nation were and no understanding of the Tudor trick of making the best of a bad job and using Parliament as a forum for explaining government policy and mobilizing public opinion. But, however he handled the problem which faced him at Christmas, 1620, he could not hope to do so unarmed and on an income barely sufficient for peace-time needs. Even if his role was to be, as he always hoped, that of mediator, he would not be listened to at all unless his words were backed by some show of force. So the writs had to go out in January of 1621 for a Parliament which turned out to be the most truculent that had yet sat in England.

Actually at the outset in 1621 there were the makings of the situation of which Winwood had dreamed seven years before: of King and Commons meeting each other half-way on grievances in order to collaborate wholeheartedly in a popular war. They desired, after all, the same objective—the restoration of Frederick and his wife at least to their hereditary dominions in the Palatinate. Feeling against Buckingham and his monopoly of power had not yet hardened into a settled hatred, and the prospect of fighting the Spaniards in a good, Protestant cause might have induced the Commons to vote really adequate subsidies. Moreover even Buckingham at this stage had joined the majority on the Council which clamoured for war, so that for once Court and Country, Council, City, and Parliament were all united. In all this unanimity, however, King James himself was a significant exception. Gondomar was back from Spain, where he had been conferring with his master on the details of the proposed marriage, and James was under the old spell. With desperate obstinacy he clung to a policy which had already broken down, adding the evacuation of the Palatinate as one more concession the Spaniards must make to achieve a marriage which they had already unmistakably shown they did not really want at all.

It is very unlikely that any combination of men or policies in London could seriously have influenced the course of events in Europe during the next few years. In spite of the economies and reforms of Buckingham's new Navy Board, the fleet was only half the size it had been at the end of Elizabeth's reign, and there were not the trained veteran naval commanders to conduct a successful maritime war against Spain. The appearance on the Continent of an English army of 12,000 men, which was about as much as the national resources could support, even if they had been fully trained and brilliantly led, could not alone clear Spinola from the Palatinate, nor would it galvanize the sluggish German Princes of the Protestant Union into action. Only the most brilliant diplomacy could have combined into an effective activity the anti-Habsburg forces available in 1621, and Parliament and country were deluded in thinking that the strength which had scored a great defensive success against the Armada would suffice for a major European offensive. But it was not for these very sound reasons that James rejected the Parliamentary policy of an all-out war. His alternative of mediation backed by a threat of force rested on the same basic fallacies, though it had the additional disadvantage that it enabled the Spaniards to pursue their objectives without detaching any forces against England. But the truth was that James, though he still showed occasional flashes of his old intellectual clarity, was by now incapable of pursuing any objective singlemindedly. The control of policy was indeed beginning to pass out of his hands altogether.

During the ten years in which he had tried to govern England without help from Parliament the King's physical and spiritual disintegration had proceeded so fast as to make a mockery of the conception of personal rule which he was seeking to illustrate. A really serious illness, exacerbated by a fit of melancholy when the Queen died of dropsy in March of 1619, had completed the effects of years of over-indulgence, and he had become a very old man, almost senile in his dependence on Buckingham and on the Villiers family circle. The fact that he had been able to reconcile Prince Charles with the favourite completed his absorption into this new domesticity. There had been a trying period when the two young men squabbled publicly, and Charles, awkward, retarded, and very much in awe of his father, had openly resented the presumption with which Buckingham asserted himself as one of the family. Then, quite suddenly, Charles's intense reserve and pride had given way. James liked to think that it was entirely due to his intervention, when he had called them together and virtually ordered them to love one another, and he congratulated Charles on setting 'a worthy example to all other kings' sons for imitation'. In all probability Buckingham saw the dangers of quarrelling permanently with the heir to the throne of an ageing king and set himself to win the Prince over. His charm and glamour and easy, splendid manners could be devastating. Charles, without intimates and never hitherto taken seriously as a person by anybody, succumbed completely, and in the end gave to Buckingham a devotion as slavish and even more disastrous than his father's.

With this one cross removed, James could sit back and wallow in all his favourite sentimentalities. He could form the minds of the two young men together: Baby Steenie and Baby Charles, who would listen lovingly while their old Dad expounded his theories of kingship and his rather hazy assessments of the European political situation. Gradually they were absorbed into the whole circle of the warm Villiers domesticity. An heiress was found for Steenie—the Lady Katherine Manners, only daughter of the Earl of Rutland, pretty, docile, a little slow and solid, but wholeheartedly adoring of her splendid husband and perfectly happy to be converted from the Roman Catholicism in which she had been brought up, to take her place as Baby Kate, and to allow the old King to share every intimacy of her marriage and motherhood. Even Steenie's tiresome, bustling busybody of a mother, Lady Compton, was woven for a time into the family circle when she came up to Court to manage the shameless fortune-hunting of her many relations.

The impact of the Villiers monopoly on Court and government was admirably exemplified by the vicissitudes it introduced into the life of Lord Chief Justice Coke. They wanted a rich wife for Sir John Villiers, Buckingham's half-witted, weakling brother, and they picked on Frances Coke, hoping that her mother, the rich Lady Hatton, would settle on her £1,000 a year and £10,000 in cash. Coke was himself at that moment in the thick of a quarrel with the King which has become famous in legal history and which was basically concerned with the Crown's right to interfere in cases which had already come before the courts. There was a celebrated scene when Coke, on his knees at the head of all the judges, had argued with James for two hours without giving way, and it is possible that he would have been dismissed anyway. But his actual fall, his removal from the Council and the Bench, certainly followed immediately on his testy rejection of the iniquitous Villiers offer for his daughter, and it was made clear to him that he could only restore his fortunes by giving way on the marriage. The end of the story was tragic farce. Coke gave way, but Lady Hatton stood firm and carried her tearful daughter off to the country, where Coke followed her and beat in his own front door with the help of his son, 'fighting Clem'. The King was away in Scotland. Bacon, as the senior Councillor left behind, thought he saw a splendid chance of completing the ruin of his oldest enemy and instituted proceedings against Coke for riot, only to find how seriously he had misjudged the situation. He only saved his own office by a series of cringing apologies to Buckingham. The marriage went through, honoured by the presence of the King and Queen and Prince Charles and the usual drunken orgy, and in due course suffered the inevitable disaster; and Coke got back his seat on the Council, though, since Lady Hatton proved much stingier than had been hoped, his restoration to favour was partial only and shortlived.

The similar campaign launched by old Lady Compton for her other son, Christopher, failed because none of the heiresses concerned would have him. In due course she herself wore out the King's patience and retired to the country, consoled by the courtesy title of Countess of Buckingham, and the worst of the campaign for endowing the Villiers tribe was over. But one undoubted effect of the Villiers supremacy was a further lowering of the whole tone of public life. The Jacobean system in Court and government was not fundamentally different from that of Elizabeth, and in some ways Buckingham's administration was an improvement. His preference for diligent, obscure officials wholly dependent on himself did bring a certain increase of efficiency in the Admiralty and in the Treasury and in the day-to-day conduct of business in the Secretary's office. But all was offset by irresponsibility and extravagance at the centre. As his hold on the King and Prince became unshakable Buckingham's vanity and caprice gradually eliminated from public life all but the lickspittles who were prepared to be entirely dependent on himself, and threw into opposition all those elements, both in Court and country, on whom the stability of government had largely depended. Moreover not even Cranfield's efficiency in the Wardrobe, and later at the Treasury, could make such a régime really solvent. It had been almost impossible to squeeze enough money out of the City to pay for the Scottish journey of 1617; and when Queen Anne died in March, 1619, her body had to be kept embalmed and unburied for nearly three months until funds could be provided for a state funeral.

The result of this was that all that the Parliamentary classes found distasteful in the conduct of government came sooner or later to be identified with Buckingham personally, while the King could find no support in his growing struggle with the House of Commons save the courtiers and time-servers who subscribed to the Villiers ascendancy. The accumulated grievances resulting from the unremedied abuses and the misgovernment of the past eighteen years were concentrated against this patently irremovable favourite. James could not do without Buckingham and, in view of the situation in the Palatinate, could not easily do without Parliament. The crisis abroad therefore produced what was for England in the long run an even more serious crisis at home.

Considering that it was the European crisis which had brought Parliament together in 1621, surprisingly little time was in fact taken up by foreign affairs. James opened the proceedings with a highly characteristic lecture in which he restated the views on Monarchy and the rights of Parliament which had already been found so distasteful by earlier Parliaments, and only touched on the foreign situation in the vaguest terms. He assured his subjects that his object was still a peaceful solution, but that he must negotiate 'with a sword in his hand', and that, if necessary, he would spend everything he had for the recovery of the Palatinate. But he asked for far too little money to make any effective threat to Spain. He had been advised that an army of 30,000 men at least was needed for intervention on the Continent. To equip and maintain this and to put the fleet on a war footing would cost £250,000 down and thereafter something like £900,000 a year—figures which James simply dared not mention to a House of Commons. In this estimate of their feeling he was, for once, quite right. They had no conception of what a continental campaign would cost and, anxious though they were to save European Protestantism, no intention of doing so at such vast expense. They would not even consider the request for £500,000, which was all that James dared ask for at first, and voted instead an interim grant of £160,000 to relieve his immediate necessities while he tried the effect of negotiations.

It was a fatal mistake not to face Parliament with the hard facts of the situation at once. For immediate war with Spain they might have voted substantial sums. The talk of preliminary negotiations cooled all their ardour, and, furthermore, gave them time to turn to grievances nearer home; and the climate of opinion favourable to any large grant of money was lost, as it proved, for good. Within a month they were embroiled in all the old difficulties and Buckingham was clamouring for the dissolution of an assembly which was pushing home an attack on monopolies, some of the most scandalous of which were held by his own family. There were no grounds of public policy which could justify patents for the levying of lighthouse tolls, or for the engrossing of wills. The exclusive right to import salmon and lobsters, and that for the manufacture of gold and silver thread, which were held by two of the Villiers brothers, could not possibly be brought within Elizabeth's celebrated definition of 'good for the subjects in general, though a private profit to some ancient servants who had deserved well', while the monopoly for the licensing of ale-houses granted to another Villiers kinsman, Sir Giles Mompesson, was actually a positive scandal, since it cut across the rights and duties of the licensing justices and caused chaos everywhere. The Commons went for Mompesson first and chose as their method the ancient procedure of Impeachment, disused for more than a century, by which they brought the accused for trial before the House of Lords.

Buckingham, once he had failed to get Parliament dissolved out of hand, decided to throw his relations over and court an easy popularity by joining in the hunt. Moreover, since all monopolies had to be reviewed in the law courts before being granted, it was possible to push Lord Chancellor Bacon forward as the judge to whom most of the worst patents had been referred, and so to make him the scapegoat for the whole Villiers family, and at the same time pay him out for having interfered with John Villiers's marriage. Surprisingly enough, the most important opposition to this highly characteristic manœuvre came from the King. James scented at once a very dangerous inroad on his prerogative if by Impeachment ministers could be made in some degree responsible to Parliament rather than to himself, and he tried to frustrate the entire proceeding. 'Those who strike at your Chancellor,' Bacon had written to him, 'it is much to be feared will strike at your Crown'; and James delivered a testy but vague speech, in which he warned the Commons off the prerogative and asked them to leave the monopolists to be dealt with by him in the ordinary courts of law. 'He that will have all done by Parliament,' he said, 'is an enemy to monarchy and a traitor to the King of England.' But he could not fight simultaneously both Buckingham and the Prince and the House of Commons. He was, moreover, still bent on co-operation with Parliament and so prepared to compromise. The Commons, anxious not to have their debates prematurely cut short by dissolution, met him half way by giving up the attack on the Chancellor in return for a free hand with Mompesson and the other monopolists, who were duly condemned.

The Commons concession did not, however, save Bacon. The Impeachment proceedings had shown that Buckingham was prepared, for the sake of a transient popularity, to throw the Chancellor to the wolves, and there were plenty of enemies in the House of Commons who would join Coke in taking advantage of Bacon's exposed position. Inquiry had already brought to light accusations of corrupt practices in the Court of Chancery which could scarcely be protected by the mantle of the prerogative. James indeed, touchy as he was about the quality of his justice, would make no attempt to cover up bribery, and, having already conceded the general principle of Impeachment, could only argue feebly that the case should be tried by a Commission appointed by himself. The Commons, however, insisted on impeaching Bacon and had little difficulty in proving that he had taken presents from interested parties in cases which he was trying, though there was no evidence that his decisions had ever been influenced by them. As he himself said, he had in fact done no more than 'partake of the abuses of the times', and the Jacobean world was riddled with corrupt practices far more scandalous than his. But he could not deny the facts. He was fined £40,000 and driven altogether from public life—the first great victim of Buckingham's volatile treachery which was soon to leave him without a friend in the world save the King and the Prince.

There was a certain symbolism in this last clash between Coke and Bacon—the climax of a bitter rivalry which went back more than thirty years. For behind all the personal jealousies and animosities there lay two opposed political theories which would ultimately find themselves face to face in civil war. Bacon saw with luminous clarity the solution of the seventeenth century's problems in terms of efficiency. He would have allowed no private liberty or parliamentary privilege to stand in the way of a beneficent monarchy and the establishment of a prosperous welfare state, with the work of the Council departmentalized and delegated to commissions of experts, while the Judges, 'Lions under the throne', enforced justice not as the Englishman's prescriptive right, but simply on the grounds that 'power is ever of greatest strength when it is civilly carried'. To Coke all the theories which lay behind divine right monarchy were anathema. The majesty and inviolability—even the sovereignty—of the law of England were his religion, and that even when the law produced situations which were unreasonable and absurd. It was Bacon who had formulated the King's case against Coke in 1616; and it was Coke who now from his seat in the House of Commons marshalled the attack on Bacon. His restoration to favour by the sacrifice of his daughter had never been more than partial; and inevitably the King's prerogative claims forced him in the end into the ranks of the Parliamentary opposition.

By 1621 that opposition was beginning to crystallize into something very much more coherent and formidable than anything seen before in England. James was paying the penalty of his own and Salisbury's neglect in the early years of the reign. Without any decisive lead from the government the Commons had found their own leadership; and they had made astonishing strides in the technique of organizing their debates and formulating the remedies for their grievances in workable legislative form. When, half way through the session, Sir Edwin Sandys fell foul of the King over the affairs of the Virginia Company and withdrew to the Tower there was a compact group ready to take his place, of whom Coke and Pym and Sir Robert

JAMES VI OF SCOTLAND AND I OF ENGLAND, IN 1621
by Daniel Mytens

Phelips were probably the most important. They dominated every debate and conducted both the attack on government policy and the defence of their own privileges along lines which were clearly thought out and co-ordinated in advance.

There was, of course, nothing yet like a political party. The rank and file of the members came up to represent the provincial grievances of remote constituencies with only the haziest idea of the problems of government. Their outlook was determined by their own economic difficulties and by basic prejudices largely inherited from the days of Elizabeth. Many of them came from that land-owning class which was struggling for solvency in a world of fixed rents and rising prices; and these would be automatically suspicious of the plans and policies of a Court where men, by contrast, achieved quick and easy riches, and of a government which they obscurely felt was to blame for their difficult situation. An increasing number were sympathetic to the Puritan grievances as embodied in the Millenary Petition, disliking both the authority claimed by the Bishops and the ritualism which they used it to enforce. Almost all detested Catholicism and wished to see it stamped out at home and re-sisted wherever possible abroad. James's methods of govern-ment at home and his policies abroad made it easy for the hand-ful of men who saw the issues more clearly to weld them into a solid and apparently compact opposition: Sandys who could bring expert criticism to bear on the fiscal expedients by which James had sought to keep his government afloat for the past ten years; Phelips who could play on their fears for a Protes-tantism 'martyred in Bohemia, wounded in France, scattered in Germany', and gravely endangered in England by the relaxa-tion of the penal laws; and Coke who could expound the legal dangers behind the sweeping claims of the royal prerogative. When, under the increasing stress of the European crisis, both the King and the Commons leaders were forced away from the studied moderation which preserved an outward harmony at least for the first session, James would find the whole House, save for a handful of courtiers and place hunters, solidly against him: as he himself said testily, above four hundred kings, bent, as far as he could see, on destroying his prerogative.

Moreover, thanks to the arrogant, touchy way in which Buckingham wielded his power, the House of Lords could no longer be counted on as a counterpoise to the growing claims of the Commons. When Lord Oxford, threatened by Buckingham with his personal enmity if he persisted in opposing him politically, retorted that 'he neither cared for his friendship nor feared his hatred', he spoke for a whole class accustomed to the hereditary use of power and deeply resentful at being excluded from it by the tribe of Villiers relations and dependants. Thus Buckingham focused on his single person all the hostile prejudices of both Lords and Commons. He stood for Spanish politics and toleration for Roman Catholics; and in due course his tiresome mother, by becoming herself a convert to Rome, still further compromised him with the Puritan opposition. The most unpopular monopolies were held by his family and friends. It was their brand-new fortunes, so largely made out of public money, which impoverished the government and drove it to the unpopular expedients of Impositions and Forced Loans. Already in 1621 he was becoming what Coke was later to call him— 'the grievance of grievances': an insuperable barrier to reconciliation between Crown and Parliament.

Thus the careful moderation which had characterized the opening session of this Parliament quickly disappeared on both sides. The Commons refused to grant any more money without some clear explanation of how James proposed to save the Palatinate, and James to their fury retorted by proroguing them. Undoubtedly he hoped by the time they met again to present them with a diplomatic triumph. For he still cherished the illusion that, without any display of force, he could persuade Philip of Spain to a joint mediation on the basis that Frederick should renounce Bohemia and Ferdinand restore him the Palatinate. As it was, Gondomar was able to free the Spanish government of any fear whatever of English action. James threatened that, if Philip broke his promises, he would find that he had roused 'a pacific lion', and sent Digby to Vienna to pursue the mediation. But neither side would listen to him, and by the autumn it was clear that Frederick was about to lose his last foothold in the Palatinate. In a brief flurry of energy James actually sent Frederick some money and for the first time brought serious pressure on him to offer reasonable terms to the Emperor. He took preliminary steps to raise an army, and he recalled Parliament.

But there the brief spurt of activity ended. With that levity which in the long run did more damage to the monarchy than all the claims of divine right, he left London on a hunting trip to Newmarket, expecting the Commons to vote him the money for a policy which he was not even present to expound and defend, and which had already proved a failure. It is not surprising that they were goaded into action which their leaders must have known was unprecedented and, by Tudor standards, unpardonable. In a great memorandum they set forth their own very simple view of the situation. They listed under fourteen headings the vile practices by which 'the Pope of Rome and his dearest son', the King of Spain, sought to destroy the true faith both in England and abroad, and under another ten headings the remedies, which in fact boiled down to two: immediate war with Spain and an increased persecution of Catholics at home. Above all the Prince should be 'timely and happily married to one of our own religion'. Such an invasion of the royal prerogative of conducting foreign policy without interference or advice would undoubtedly have provoked Elizabeth, as it did James, to cry aloud, 'God give me patience'; and the tone of his answer was authentically Elizabethan, ordering the House 'that none therein shall presume henceforth to meddle with anything concerning our Government or deep matters of State, and namely, not to deal with our dearest son's match with the daughter of Spain'. But Elizabeth had never had to face her Commons with a demand to finance a policy in which the whole nation had lost confidence, nor would she have had to introduce a dishonest preamble, as James did, ascribing his absence to 'indisposition of health'. In any case James had given way too often before to persistent Parliamentary opposition for his protest to have any effect. Characteristically, too, instead of sticking to the point at issue, on which he was certainly within his constitutional rights, he raised at once the basic questions which had so much better have remained undiscussed. 'Resolve then in our name,' his letter to the Speaker ended, 'that we find ourself very free and able to punish any man's misdemeanours in Parliament, as well during their sitting as after. Which we mean not to spare hereafter upon any occasion of any man's insolent behaviour there that shall be ministered unto us. And if they have already touched any of these points which we have forbidden in any petition of theirs . . . except they reform it before it come to our hands we will not deign the hearing nor answering of it.' Inevitably from this point each side moved to an extreme position which astounded and alarmed the other. James saw clearly that to extend the conception of free speech as the Commons were doing was to claim a sovereignty rivalling his own, as he showed by his ironical order to 'bring stools for the ambassadors' when the next delegation waited on him at Newmarket to renew their petition in more moderate terms, but with a protest added against the attempt 'to abridge us of the ancient liberty of Parliament for freedom of speech . . . the same being our undoubted right and an inheritance received from our ancestors'. James found this repetition of the attempt of 1604 to give him a constitutional lesson quite infuriating. 'We are an old and experienced King,' he told them, 'needing no such lessons.' He objected strongly to the 'great complaints of the danger of religion within this kingdom, tacitly implying our ill-government in this point'; and he denounced the claim of unfettered freedom of criticism and advice as a 'plenipotency' calculated, like those of the Pope and 'the Puritan ministers in Scotland', to 'bring all kinds of causes within their compass and jurisdiction'. His final conclusion that their privileges were only 'derived from the grace and permission of our ancestors and us' so shocked the Commons that they drew up on December 18th a Protestation in which their dispute with the King ceased to be a mere aftermath of Elizabethan wranglings and became the full-dress constitutional battle of the seventeenth century. For they claimed an unfettered freedom of debate and freedom from arrest as 'the ancient and undoubted birthright and inheritance of the subjects of England' in revolutionary terms which overrode all the traditional restrictions.

James's situation had never been comfortable since the Bohemian revolt landed him between a clamorous English opinion and the hard realities of European politics. But now, by letting his difference of opinion with the Commons broaden into a debate on the fundamentals of sovereignty, he had made his position impossible. Gondomar, who had throughout been trying simply to prevent James from intervening in the war, had played cleverly on his feelings to exacerbate the dispute, seeing clearly that a dissolution of Parliament would leave England diplomatically at Spain's mercy. A king who had to tolerate such insolence from a popular assembly was not, he had written, properly a king at all. With a government so hampered the King of Spain could not really negotiate at all, still less trust an Infanta to a throne which visibly trembled on the edge of disaster. To this were added the persuasions of Buckingham and Prince Charles: Buckingham's because his bid for popularity by throwing the monopolists and Bacon to the wolves had so conspicuously failed; the Prince's because Buckingham could do no wrong and he had begun to fancy himself as anxious for the Spanish match as his father.

James still had intelligence enough to see the dilemma in which he had landed himself. He must now either become a diplomatic dependant of Spain, or surrender to the English Commons a vital part of that precious kingship which he had fought all his life to preserve from Kirk and Pope. Inevitably he felt that at all costs he must save his kingship. With great formality he sent for the Journal of the House of Commons and in the presence of his Privy Council he tore out the page which recorded the offensive Protestation. In a long Proclamation he sought to explain to the nation at large how excellent had been his intentions and how vilely he had been used by the Commons, so that he was forced to dissolve the Parliament with nothing achieved. But English opinion was more likely to agree with Gondomar's gleeful report to the King of Spain that this was 'the best thing that has happened in the interest of Spain and the Catholic religion since Luther began to preach heresy a hundred years ago'. Deprived of any hope of effective English aid, the Elector Palatine lost the rest of his dominions, including his capital of Heidelberg, and the Emperor Ferdinand, though he kept James in play with desultory negotiations through the court of Brussels, made it clear at the end of 1622 that he intended to give Frederick's Electorate to his cousin, Maximilian of Bavaria. Once Parliament was dissolved there was no way of bringing pressure to bear on Spain, save through the marriage negotiations, and perforce James concentrated on them for the next two years, hoping against hope that at the last minute King Philip would save his face for him.

CHAPTER XIV

The End of King James's Peace

*

King James cannot be fairly held personally responsible for the vagaries of English policy during the last three years of his reign, for he was fast sinking into dotage. It was, of course, largely his own fault that it was so premature and unattractive a dotage; the direct result of idleness and over-indulgence. He had always been afraid of death and had deliberately avoided the death-beds of his wife and son. Now he was haunted by the fear of his own, by the pains of gout and arthritis, and the dread of a return of the agonies he had suffered when he all but died of a stone in his kidneys in 1619. He was corpulent and feeble and less attractive than ever in his personal habits; and he sat alone for long periods, weeping and muttering to himself, the constant prey, so all the foreign ambassadors reported, to fear: fear of what the Emperor or the King of Spain might do next to wound and humiliate him; fears for his beloved Steenie and his Baby Charles whenever they were out of his sight; fears, even, after the manner of his youth, for his own safety, so that one night he roused the whole of Whitehall with cries of 'treason' when some banqueting lawyers at Gray's Inn woke him by letting off a cannon. In the end he came even to fear sometimes that Buckingham and Charles were plotting against him. Only when he was drunk could he recover his old cheerfulness, and in his last years he seldom went to bed sober. 'All things,' the French ambassador wrote at the end of one of his despatches, 'end with the goblet.'

Except for occasional fits and starts of energy, when he would still deliver one of his old pungent, commonsensical judgements, he dropped more and more out of political life altogether. Cartoons in the shop windows of Catholic Europe might show him as a figure of fun, with empty pockets turned inside out and flourishing an empty scabbard; libellous pamphlets could be sold in London castigating his drunkenness and vice and assuring him that ten healths were drunk in his own capital to the Elector Palatine to every one that was drunk to him; even his daughter wrote to reproach him for neglect and incompetence; but he could not rouse himself to action. Absorbed in the domesticities of the Villiers ladies, fussing over their pregnancies and prescribing for the weaning of their babies, he escaped from an unkind world which would not dance to the tunes he had piped. His debts had risen, in spite of Middlesex's economies, to £900,000, but the only urgency was to relieve Buckingham of the need to borrow £13,000 for the expenses of Kate's first lying-in, which must have been on a very grand scale. 'If he once run in arrear,' James wrote to the harassed Middlesex, 'he will go ever backward. Do quickly therefore what ye are to do for him and remember that a thing done in time is a thing twice done. Comfort me with some present good news in this point for till then I protest I can have no joy in the going well of my own business. And so I conclude either now or never. God bless your labours.'

In spite of ceaseless pressure of this kind, sometimes very cunningly applied, Middlesex did manage to get the deficit gradually under control. But without a King and without a policy, the government simply drifted down the apparently interminable road of the negotiations for Charles's marriage. A curious air of unreality had pervaded them ever since they had first been initiated ten years before under the aegis of Carr and the Howards, when Gondomar had first presented his credentials at the Court of King James. It was a different Prince, now, and he sought the hand of a different Infanta. But the misunderstandings, the false hopes, and the miscalculations on both sides remained obstinately the same. Gondomar still nursed the dream of a predominantly Catholic England coming out into the open and acknowledging its old allegiance as a result of the public reconversion of the royal family. James, in his moments of coherence, still believed that he could gain all the diplomatic advantages of a Spanish alliance without sacrificing the Church of England or his own unshakeable convictions. He continued to make large half-promises of complete relaxation of the penal laws, of toleration for public worship by the Infanta and for the

Catholic upbringing of her children, which he knew in his heart English opinion would never allow him to concede. The certain refusal of Parliament to repeal the anti-Catholic laws was the card which James kept up his sleeve. King Philip and his all-powerful minister, Olivares, more sceptical than Gondomar about the seriousness of James's intentions and the possibilities in England, kept one up theirs, too: the certain refusal of the Pope to issue a dispensation for the marriage except on terms quite unacceptable to an English Parliament, or even to James himself. In the purely diplomatic sphere the negotiations were equally unreal. The Spaniards had no intention of sacrificing their whole European policy by surrendering the solid gains already made for Catholicism in Germany for anything less than a certainty of English re-conversion, while the recovery of the Palatinate was, from the English point of view, the only object worth working for at all.

Nevertheless the negotiations went on. The Spaniards had every advantage in delaying an English declaration of war by dangling promises which they never meant to fulfil; and James could not withdraw without publicly admitting in Parliament the bankruptcy of a policy which had all along been mistrusted and disapproved by an overwhelming majority of his subjects. More curiously still, there even came a moment when both sides seemed to have gone so far in this elaborate make-believe that it would be impossible to draw back. The professional diplomats—Lord Bristol in Madrid and Gondomar in London—had worked away so skilfully and patiently at the details of the agreement that the governments were caught in the toils of their own disingenuousness. Philip and Olivares gloomily recognized that they might have, after all, to 'sacrifice' the Infanta and allow the marriage. James could not bring himself to admit the impossibility of the Spanish demands in their final form and, still dazzled by the thought of the dowry and of the possibility of a bloodless recovery of the Palatinate which might even lead to a general pacification of Europe, shut his eyes to the certain complications in England and pushed doggedly on. It was at this point that his gradual surrender of his will to the caprices of his favourite produced its first really disastrous consequence.

It is never possible to say that Buckingham had any coherent and definable policy at home or abroad. He was driven by pique, by the opportunism engendered by a too-successful career at Court, and by his own overwhelming desire for spectacular success. He had taken on the Spanish negotiations as part of Somerset's legacy and had presumably backed them in the first place because they were obviously dear to James's heart and his bread was therefore buttered on that side. By the end of the 1621 Parliament he had become an enthusiast, partly, perhaps, out of pique that his bid for popularity with the Commons had failed. In any case Gondomar listed both him and the Prince as good friends working for the match and against Parliament, and the French Ambassador reported disgustedly that Buckingham was scarcely behaving like an Englishman, he was so deeply involved in Spanish intrigues. When Gondomar went back to Spain in 1622 to help hammer out acceptable terms, Buckingham and Charles both kept in touch with him; and, while the King and Council were seriously discussing war to recover Heidelberg, they were secretly writing of the possibility of the Prince's coming to Madrid to force a speedy conclusion. This had been Gondomar's suggestion in the first place, and it had now caught the imagination of Charles. Buckingham, convinced that he could do better than the professional diplomats and seeing a chance of scoring a spectacular personal triumph, took it up with enthusiasm; and in February of 1623, when the negotiations were again flagging, the two of them broached the plan to the King. They proposed to cross France without a formal pass, incognito and largely unattended, and to take the Spanish government entirely by surprise.

Charles's boyish desire to emulate the romantic feat of his father by bringing back his bride from over the sea is understandable. But Buckingham, with five years of supreme political power behind him, should certainly have perceived the criminal folly of the project. Not only was he proposing to expose the King's only son to the very real and quite unnecessary dangers of a journey half across Europe unguarded and unattended. He would also destroy at a blow the delicate bargaining position built up by Bristol and would give the Spaniards the chance to raise their terms as high as they pleased, while the impact on an already hostile English public opinion was certain to be disastrous. All this James himself could see clearly enough. But drink and illness and his doting fondness for the two young men had so sapped his will power by now that he had at last surrendered to Buckingham what he had never surrendered before—his own royal freedom of action. His initial consent was surprised out of him one night when he was tired and ill and not thinking very much of what he was saying. But when the next morning, tearful and protesting, he changed his mind, he was treated to the sort of scene which he could no longer resist. The servile, extravagant self-abasement with which Buckingham had at first invariably met the King's doting preoccupation could safely be abandoned occasionally now that he was securely established in the affections of the Prince, and both he and Charles treated the King's change of mind with insolent contempt, accusing him of listening to other advice behind their backs, and telling him that if he broke his promise now he would never be believed again. To stiffen his own weakening will James sent for Francis Cottington, just back from Madrid, and an expert on Spanish affairs; and Cottington confirmed all his worst fears, thereby diverting on to his own head the abuse and recriminations of the two young men. Since the two were capable of a prolonged sulk, every minute of which would be unbearable to James, they were bound to win in the end, and on February 17th, still weeping hysterically and screaming that he would 'lose Baby Charles', he let them go.

The most lurid of the King's fears did not materialize. Attended by Cottington and Endymion Porter, the two 'babes', whom James liked to think of as 'dear adventurous knights worthy to be put in a new romanso', safely crossed France as Tom and John Smith, calling incognito at the French court on the way, and surprised Bristol from his bed late one night. But, apart from that, the impact of their arrival in Madrid was every bit as disastrous as Cottington had foretold. While Bristol was still pondering how he was formally to announce to King Philip the embarrassing arrival of the Prince, Gondomar had already rushed round to Olivares with the joyful news which to both of them could only mean that Charles had decided to turn Catholic. This belief Buckingham and Charles at first foolishly encouraged, thinking that it would bring down the Spanish terms, and a series of meetings was arranged in which the Catholic theologians formally set out their case. But even when the Spaniards were finally disillusioned on this point they could still see that for the Prince to go home without his bride would involve so fearful a loss of face that they could well afford to stiffen their terms. They refused to allow the Anglican chaplains whom James sent out even to enter the royal palace; they secretly begged the Pope to refuse the dispensation which they now felt obliged to apply for formally; and they wore away the whole spring and summer in haggling. For they, too, had to face certain unpleasant facts. Unless they could tire out Charles's obstinate patience they would have to let the marriage go through or accept a complete diplomatic break with England, and the Infanta, who had once told her brother that she would go into a nunnery rather than marry a heretic, was set to learning English grammar.

Meanwhile Charles's wooing of the Infanta steadily degenerated into farce. From the moment that he was allowed his first glimpse of her in the boot of the King's coach, with a blue ribbon on her arm for identification, he imagined himself to have fallen deeply in love. Buckingham, still under the heady delusion that he was about to score a resounding diplomatic triumph, and much impressed by the 'real courtesy' of Olivares, wrote to James that there was 'not a sweeter creature in the world' than the Infanta, and that 'Babie Charles himself is so touched at the heart, that he confesses all he ever yet saw is nothing to her'. But any attempt to get on more intimate terms was frustrated by the rigid Spanish court etiquette. He could never see her alone and could only make himself ridiculous by gazing at her across the royal box at the theatre 'half an hour together in a thoughtful posture', with a concentration which reminded Olivares of a cat watching a mouse. The only time he ventured to speak to her of his feelings he was stopped at once by the Queen; and when in June, exasperated by all this and by a fresh set of impossible Spanish demands, he leapt the wall of her orchard to force an interview with her, he merely succeeded in frightening her badly and in offending the Spanish sense of decorum unbearably.

Though he was for some months only imperfectly informed of the difficulties arising in Spain, James was none the less having a miserable time of it at home dealing with an alarmed Privy Council and an outraged public opinion which he could not silence, and worst of all with his own doubts and fears. He put a brave face on it to the Court, talking with cheerful confidence of his high hopes of the negotiations and refusing to discuss doubts or dangers. The same note of confidence and reassurance was struck in the set of indifferent verses in the pastoral manner which he produced, addressed to his son:

> *'Love is a world of many Spains,*
> *Where coldest hills and hottest plains,*
> *With barren rocks and fertile fields*
> *By turns despair and comfort yields;*
> > *But who can doubt of prosperous luck,*
> > *Where love and fortune doth conduct.'*

To the Council he was forced to admit that he had given way to the importunity of his son and his favourite, but he tried hard to mitigate the outburst of public hatred against Buckingham by muzzling the preachers, who were the most dangerous source of such propaganda. He forbade prayers for mercy to the Prince 'now that he was going into the House of Rimmon', which were becoming extremely popular in the City churches, and all mention of the subject in sermons; and he had the bells rung for compulsory rejoicing when he got news of Charles's safe arrival in Madrid. His private fears and all his affection and longing for the young men he poured out in a series of letters whose tenderness would be moving if it were not so grotesque.

'God bless you, my sweet Baby,' one characteristic letter ended, 'and send him good fortune in his wooing, to the comfort of his old father, who cannot be happy but in him. My ship is ready to make sail, and only stays a fair wind. God send it her; but I have, for the honour of England, curtailed the train that goes by sea of a number of rascals. And, my sweet Steenie gossip, I must tell thee that Kate was a little sick these four or five days of a headache, and the next morning, after a little casting, was well again. I hope it is a good sign that I shall shortly be a gossip over again, for I must be thy perpetual gossip; But the poor fool Kate hath, by importunity, gotten leave for me to send thee both her rich chains; and this is now the eighth letter I have written for my two boys, and six to Kate. God send me still more and comfortable news of you both, till I may have a joyful, comfortable, and happy meeting with you; and that my Baby may bring home a fair lady with him, as this is written upon our Lady-day.'

In another letter he assured Steenie that he was wearing his picture 'in a blue ribbon under my wash-coat, next my heart'. But there were doubts and alarms even in those early months. In spite of his many writings on the subject, James had never yet managed to make his religious position clear to other men and, twenty years after the Bye Plot, there was still the delusion in the Catholic world that his conversion was a possibility. 'I know not what ye mean,' he wrote in answer to Buckingham on March 25th, 'by my acknowledging the Pope's spiritual supremacy. I am sure ye would not have me renounce my religion for all the world; but all that I can guess at your meaning is, that it may be ye have an allusion to a passage in my book against Bellarmine, where I offer, if the Pope would quit his godhead, and usurping over kings, to acknowledge him for the chief bishop, to which all appeals of churchmen ought to lie *en dernier resort*, the very words I send you here inclosed, and that is the farthest my conscience will permit me to go upon this point. For I am not a monsieur that can shift his religion as easily as he can shift his shirt, when he cometh from tennis.'

It is not surprising that he refused to show anybody Buckingham's letters or his answers to them. But his confidence was not seriously shaken, and when Charles asked him for 'somewhat under your Majesty's hand to show whereby that ye engage yourself to do whatsomever I shall promise in your name', he recklessly sent the *carte blanche* required, remarking only that, 'it were a strange trust that I would refuse to put upon my only son and upon my best servant'. He sent out a shipload of companions and attendants, and all the jewels and presents they asked for. He fitted out an expensive fleet to fetch home the bridal pair, and he set about redecorating and enlarging St James's Palace for the Infanta's reception.

Then in the middle of June the blow fell. Cottington arrived from Madrid with the precise terms on which the Pope was prepared to grant the dispensation. The Infanta was to have control of the education of her children and was to be allowed to open her church in London for public worship. There must be complete freedom of worship for Catholics, and the Oath of Allegiance was to be altered to suit them. To all this James and

269

his whole Council must agree on oath, and the King must further swear to obtain Parliamentary confirmation of these terms within a year. Finally, Philip of Spain had also to bind himself under oath to see that these terms were kept, and this in turn provoked a further Spanish demand that the Infanta should remain in Spain for a year after the marriage, lest England break her word. It is not surprising that James said that the news had stricken him dead. Confidence gave way to hysteria. He was convinced that his babes were prisoners, and to recover them he was prepared to sign anything the Spaniards asked.

'Come speedily away,' he wrote, 'and if ye can get leave, give over all treaty. And this I speak without respect of any security they can offer you, except you never look to see your old dad again, whom I fear ye shall never see, if you see him not before winter. Alas, I now repent me sore that I ever suffered you to go away. I care for match, nor nothing, so I may once have you in my arms again. God grant it, God grant it, God grant it; amen, amen, amen! I protest ye shall be as heartily welcome as if ye had done all things ye went for, so that I may once have you in my arms again; and God bless you both, my only sweet son, and my only best, sweet servant, and let me hear from you quickly, with all speed, as ye love my life; and so God send you a happy and joyful meeting in the arms of your dear dad.'

At all costs now the marriage treaty must go through. The vital thing was to get his boys home, with or without the Infanta, and salvage what could be salvaged afterwards. In a tormented gloom which he could no longer conceal from the world James signed and promised all that was asked of him, and even, by a last exertion of his royal authority, persuaded his reluctant Council that the seriousness of the crisis made it imperative that they should sign and promise too. In Madrid, meanwhile, on July 25th, the marriage treaty was actually signed. The Spaniards were astounded and not best pleased to find their most outrageous demands, put in largely to make the treaty unacceptable, agreed without protest. Charles's surrender was abject and unconditional. There was no mention of the £500,000 dowry, to which the Spaniards had whittled the million which had been dazzling James's imagination for the past ten years, and without which, so he had assured Buckingham, he must go bankrupt. There was no mention of Spanish help to restore Frederick and

Elizabeth in the Palatinate. In his own words, James was 'marrying his son with a portion of his daughter's tears'. Moreover Charles in his folly was proposing to consummate the marriage and then sail home without the Infanta, who was to follow a year later, so that he might be leaving behind an heir who would make it almost impossible for James to do as he intended—have the marriage dissolved by the Church of England as soon as his babies were safely home.

Buckingham's vanity, as much as anything, saved the nation from what must have been, in the existing state of public opinion, a major disaster. Promoted a Duke by his adoring master to put him on an equal footing with the grandees of Spain, he had expected to lord it in Madrid as he did in Whitehall. Faced by the unaccustomed hostility of men who would neither defer to his whims nor tolerate his bad manners, he became touchy and petulant, and imagined slights even where none were. He broke out in fury at the 'trickery and deceit' with which the Spaniards had conducted the negotiations and was told coldly by Olivares that he had much better have left the matter to professional diplomats like Bristol who understood it; and he flew into a rage when he heard that the Spaniards resented the familiarity with which he treated the Prince, sitting on his table and remaining hatted in his presence. On their side the Spaniards, too, were hostile and resentful after a summer of tolerating the atrocious manners and the arrogance of the English courtiers who had swarmed out after the Prince. There was an ugly incident when Sir Edmund Verney struck a priest; and the Spaniards let it be known that they would not allow Charles to keep his Protestant attendants in Madrid over the winter. By the beginning of August only the obstinate determination of Charles not to go home unwed kept the negotiation open at all, and under the double influence of Spanish coldness and Buckingham's resentment that, too, was being worn down. It was King Philip in the end who suggested that there was little point in his waiting on for the final approval of the Pope, since he was anyway to leave his bride behind. So in the end, on September 2nd, the pair left Madrid almost as hastily and unceremoniously as they had entered it. Charles had sworn to the marriage contract and left a proxy with Lord Bristol. But Bristol was not to use it until instructed from England and the Spaniards, anyway, showed little serious intention of going through with the matter.

Their return, still Protestant and without the Princess, provoked the greatest spontaneous public rejoicing King James's England ever saw. The bells rang everywhere and there were bonfires all along the Portsmouth road. In London rich men showed their satisfaction by providing banquets in the streets and setting debtors free from prison. There was a *Te Deum* in St Paul's, and Charles himself reprieved a batch of condemned felons whom he met on the road to Tyburn as he rode through. The pair had landed on October 5th. On the 6th they were met at last, half way down the stairs at Royston, by their old Dad and Gossip, who hugged them to him while all three wept in joy and relief. James had been made to look more of a fool than ever in the eyes of Europe. The policy he had tenaciously pursued in the teeth of the facts and of his subjects' most deeply-rooted prejudices was in ruins. He was all but bankrupt and could do nothing to help his exiled daughter. But Steenie and his Babe were back, and for a week or two nothing else mattered.

But as the excitement died down James found that he was faced by much more than the mere failure of a diplomatic negotiation. In spite of his feebleness, his gout, and his maudlin hysteria, he had managed to draw on enough reserves of energy to keep the threads of policy in his hands while the young men were away. Now they slipped from his hands altogether. Nothing now would satisfy Buckingham's hurt vanity and his rage against the Spaniards but war; and war with Spain alone offered him the chance to keep the popularity which he had so briefly and unexpectedly enjoyed when he got back from Madrid. To achieve this he was prepared to go to any lengths, supported as he was by the Prince. Parliament must be called, Councillors hostile to the war policy silenced or ruined, the King himself coerced and deceived. There were grotesque intrigues to prevent any Spanish representative from seeing James, or getting word to him, and the King's apartments, wherever he might be, were continuously picketed by the Duke or the Prince or by the Villiers ladies.

James defended the shreds of his policy obstinately and noisily, but quite ineffectually. The occasional outbursts of temper with which he attempted to assert his will in private were treated by his favourite and his son either with indulgent contempt or with open rudeness and reproaches. His frequent illnesses and absences from London were exploited by the suppression of information and by ignoring or distorting the instructions he did give; and the influence of the anti-war party on the Council was steadily undermined as men realized that effective decisions could only be got now from Prince Charles. The Spanish ambassadors could scarcely get to see him, and he allowed himself to be talked into a peremptory demand for the restitution of the Palatinate as a condition of proceeding further with the proxy marriage arranged with such difficulty at Madrid. Spanish pride did the rest. Insulted by the demand for an immediate answer, Philip of Spain drew back from a marriage he had never really wanted, and James was left altogether without a policy. He must either acquiesce in the loss of the Palatinate, which he had vowed never to do, or try to recover it by war, which he rightly believed to be impossible. Wearily he assented to the transfer of Charles's marriage negotiations from Madrid to Paris, since he could not quarrel simultaneously with both the great Catholic powers, and to the calling of a Parliament which was certain to clamour for war, though he told Charles roundly that 'he would live to have his bellyful of Parliaments'. When Buckingham determined to punish Lord Middlesex for supporting the King's peace policy in the Council by organizing his Impeachment, James showed the same testy prescience. 'By God, Steenie,' he said, 'you are a fool and will shortly repent this folly and will find that in this fit of popularity you are making a rod with which you will be scourged yourself.' But he gave way, and in February, 1624, opened his last Parliament.

James's opening speech was in fact a public confession that his policy and his government had broken down. He put up a feeble, disingenuous defence of his negotiations, denying that he had in any way endangered the interests of English Protestantism, and ended by asking openly for their advice, thereby abjectly surrendering that exclusive prerogative of handling foreign affairs for which both he and Elizabeth had fought so long and so tenaciously. He must have known in advance what Parliament's answer would be, for their simple, twofold solution never varied: war with Spain and an immediate tightening-

T

up of the anti-Catholic measures at home. But this advice when they gave it infuriated him. Illogically he protested that they were meddling with matters which did not concern them. But, since he had not the energy to take up the fight himself and could not prevent Buckingham and Charles from pursuing policies of which he disapproved, he withdrew protesting into the country and left events to take their course. Middlesex, one of the best servants James ever had, was duly impeached and condemned. The treaties with Spain were annulled, and subsidies to the value of over £400,000 were voted to put the nation on a footing for war: 'the greatest aid which was ever granted in Parliament to be levied in so short a time'. It is true that these sums were not to be paid into the Treasury, but into a special fund which could only be disbursed on the authority of a Council of War nominated by the Commons. But for the moment that mattered little, since Buckingham and Charles were temporarily popular heroes. The blame for anything that had gone wrong at Madrid had been adroitly thrown on to Bristol, and Commons and government were apparently pursuing a common policy against which the King had scarcely the energy to protest.

Henceforward James in effect dropped out of political life altogether. Once the Spanish ambassadors managed to break through to him with an accusation that Buckingham was engaged in treasonable plots to dethrone him, but they only provoked one of those tearful, stormy scenes of reproach and reassurance which marked this last phase of James's relationship with his beloved Dog, whom he had begun to think of now as, in some mystical way, his 'sweet child and wife'. He made a half-hearted effort in September to oppose the terms of the marriage treaty with France, whose concessions to English Catholics were, as Chamberlain remarked, 'every way as heavy at least as the Infanta's' and at the same time a clear breach of faith with Parliament. But he had to give way. The two young men were all he had left, the only comfort to their 'dear dad and husband'. Rather than lose them he would surrender all political power, and even close his ears to accusations of treason which, in his heart, he sometimes believed to be well founded.

It was the young men who set about preparing an unwieldy England for large-scale war, refitting ships, and conscripting an army of 12,000 men for direct intervention on the Continent. They brought over a German soldier of fortune, Count Ernest of Mansfeld, to command the army, to the fury of the English professional soldiers, and inflicted a final insult on Spain by lodging him in the chambers prepared for the Infanta in St James's Palace; and they revolved grandiose plans for European grand alliances against the Habsburgs which took no account at all of diplomatic and military realities. But their disastrous planning, culminating in the destruction of Mansfeld's army by famine and disease on the island of Walcheren, belongs properly to the beginning of the reign of King Charles. James, though he still lived, had ceased altogether to rule. He was wholly preoccupied with his few remaining pleasures, his diseases, and his tantrums. He was able to gorge himself on melons at the beginning of July, and even to set out on a modified Progress in the late summer. But he did not emerge from his chamber that Christmas, 'not coming once to the chapell, nor to any of the playes'. In the end it was his own characteristic lack of self-discipline which, as much as anything else, carried him off. The tertian ague which attacked him in the first week of March in 1625 was by universal agreement 'without any manner of danger if he wold suffer himself to be ordered and governed by phisicall rules'. But that was one vital thing which Buchanan had failed to teach him, and he owed many of his troubles in England to that lack. He refused now to do as he was told, drank vast quantities of beer to cool himself, and absorbed indiscriminately and in the teeth of the advice of his official doctors, the remedies offered by the old Countess of Buckingham, who had emerged from her semi-retirement to take fussy charge of his sick bed. A series of painful convulsions and fainting fits culminated in what was apparently a slight stroke which left him unable to control the muscles of his face and almost suffocating from the vast quantities of his own phlegm. A violent attack of dysentery completed his misery and degradation, and on March 27th, having sunk into merciful unconsciousness, he peacefully died.

Politically speaking, when it came at last, James's death was almost without significance. Since he had ceased gradually to rule long before he ceased to reign, the situations and policies of his last years had been those of the new men and a new age.

The conduct of foreign affairs had passed practically out of his control, and the overwhelming domination of Buckingham had already begun the long story of Charles I's struggle with the House of Commons. Nevertheless the scene round the death-bed at Theobalds marked the end of an age in England at least as decisively as had the death of Elizabeth twenty-two years before. Archbishop Abbot and Lord Keeper Williams, Bishop of Lincoln, the prelates who had knelt beside him and helped him to make a devout and godly end before he lapsed into uncon-sciousness, were men who would find themselves fish strangely out of water in Laudian England. They, and indeed all those who flourished at James's Court, had about them qualities pecu-liarly Jacobean: a large tolerance which kept them easily on terms with the rich, corrupt, extravagant world in which they had to live. They represented an Elizabethan England grown up and come into its own, which had weathered the anarchy of the Reformation and the Catholic attack from abroad, but had as yet no serious need to fear the threat of Puritan rebellion and evolutionary political claims. In their eating and their drinking, in their architecture and in the great rolling, involved sentences of their prose they displayed the same flamboyance which so easily degenerated into vulgarity and bad taste; the easy accept-ance of things as they were which all too often meant condoning scandal and excess, all of which were characteristic of the King round whom their world revolved. The luxury, the wild, dis-orderly hunting, the great feasts and the drunken horseplay far into the night—all would be wholly repugnant to King Charles's fastidious taste and icy decorum. The new reign would set a new tone, not only at Court, but in the nation at large.

James had certainly not been a great or a spectacular king, nor had he been a very good one. The rickety financial system bequeathed him by Elizabeth he passed on to Charles un-remedied and with an even larger current deficit. The rift within the Anglican Church was wider and more threatening at the end of his reign than it had been at the beginning. Though he had on the whole successfully defended the prerogatives which he had inherited from Elizabeth and passed on to his son a power theoretically undiminished, a tradition of collaboration in government between Crown and Council and Parliament had been broken largely by his own idleness and negligence; and by sheer ineptitude he had added unnecessary grievances, economic and social, to those already existing in 1603. The tone of his court had degenerated, and government by the end of his reign had become both less competent and more corrupt.

But there had been many compensations, even in his personal faults. His best claim he made for himself in the long, rambling speech with which he opened the Parliament of 1621. 'I will not say,' he said, comparing himself to Queen Elizabeth, 'I have governed as well as she did, but I may say we have had as much peace in our time as in hers'; and Bishop Williams picked up the same theme in the funeral oration which he subsequently published under the title of *Great Britain's Salamon*: 'Surely actions of Peace (what ever debauched people say to the contrarie), set out a Prince in more orient colours than those of War and great combustions.' In the teeth of the romantics who dreamed of Drake, and of Puritans who would have plunged England into a continental struggle with the Counter Reformation, James had given England a jovial interlude of twenty years of peaceful prosperity. His coarse, friendly lack of dignity spared Englishmen any approach to the apotheosis of Monarchy which was to ruin France, and his laziness had prevented him from making good the large claims to divine right which he loved to make in theory. All in all, his impact on men and events was a good deal less disastrous than that of his far more conscientious son. A curious note of sincerity pervades many of the conventional panegyrics which marked his death, and certainly he was not such a figure of scorn to his contemporaries as he has become to historians. They buried him magnificently after a month's lying in state, though appropriately enough the proceedings were 'confused and disorderly', and the whole cost three times what had been spent on burying Elizabeth. It was a fitting final commentary on the Jacobean Age.

Sources and Authorities

This does not pretend to be an exhaustive or authoritative list of sources for a life of James VI and I, but only of those which have been used or quoted in the preparation of this particular book, and in which a specialist might search for more detailed information on any part of the subject. I hope that the arrangement of these by chapters will give a sufficient clue to my authorities to justify me in eschewing footnotes, which seem to me, in the hands of many modern historians, to have become a tedious nuisance even to the serious student.

Chapter I

Of the general histories of Scotland that of Hume Brown has probably the most enduring value. For Mary's reign in particular and the birth of James VI the relevant passages of Calderwood's *History of the Kirk of Scotland* and of Spottiswoode's *History of the Church of Scotland* are good contemporary sources, as are Sir James Melville of Halhill's *Memoirs of his Own Life*, and Herries's *Historical Memoirs of the Reign of Mary, Queen of Scots and of King James VI*, published by the Abbotsford Society in 1836. Stephan Zweig, *The Queen of Scots*, T. F. Henderson, *Mary, Queen of Scots*, and F. A. Macunn, *Mary Stuart*, are comparatively modern biographies. Agnes Mure Mackenzie, *The Scotland of Queen Mary and the Religious Wars*, 1513–1638 (Maclehose, 1936), gives an excellent account of the whole period, though slightly coloured by excessive nationalist prejudice.

Chapter II

Apart from the authorities already quoted for Chapter I, there is Melville's *Historie and Life of King James the Sext*. The *Letters and State Papers of King James VI* have been published by the Abbotsford Club, and there are valuable contemporary sources scattered through the publications of the Bannatyne and Maitland Clubs and of the Scottish Historical

SOURCES AND AUTHORITIES

Society. There are, of course, the *Calendars of State Papers, Scottish*, and the *Register of the Privy Council of Scotland*. The best modern accounts of James's youth, which have made use of all the above, are in Steeholm, *James I of England* (Michael Joseph, 1938), which is highly coloured, but readable, and Charles Williams's *James I* (Arthur Barker, 1934), which concentrates largely on the Scottish part of the story, unlike the most recent, and perhaps the most scholarly of all the biographers, D. Harris Willson, who, in *King James VI and I* (Cape, 1956), passes comparatively rapidly over James's early life.

Chapter III

The Correspondence of Robert Bowes, the English Ambassador, was published by the Surtees Society in 1842. James's own poems and writings were collected and published by James Montagu in 1616 in *The Works of the Most High and Mightie Prince, James*, and have mostly been re-edited and republished since. The contemporary letters and documents concerning Mary Stuart have all been summarized and brought together in readable form by Robert S. Rait and Annie I. Cameron in *King James's Secret: Negotiations between Elizabeth and King James VI Relating to the Execution of Mary, Queen of Scots* (1927), which, with details from Conyers Read's *Sir Francis Walsingham* (O.U.P. 1925, 3 vols.), have formed the basis of every modern account of these transactions. The *Papers Relative to the Marriage of King James VI* were published by the Bannatyne Club in 1828.

Chapter IV

All the available contemporary sources, the *Letters of Gray*, the *Letters of Elizabeth and James VI*, and the *Correspondence of James VI with Sir Robert Cecil* have all been used with brilliant effect by Helena G. Stafford in her *James VI of Scotland and the Throne of England* (New York, 1940), which has been the almost exclusive source of the account of Anglo-Scottish relations given here. There is also some good contemporary material in Logan Pearsall Smith's *Life and Letters of Sir Henry Wotton* (O.U.P., 1907, 2 vols.).

280

SOURCES AND AUTHORITIES

Chapter V

On the situation bequeathed to James by Elizabeth the most useful general works are probably A. L. Rowse, *The England of Elizabeth*, J. E. Neale's *Queen Elizabeth*, G. R. Elton's *England under the Tudors*, and the opening chapters of Trevelyan's *England under the Stuarts*. For administrative details and Parliamentary procedure and debates the classic collections—Prothero's *Statutes and Documents, 1558–1625*, and J. R. Tanner's *Tudor Constitutional Documents* are still irreplaceable, though there is much of supplementary value in Neale's *Elizabethan House of Commons* and *Elizabeth I and her Parliaments*, and the rival theses in R. H. Tawney's *The Rise of the Gentry* (Economic History Review, 1941) and H. R. Trevor Roper's *The Gentry, 1540–1640* (Cambridge, 1953), have thrown much new light on the economic situation and political attitudes of the Parliamentary classes. The feeling of decline which hung over the last years of Elizabeth is well revealed in Sir Julian Corbett's *The Successors of Drake*, and to some extent in Lytton Strachey's *Elizabeth and Essex*.

Chapter VI

The Court and social background of James I's reign is very well documented by diarists, gossips and letter-writers. The most continuously useful collection is the definitive, 2-volume edition by N. E. McClure of the *Letters of John Chamberlain* (Philadelphia, 1939). There are also *The Commonplace Book of Sir John Oglander* (ed. Francis Bamford, 1936), *The Diary of the Lady Anne Clifford* (ed. V. Sackville-West, 1923), and the *Journal of Sir Roger Wilbraham* (Camden Misc., 1902). For James's movements in general there is John Nichols's *Progresses of King James I*, while for the journey south there is the *True Narrative of the Entertainment of his Majesty from his Departure from Edinburgh till his receiving in London*, printed in Firth's *Stuart Tracts*, which also contains John Savile's eyewitness account of the meeting with Cecil at Theobalds. The gossipy and unreliable *History of Great Britain* by Arthur Wilson and *The Court of King James I* by Sir Anthony Weldon, printed during the Commonwealth, but based on the anecdotage of James's contemporaries, are worth dipping into for some of the authentic atmosphere of the period, as are Goodman's *Court and Times of King James I* and Roger North's *Detection of the Court and State of England*. Perhaps most valuable of all for the Jacobean background is the series of studies collected by David Mathew under the title of *The Jacobean Age*.

Chapter VII

For the Spanish Peace negotiations, apart from the *Calendars of State Papers*, there are the miscellaneous documents in the *Winwood Memorials*. The religious problems are well surveyed in Frere's still very valuable *The English Church in the Reigns of Elizabeth and James I*. Izaak Walton's *Lives* of Hooker and Donne are excellent and John Aubrey's *Brief Lives* are well worth pottering through for personal details. Bishop Hacket's *Scrinia Reserata* gives a good account of a somewhat different type of Jacobean churchman. For the economic difficulties facing the Church, C. Hill, *The Economic Problems of the Church from Archbishop Whitgift to the Long Parliament* is invaluable. The contemporary *Summe and Substance of the Conference at Hampton Court*, by William Barlow, is full of good detail, but an official, and therefore anti-Puritan account, and James Montague's *Letter to his Mother concerning the Conference at Hampton Court*, printed in *Winwood Memorials*, Vol. 2, is also too subservient to authority.

Chapter VIII

J. R. Tanner's two books, *English Constitutional Conflicts of the Seventeenth Century*, and *Constitutional Documents of James I* are still the best documented accounts of James's disputes with his Parliaments. Modern research has done little to lessen the value of S. R. Gardiner's *History of England*, 1603–1642, of Figgis, *The Divine Right of Kings*, or of Spedding's monumental *Letters and Life of Sir Francis Bacon*; but there are some good modern special studies: *The Privy Councillors in the House of Commons*, 1603–1610 by D. Harris Willson (Minnesota Press), Allen's *English Political Thought*, 1603–1644 (Methuen, 1938), and Judson, *The Crisis of the Constitution* (Rodgers, 1939). *The Journals of the House of Commons* are often illuminating, and W. Notestein's lecture on *The Winning of the Initiative by the House of Commons* (London, 1924), is irreplaceable. Nothing much has been added to the literature of the Gunpowder Plot since Gardiner answered Father Gerrard's *What was Gunpowder Plot?* with *What Gunpowder Plot was* in 1897.

Chapter IX

To the general works already quoted may be added Innes, *The Maritime and Colonial Expansion of England under the Stuarts* and *The Ocean in British History* by J. A. Williamson: to the contemporary commentaries on the declining tone at Court Sir John Harington's *Nugae Antiquae* and the *Autobiography of Sir Symonds D'Ewes*.

Chapter X

For a sound factual analysis of the breakdown of 1610, and indeed of much else in the reign, the best authority is Godfrey Davies, *The Early Stuarts*, in the *Oxford History of England*. The classical source for the details of the dispute is still Gardiner's *Parliamentary Debates of* 1610. Most of the available fiscal information is to be found in F. C. Dietz, *English Public Finance*, 1558–1641 (1932).

Chapter XI

The Letters of Elizabeth, Queen of Bohemia have been edited by L. M. Baker, but unfortunately without any explanatory commentary. P. M. Handover, *Arabella Stuart* (Eyre & Spottiswoode, 1957), has probably said the last word on that subject. The whole story of the rise of Somerset, the Essex divorce, and the eventual crash is told in *The Murder of Sir Thomas Overbury* by William McElwee (Faber, 1952). Archbishop Abbot's own account of his share in these transactions and in the rise of George Villiers is printed in Rushworth, *Historical Collections*.

Chapter XII

There are full official accounts of all the trials connected with the Overbury murder in Howell's *State Trials,* and the gossip is to be found in the books already quoted. There is V. T. Harlow, *Raleigh's Last Voyage*, and the most recent of the many biographies of Buckingham is D'Erlanger, *George Villiers, Duke of Buckingham.*

SOURCES AND AUTHORITIES

Chapter XIII

Professor Notestein has published seven volumes on *The Commons' Debates of* 1621, and of other modern work on the constitutional crisis there is material in Thompson's *History of Parliament*, 1295–1642 (Minnesota, 1954), in Willson, *The Privy Council and the House of Commons*, 1603–1625, and in Rosse, *The Struggle for Sovereignty*, 1558–1628. The classic work on the European crisis of 1618 is, and is likely to remain, C. V. Wedgewood's *The Thirty Years' War*.

Chapter XIV

There are no works to add dealing specifically with the last years of the reign, except perhaps the racy, rather written-up account of the Prince's visit to Madrid to be found in Howell's *Familiar Letters*, and the somewhat different account in the *Narrative of the Spanish Marriage Treaty* by Francisco de Jesus, (Camden Society Misc.).

Index

INDEX

Beauchamp, *see* Seymour

Beaulieu, 200

Beaumont, Comte de, French Ambassador, 173

Belgium, 77, 117

Bellarmine, Cardinal, 129, 144

Belvoir Castle, 109

Bermuda, 101

Berwick, 57, 62, 89, 107–8

Bilson, Thomas, Bishop of Winchester, 219

Bingley, Sir John, 241–2

Black Acts, The, (1584), 77

Black, Dr David, 83

Blackness, 76

Blount, Charles, Lord Mountjoy, 113, 118

Bohemia, 247, 257–8

Book of Common Prayer, 130, 132, 137, 139

Book of Rates, 190, 193

Borthwick, 29

Bossuet, Bishop, 101

Bothwell, Earl of, *see* Hepburn

Bourbon, Catherine de, 63

Bowes, Sir Robert, and Ruthven Raid, 52, 54–56; other refs., 44, 48–49, 64, 82

Brazil, 236

Brienne, Comte de, French Ambassador to Scotland, 23

Brig o' Dee, 64, 75–76, 82

Bristol, Earl of, *see* Digby

Brooke, Henry, 8th Lord Cobham, 87, 112, 119, 120–21, 202–3

Brooke, George, 119–20

Browne, Anthony, 2nd Viscount Montague, 205

Bruce, Edward, 1st Lord Kinloss, 87, 185

Brussels, 85, 219

Buchan Castle, 82

Buchanan, George, 33, 37–42, 44, 46, 275

Buckingham, Duke of, *see* Villiers

Buckinghamshire, disputed election, 150–51

Burleigh, Lord, *see* Cecil

Bye Plot, 119, 132, 137, 139

Cadiz, 91, 98, 99, 102, 104, 211

Caesar, Sir Julius, 191, 196, 207

Caithness, 78

Calderwood, David, 238

Calvert, Sir George, 1st Lord Baltimore, 242

Calvin, John, 59

Cambridge, 110, 131, 134

Campbell, Archibald, 5th Earl of Argyll, 14, 23, 25, 27, 43, 82

Campion, Dr Thomas, 100, 122, 174, 209

Canons of 1604, The, 155, 157

Carberry Hill, Battle of, 29, 31, 34–35

Carey, Henry, 1st Lord Hunsdon, 49

Carey, Sir Robert, 62, 89, 100, 108

Carleton, Sir Dudley, 106, 117, 172–3, 178

Carlisle, 239

Carr, Robert, Earl of Somerset, and his rise to favour, 171–2, 176–80, 197, 205; involved in Essex divorce, 206–7, 209, 211; marriage, 212, 221; rels. with Villiers, 214–18, 225; and Overbury's murder, 219, 222, 224–8; his trial, 228–32; other refs., 193, 199, 202, 236, 242

Carrara, 164

Casket Letters, 31, 34, 38, 41

Catesby, Robert, 159, 162

Catherine de Medici, Queen Consort of France, 221

Cecil, Frances (*b.* Drury), Countess of Exeter, 241–2

Cecil, Sir Robert, 1st Earl of Salisbury, and James's accession, 103–6, 112–14, 116, 124; and Main Plot, 119–22; and Gunpowder Plot, 150–61; his rels. with Parliament, 151–2,

286

INDEX

INDEX

Donne, John, Dean of St Paul's, 100, 135

Dorset, Earl of, see Sackville

Dorsetshire, 163

Douai, 118

Douglas, Archibald, Scottish Agent in London, 60–61

Douglas, Archibald, 8th Earl of Angus, 49–50, 57, 70, 77–78, 82

Douglas, James, 4th Earl of Morton, as Regent of Scotland, 43–49; other refs., 21, 32, 34–5, 50

Drake, Sir Francis, 91, 97, 102–4, 125, 277

Drayton Beauchamp, 131

Dudley, John, Duke of Northumberland, 131

Dudley, Robert, Earl of Leicester, 27, 58, 60, 62, 103

Dumbarton, 47, 49

Dunbar, 22, 28, 29

Duncan, Geilie, 72

Dundee, 82, 238

Dunkirk, 110

Dunne, Sir Daniel, 207

Durham, 108, 134

Durham, Bishop of, see Mathew and James

Durham House, 87, 109

Durie, John, 51

East India Company, 101, 164–5

East Lothian, 71

Ecclesiastical Polity, by Hooker, 131

Edinburgh, riots of 1596, 83–84; James's visit in 1617, 238; other refs., 13, 15, 19, 22, 26–27, 30–31, 35–36, 38, 43–44, 47–48, 61, 63–64, 68, 73–74

Edward III of England, 69

Edward IV of England, 62

Edward VI of England, 17, 106, 180

Egerton, Thomas, Lord Ellesmere, Lord Chancellor, 226–7

Elector Palatine, see Frederick

Elizabeth I of England, and the Raid of Ruthven, 53–56, 58; dealings with Bothwell, 74–77, 80–81; attitude to the 'Spanish Blanks', 77–78; her pension to James, 59–60, 62–65, 68–69; and the succession question, 83, 85–87; attitude to religion, 129–31, 133–4, 139, 154–5, 158; death, 89; funeral, 115–16; other refs., 13, 17, 19, 27, 30, 34, 38–40, 48–49, 90, 96–99, 102–4, 106, 109–10, 112, 116, 123–7, 146–8, 151–2, 167, 174, 186, 200, 202, 234, 245, 249, 259, 273, 276–7

Elizabeth, Princess, Electress Palatine, Queen of Bohemia, marriage, 204–5, 245; other refs., 172, 198, 248–9, 271–2

Ellesmere, Lord, see Egerton

Elwes, Sir Gervase, Lieutenant of the Tower, 221–4

Ely, 131

Enfield Chase, 115

Errol, Earl of, see Hay

Erskine, Sir Alexander, Master of Mar, 43–44

Erskine, Annabella, (*b*. Murray), Countess of Mar, 23, 27, 33, 40–42, 66, 79

Erskine, John, 6th Earl of Mar, Regent of Scotland, 14, 22, 27–28, 33, 35–36, 40, 42

Erskine, John, 7th Earl of Mar, as James's playmate, 40, 43; as guardian of Prince Henry, 79–80, 115; other refs., 44, 50, 57, 74, 77, 87–88, 113, 156

Erskine, Sir Thomas, of Gogar, Viscount Fenton, 113, 218

Essex, Earl of, see Devereux

Falkland Palace, 37, 238

Farnese, Alexander, Prince of Parma, 64

Fawkes, Guy, 159–61

INDEX

Ferdinand, II, Holy Roman Emperor, 244, 247, 258, 261

Flanders, 164

Fleming, Chief Baron Sir Thomas, 194

Flodden Field, 16

Flushing, 219

Forman, Dr Simon, 222

Fotheringay Castle, 59

Foxe's *Book of Martyrs*, 161, 248

Franklin, James, 222, 228

Frederick II of Denmark, 63, 65

Frederick, Elector Palatine, King of Bohemia, marriage, 198, 204–5; accepts and loses Bohemian crown, 245, 247–9, 258, 261–3, 270

Garnet, Father Henry, 118, 162

Geneva, 17, 135

Gerard, Father, 119

Gibbe, Henry, 52, 121, 219

Gilbert, Sir Humphrey, 165

Glamis, Master of, *see* Lyon

Glasgow, 25–26, 239

Glenlivet, Battle of, 82

Gloucestershire, 200

Godmanchester, 110

Golden Act of 1591, 77

Gondomar, Count, *see* Acuña

Goodman, Bishop, 67

Gordon, George, 5th Earl of Huntly, 21–22, 25, 27, 30, 35

Gordon, George, 6th Earl of Huntly, and Catholic plots, 64, 66, 70, 77–79, 81–82; murders Moray, 75–76; other refs., 55, 83

Gordon, Lady Janet, Countess of Bothwell, 21, 29

Gordon, Father James, 77

Gordon, Sir Patrick, of Auchindoun, 77

Gowrie Conspiracy, 87–89, 173

Gowrie, Earl of, *see* Ruthven

Graham, John, 3rd Earl of Montrose, 55

Graham, Sir John, 213

Gray, Patrick, Master of, 57–58, 60–61, 66

Grays, 232

Gray's Inn, 174, 262

Great Britain's Salamon, by Bishop Williams, 277

Great Contract, The, 190–6

Greenway, Father Oswald, 162

Greenwich, 13, 101, 115

Grenville, Sir Richard, 102

Grey of Wilton, Thomas, 15th Lord, 119, 120–21

Grimstone Hall, 109

Grotius, Dr Hugo, 134

Guise, Henry, 3rd Duke of, 50, 62

Gunpowder Plot, 143–4, 159–163, 166, 168, 181–2, 184, 188

Gustavus Adolphus of Sweden, 245

Guzman, Gaspar de, Count of Olivares, 264, 266–7, 271

Haddington, Viscount, *see* Ramsay

Hakewill, William, 194

Hamilton, Archbishop, of St Andrews, 23, 26, 29

Hamilton, family, 18, 34

Hampshire, 200

Hampton Court Conference, 134–140, 144–5, 153, 155, 199

Harington, Sir John, 110, 174–5

Hastings, Sir Francis, 185

Hastings, Henry, 3rd Earl of Huntingdon, 62, 85

Hatfield House, 164, 198

Hawkins, Sir John, 97, 104

Hay, Francis, 9th Earl of Errol, and the 'Spanish Blanks', 77–79; final rebellion and pardon, 82–83; other refs., 64, 70, 75

Hay, James, Viscount Doncaster, 173, 176, 247–8

Heidelberg, 261, 265

Henderson, involved in the Gowrie Conspiracy, 88

INDEX

Henry VII of England, 16

Henry VIII of England, 92, 99, 106, 130, 146, 202

Henry III of France, 62

Henry IV of France, King of Navarre, 18, 39, 62–63, 78, 166

Henry, Prince of Wales, birth and christening, 79–81; and the Spanish match, 198; relationship with James, 169–72; death, 198, 204, 210, 211; other refs., 112, 118, 178, 180, 222, 242

Hepburn, Francis Stewart, 5th Earl of Bothwell, implicated in witchcraft, 70–74; raids on Holyrood, 73–75; plots, 76–78, 80–82; other refs, 57, 61–62, 64, 66

Hepburn, James, 4th Earl of Bothwell, and Darnley's murder, 24–28; marriage to Mary Stuart, 29–31; other refs., 21–23, 32–33, 37, 45, 47, 60, 70

Herbert, Sir John, Secretary of State, 152

Herbert, Philip, Earl of Montgomery, 173, 176, 213, 233

Herbert, William, 3rd Earl of Pembroke, 176, 213, 224

Heriot, George, 172

High Commission, Court of, 192, 195

Hinchinbrooke, 93, 109–10

Hindlip House, 162

History of the World, by Raleigh, 122, 237

Holbeche House, 162

Holland, 101

Holyrood, Bothwell's raids on, 73–75; other refs., 20, 22, 29, 32, 48, 64, 90, 238

Home, Elizabeth, *see* Howard

Home, Sir George, Earl of Dunbar, 111, 113

Hooker, Richard, 131

Howard, Charles, Lord, of Effingham, Earl of Nottingham, Lord High Admiral, 91–92, 104, 113, 165, 198, 242

Howard, Elizabeth, (*b.* Home), Countess of Suffolk, 206, 241–2

Howard, Frances, Countess of Essex and Somerset, divorced, 206–8; second marriage, 173, 211–12; murders Overbury, 219, 221–2, 224–5, 228; her trial, 228–32

Howard, Lord Henry, Earl of Northampton, letters to James, 87, 104–5, 112; part in Essex divorce, 206–9, 221–2; disgraced, 213–14; death, 219, 225; other refs., 113, 197, 199–200

Howard, Theophilus, Lord, de Walden, 242

Howard, Thomas, Duke of Norfolk, 35, 104, 112

Howard, Thomas, Earl of Suffolk, part in Essex divorce, 206–9, 222; his downfall, 241–2; other refs., 91–92, 95, 101–2, 104, 113, 161, 205, 228, 237

Hudson's Bay, 101

Hull, 110, 150

Hunsdon, Lord, *see* Carey

Huntingdon, Earl of, *see* Hastings

Huntingdonshire, 110–11

Huntingtower, 50

Huntly, Earl of, *see* Gordon

Ignoramus, play, 213

Impeachments: Sir Giles Mompesson, 254–5; Sir Francis Bacon, 255–6; Lord Middlesex, 273–4

Impositions, (*see* also Book of Rates), 193, 195, 248

Infanta, *see* Isabella and Maria Anna

Ingram, Sir Arthur, 95

Inquisition, Spanish, 161

INDEX

Lennox, Earl and Duke of, *see* Stuart

Lerma, Duke of, 183

Lethington, *see* Maitland

Levant Company, 101, 190

Lincoln, 237

Lindsey, Sir David, 65–66

Linlithgow, 28, 35, 48, 84

Litell, Helen, 22

Lochleven Castle, 30, 33, 37, 43, 74

London, 156–7, 166, 168, 183, 211, 227, 259, 263–4, 272. *See* also Tower

Louis XIII of France, 245

Louis XIV of France, 100

Lulworth, 218, 227

Lyle, Lawrence, 209

Lyon, Sir Thomas, Master of Glamis, 50, 57

Madrid, 183, 239; visit of Charles and Buckingham, 264–71, 273

Main Plot, 119, 141, 202

Mainwaring, Sir Arthur, 222

Maitland, Sir John, of Thirlstane, 58, 64–65, 73, 75, 79–80, 84, 201

Maitland of Lethington, William, 21, 25–26, 29, 34–35

Manners, Lady Katherine, *see* Villiers

Manners, Roger, 5th Earl of Rutland, 109, 251

Manoa, 236

Mansfeld, Count Ernest of, 275

Maria Anna, Infanta of Spain, 236, 246, 267, 269–70, 274–5

Marie de Medici, Queen Consort of France, 166

Mar, Earl and Countess of, *see* Erskine

March, Earl of, *see* Stuart

Markham, Sir Gervase, 119, 121

Marlborough, 198

Mary I of England, 106, 130, 188

Mary, Princess, infant daughter of James I, 169

Mary of Guise, Queen Consort of Scotland, 17

Mary Stuart, Queen of Scots, and birth of James, 13–14; political struggles, 16–17, 19–34; imprisoned in England, 35–36, 38, 40–41, 44–45, 53; events leading up to her death, 56–61; other refs., 46, 50, 70, 85, 89, 104, 112

Mary Tudor, Duchess of Suffolk, 202

Masques: *of Blackness*, by Ben Jonson, 172; *of Flowers*, 174; *of Solomon and Sheba*, 174–5

Mathew, Dr Tobie, Bishop of Durham, Archbishop of York, 70, 108–9, 134

Maximilian of Bavaria, 261

May, Sir Humphrey, 218, 227

Medici, *see* Catherine and Marie

Melville, Andrew, 56, 77, 82–84, 238

Melville, Sir James, 13, 24, 54

Melville, Sir Robert, 60–61

Merchant Adventurers, 101, 235

Middlesex, 228

Middlesex, Earl of, *see* Cranfield

Millenary Petition, 1603, 132, 134–5, 155, 257

Molière, 100

Mompesson, Sir Giles, 254–5

Monopolies, 97–98, 146, 234, 248

Monson, Sir Thomas, 221

Monson, William, 240–41

Montacute, 93

Montague, James, Bishop of Bath, 137

Montague, Lord, *see* Browne

Montaigne, 37

Monteagle, Lord, *see* Parker

Montrose, Earl of, *see* Graham

Moore, Francis, 146

Moray, Earl of, *see* Stuart

More, Sir George, 229–31

Morton, Earl of, *see* Douglas

Mountjoy, Lord, *see* Blount

INDEX

Murray, David, 204

Murray, John, playmate of James VI, 40

Muscovy Company, 101

Napier, Barbara, 72

Naunton, Sir Robert, 242

Neile, Richard, Bishop of Coventry, 207

New Forest, 200

Newark, 111

Newcastle, 21, 108

Newmarket, 200, 213, 259–60

Neville, Sir Henry, 112, 193

Nombre de Dios, 102

Norfolk, Duke of, *see* Howard

North Berwick, 72

Northampton, 158

Northampton, Earl of, *see* Howard

Northamptonshire, 157–8

Northumberland, Earl of, *see* Percy

Nottingham, Earl of, *see* Howard

Ochiltree, *see* Stewart, Captain James

Olivares, Count of, *see* Guzman

O'Neill, Hugh, Earl of Tyrone, 86

Orinoco, River, 211, 233, 236–7, 239

Oslo, 65

Ostend, 203

Overbury, Sir Thomas, rels. with Somerset, 179–80; and Essex divorce, 206–9, 212; inquiry into his death, 219–21; his murder, 222–6, 232, 241; other refs., 214, 228–9

Oxford, 131, 134, 193

Oxford, Earl of, *see* Vere.

Palatinate, 248–50, 258, 264, 273

Palsgrave, *see* Frederick

Paris, 213, 273

Parker, William, Lord Monteagle, 160–61

Parma, *see* Farnese

Parsons, Father Robert, 85, 142, 159

Paulet, William, 4th Marquis of Winchester, 200

Percy, Henry, 9th Earl of Northumberland, 87, 121

Percy, Sir Thomas, 159–61

Perth, 41, 88, 238

Peru, 244

Pett, Phineas, Master Shipbuilder, 170

Peyton, Sir John, 106

Phelips, Sir Robert, 256–7

Philip II of Spain, 53–54, 59, 69, 188

Philip III of Spain, 85, 127–8, 183, 246, 258, 261

Philip IV of Spain, 264, 267, 270–1, 273

Pocahontas, Princess, 165

Poems, by Overbury, 219, 223

Poetical Exhibition, by Jonson, 164

Porter, Colonel Endymion, 266

Prague, 247

Purveyance, 116, 154, 186, 191, 196, 200

Pym, John, 256–7

Queensferry, 75–76

Racine, 100

Radcliffe, Robert, 5th Earl of Sussex, 80

Raleigh, Sir Walter, attitude to Scottish succession, 102–3, 105; involved in Main Plot, 109, 112, 131, 171, 178, 198; colonization in Virginia, 165–6; in the Tower, 202, 204, 211, 233; his Orinoco expedition, 233–4, 236–7, 239; trial and execution, 240; other refs., 87, 109, 112, 131, 171, 178, 198

Raleigh, Walter, the younger, 239

Ramsay, Sir John, Viscount Haddington, Earl of Holderness, 88, 173

293

INDEX

Villiers, George, 1st Duke of Buckingham, rise to power, 213–15, 217–19, 225–6, 229, 233–4; attitude to Spanish match, 244, 249, 261, 264–5; Madrid journey, 265–72; insists on war, 273–4; other refs., 202, 237–40, 242, 250, 254, 257–8

Villiers, Sir John, Viscount Purbeck, 251, 254

Villiers, Katherine, (b. Manners), Duchess of Buckingham, 251, 263, 268

Villiers, Mary, (b. Beaumont), Lady Compton, Countess of Buckingham, 251–2, 275

Virginia, 101, 164–5

Virginia Company, 250

Walcheren, 275

Walsingham, Sir Francis, Secretary of State, 56, 58–59, 62, 77, 103, 160

Walton, Izaak, 131

Wards, Court of, 154

Ware Park, 163–4

Warwick, Earl of, see Rich

Watson, Father William, 119–120, 141

Wemyss, 19

Wentworth, Thomas, Earl of Strafford, 99, 171

Westminster, 34, 38, 115, 131, 161, 230–1

Weston, Richard, 221–4, 226, 228

White Mountain, Battle of the, 248

Whitehall, 101, 112, 114–15, 174, 176, 179, 200, 230–2, 262, 271

Whitelocke, Sir James, 193–4

Whitgift, John, Archbishop of Canterbury, 131, 139–40, 157

Widdrington, 108

Wife, The, poem by Overbury, 209

William the Silent of Holland, 58

Williams, John, Bishop of Lincoln, Lord Keeper, 135, 276–7

Wilton, 93

Wiltshire, 260

Wimbledon, 242

Winchester, 121, 131

Winchester, Marquis of, see Paulet

Windsor, 115, 218

Winwood, Sir Ralph, Secretary of State, part in rise of Villiers, 213; the discovery of the Overbury murder, 219–21, 223–4; part in Raleigh's release, 233–4, 239–40; other refs., 121, 211, 249

Wittenberg, 135

Woolwich, 170

Worcester, Earl of, see Somerset

Worcestershire, 162

Worksop, 109–10

Wotton, Sir Henry, 128, 142, 217

Wotton, Lady, 205

Wriothesley, Henry, Earl of Southampton, 87, 101, 112, 184, 200

Yelverton, Sir Henry, Attorney General, 150

York, 34, 108–9, 237

Young, Peter, 37–39, 44, 62

Zouche, Edward, Lord, 219, 227